# Get a FREE eBook

To register this book, scan the code or go to
**www.manning.com/freebook/peixeiro2**

---

## By registering you get

- **FREE eBook copy**
  download in PDF and ePub
- **FREE online access**
  to Manning's liveBook platform
- **FREE audio**
  read and listen online in liveBook
- **FREE AI Assistant**
  it knows the contents (and your exact location) when it answers
- **FREE in-book testing**
  fun tests to lock in your knowledge

In Manning's liveBook platform you can share discussions and comments with other readers, add your own bookmarks and highlights, insert personal notes anywhere on the page, see color versions of all the book's graphics, download source code and other resources, and more!
To register, scan the code or go to www.manning.com/freebook/peixeiro2

---

# *Time Series Forecasting Using Foundation Models*

MARCO PEIXEIRO

For online information and ordering of this and other Manning books, please visit www.manning.com. The publisher offers discounts on this book when ordered in quantity.

For more information, please contact

Special Sales Department
Manning Publications Co.
20 Baldwin Road
PO Box 761
Shelter Island, NY 11964
Email: orders@manning.com



Manning Publications Co.
20 Baldwin Road
PO Box 761
Shelter Island, NY 11964

Development editor: Sarah Harter
Technical editor: Anurag Lahon
Review editor: Dunja Nikitović
Production editor: Andy Marinkovich
Copy editor: Keir Simpson
Proofreader: Melody Dolab
Typesetter: Tamara Švelić Sabljić
Cover designer: Marija Tudor

ISBN 9781633435896

*To my wife, my parents, and my sister. Please read it this time.*
*And to my little peach, may this book put you to sleep.*

# brief contents

# contents

# *preface*

In October 2023, I used TimeGPT, one of the foundation forecasting models that we explore in this book, for the first time. After running it for a project, I found that it made better predictions than the models I'd carefully built and tuned on my data.

That's when I knew that large time models were about to change the field of time-series forecasting. A pretrained model not only performed better than my own but also was much faster and more convenient. This is the ultimate promise of foundation models: a single model enables you to deliver state-of-the-art forecasting performance without the hassle of training a model from scratch or maintaining multiple models for each use case.

Since then, many models have been proposed and developed, and a big shift has occurred in the scientific community, where a great deal of effort is now spent building better foundation forecasting models. Just as data professionals are expected to know large language models (LLMs), I anticipate that large time models will be must-know technology for practitioners, so I set out to write a book to bring readers up to speed.

This book explores the major contributions to large time models. It can't cover all that has been done or anticipate all that will happen next, of course, but it will enable you to use and optimize current large models. I included the most recent modifications to methods covered in the book to ensure that what you read is as up to date as possible.

The book focuses on practicality and hands-on work with each model. The idea is that you'll master new tools and adapt them to your own scenarios. In a dedicated capstone project at the end, you compare large time models with more traditional approaches and evaluate their performance.

I had the chance to join Nixtla and have worked on TimeGPT since 2024, which gave me the opportunity to study other foundation models and work with them extensively, putting me in a particularly good position to write this book. I remain impartial in my evaluations, as you'll see throughout the chapters.

# *acknowledgments*

First, thanks to my lovely wife for her patience during this project, although I think she was enjoying the quiet evenings without me toward the end.

Special thanks to Brian Sawyer. He allowed me to write my first book, and writing a second one is more than a dream come true. I thank him for his trust, and let's hope for a third book.

Huge thanks to Sarah Harter for her amazing work as my development editor. She helped me get organized and improve the book throughout the months. Working with her was an absolute pleasure.

A big "thank you" to Jonathan Gennick for trusting my expertise and for going above and beyond to make this book a reality. Thanks also to my technical editor, Anurag Lahon, for his careful review of the code.

Many thanks to everyone I haven't met who worked in the background to make this book come true.

To all the reviewers—Ako Heidari, Alireza Aghamohammadi, Anne Katrine Falk, Arjun Ashok, Ashish Patel, Aushim Nagarkatti, Avinash Tiwari, Chalamayya Batchu, Christoph Bergmeir, Felipe Coutinho, Gaurav Pandey, Guillermo Alcantara, Hardev Ranglani, Hatim Kagalwala, Jay Shah, Jeffrey Tackes, Johannes Stephan, Karanbir Singh, Kaushik Dutt, Kaushik Ruparel, Kavin Soni, Manu Joseph, Mariano Junge, Mariia Bulycheva, Meetu Malhotra, Natapong Sornprom, Olena Sokol, Peter Gruber, Prashanth Josyula, Ritwik Dubey, Saikrishna Chinthapatla, Sana Hassan, Sathya Narayanan Annamalai Geetha, Sharmila Devi Chandariah, Shubham Patel, Sofiia Shvets, Steven Edwards, Sudarshan Anand, Tony Dunsworth, and Vojta Tůma—your suggestions helped make this book better.

Finally, thank you to all my teammates at Nixtla, who built amazing open source software for the forecasting community and gave me the chance to contribute to it. Thanks to them, writing the code for this book was a breeze.

# *about this book*

This book is meant to give you all the necessary knowledge to use large time models in the most optimal way and adapt them to your own use cases. We begin by exploring the transformer architecture, which still powers most foundation forecasting models. Then we attempt to build a tiny foundation model to experiment with concepts such as pretraining, fine-tuning, and transfer learning. This experience is a great way to appreciate the challenges of building a truly foundational model for forecasting.

Next, we explore foundation models specifically built for time-series forecasting, from TimeGPT to TimesFM. Then we experiment with LLMs applied to forecasting. We explore each method's inner workings and pretraining procedures, which dictate the model's capabilities and optimal use cases. That way, you'll understand when to use a particular model and how to use it optimally. The book concludes with an experiment that draws on all the methods we explored throughout the book.

## *Who should read this book?*

This book is meant for practitioners who have some experience in time-series forecasting using Python, possess foundational knowledge of time-series forecasting concepts, and know how to train forecasting models. The book assumes knowledge of basic forecasting concepts such as seasonality, trend, and autoregression. It also assumes some knowledge of statistical models such as ARIMA, which we use in the last chapter to compare the performance of traditional models and foundation models.

By the end of the book, you'll have the skills and knowledge to apply the major available large time models to your own projects, making sure that the models are adapted and fine-tuned to your use cases.

### How this book is organized: A roadmap

This book is divided into four sections covering 10 chapters. In part 1, we explore the concept of foundation models and build a tiny foundation model:

- Chapter 1 explores the transformer architecture, which is the backbone of many large time models that we use throughout the book. We also study the benefits and drawbacks of using foundation models for forecasting.
- Chapter 2 details the technical steps and concepts involved in building a foundation model, such as pretraining, transfer learning, and fine-tuning. We apply those concepts in a hands-on experiment by building a small time model.

In part 2, we explore foundation models built specifically for time-series forecasting:

- Chapter 3 introduces TimeGPT, one of the first foundation models proposed. We learn how it works, how it was pretrained, and how to use it for forecasting. We also fine-tune the model, include exogenous features, and produce explainability plots using `shap`. As a bonus, we use it for anomaly detection.
- Chapter 4 explores Lag-Llama, a probabilistic model mostly geared toward research. We learn how its parameters affect its performance and how to fine-tune it.
- Chapter 5 dives into Chronos, a framework that can adapt any LLM for forecasting tasks. After studying its architecture and pretraining protocol, we learn how to use it optimally. We also perform fine-tuning and anomaly detection.
- Chapter 6 explores Moirai, a model built to handle exogenous features natively. We discover its architecture and learn to perform inference both with and without covariates.
- Chapter 7 explores TimesFM, a deterministic model that is ideal for point forecasts.

In part 3, we experiment with LLMs in forecasting because the task of completing sentences with text can be analogous to forecasting with numbers:

- Chapter 8 explores the use of Flan-T5 and Llama models for time-series forecasting. We use Flan-T5 as a local model and access Llama through an API. We learn how to adapt LLMs for forecasting and use techniques such as few-shot and chain-of-thought prompting to guide the models.
- Chapter 9 introduces Time-LLM, a model that effectively reprograms LLMs for time-series forecasting. It can't perform zero-shot forecasting but can be a better choice than using LLMs directly.

The single chapter in part 4 is a capstone project:

- Chapter 10 gives you the perfect opportunity to solidify your learning and implement your knowledge in a self-guided project. I provide a proposed solution and analysis of the results, but the goal is to let you experiment and come up with your own results.

**TIP** To get the most value from chapters 3 through 7, readers who have never worked with foundation models should read the first two chapters to understand their capabilities and concepts.

## About the code

All the code in this book is in Python. You may not reproduce the same results because there is always some variability in the output of models, especially probabilistic models.

This book contains many examples of source code both in numbered listings and in line with normal text. In both cases, source code is formatted in a `fixed-width font like this` to separate it from ordinary text. Sometimes code is also **`in bold`** to highlight code that has changed from previous steps in the chapter, such as when a new feature adds to an existing line of code.

In many cases, the original source code has been reformatted; we've added line breaks and reworked indentation to accommodate the available page space in the book. In rare cases, even this was not enough, and listings include line-continuation markers (➥). Additionally, comments in the source code have often been removed from the listings when the code is described in the text. Code annotations accompany many of the listings, highlighting important concepts.

You can get executable snippets of code from the liveBook (online) version of this book at https://livebook.manning.com/book/time-series-forecasting-using-foundation-models. The complete code for the examples in the book is available for download from the Manning website at https://www.manning.com and from GitHub at https://mng.bz/a9Q9.

## liveBook discussion forum

Purchase of *Time Series Forecasting Using Foundation Models* includes free access to liveBook, Manning's online reading platform. Using liveBook's exclusive discussion features, you can attach comments to the book globally or to specific sections or paragraphs. It's a snap to make notes for yourself, ask and answer technical questions, and receive help from the author and other users. To access the forum, go to https://livebook.manning.com/book/time-series-forecasting-using-foundation-models/discussion.

Manning's commitment to our readers is to provide a venue where meaningful dialogue between individual readers and between readers and authors can take place. It is not a commitment to any specific amount of participation on the part of the author, whose contribution to the forum remains voluntary (and unpaid). We suggest that you try asking the author some challenging questions lest his interest stray! The forum and the archives of previous discussions will be accessible on the publisher's website for as long as the book is in print.

# about the author

**MARCO PEIXEIRO** is the author of *Time Series Forecasting in Python*, published by Manning Publications. He works at Nixtla, actively developing TimeGPT and maintaining open source forecasting libraries such as `neuralforecast`. He conducted time-series forecasting workshops for the Open Data Science Conference (ODSC) and is a guest lecturer at Harvard Business School. He also writes blog articles for his Medium publication The Forecaster (https://medium.com/the-forecaster) and hosts online courses on forecasting and other subjects on his website (https://www.datasciencewithmarco.com).

# *about the cover illustration*

The figure on the cover of *Time Series Forecasting Using Foundation Models,* captioned "Tartare de Crimée," or "Crimean Tatar," is taken from a collection by Jacques Grasset de Saint-Sauveur, published in 1784. Each illustration is finely drawn and colored by hand.

In those days, it was easy to identify where people lived and what their trade or station in life was by their dress alone. Manning celebrates the inventiveness and initiative of the computer business with book covers based on the rich diversity of regional culture centuries ago, brought back to life by pictures from collections such as this one.

# Part 1

# The rise of foundation machine learning models

This part gently introduces the concept of foundation models. In chapter 1, we explore the transformer architecture from a time-series forecasting perspective; this deep learning architecture powers most of the foundation models we explore in the following chapters. We also highlight the benefits and drawbacks of foundation models. In chapter 2, we experiment with the fundamental concepts of foundation models—pretraining, transfer learning, and fine-tuning—by building our own tiny foundation model and realizing how big a challenge it is.

# Understanding foundation models

**This chapter covers**

- Defining foundation models
- Exploring the transformer architecture
- Understanding the advantages and drawbacks of foundation models
- Using foundation models for time-series forecasting

Foundation models represent a major paradigm shift in machine learning. Traditionally, we build data-specific models, meaning that each model is trained on a dataset specific to a particular scenario. Thus, the model specializes in a single use case. In another situation, another model must be trained with data specific to that situation.

We are finding more ways to apply and interact with foundation models. Video meeting applications such as Microsoft Teams use foundation models to summarize the key points of a presentation. Canva, which builds web-based design tools, enables users to create an image from a text input using the DALL-E model developed by OpenAI. Also, millions of people have interacted with ChatGPT; the free version uses the GPT-5 model to generate text and code. Finally, Toys"R"Us created a video ad using Sora, a foundation model that generates video from text [1]. This book, however, focuses on foundation models applied to time-series forecasting, which itself can be applied to a wide range of applications, including weather forecasting and demand planning.

Foundation models remove the need to build models for specific tasks or use cases. Now we can use the same model for many tasks and situations, which can greatly simplify and speed up our workflow.

In time-series forecasting, a single foundation model can forecast series with different frequencies and temporal properties, such as seasonality or holiday effects. Also, advanced foundation models can perform tasks such as anomaly detection and time-series classification.

This chapter defines foundation models and explores the advantages and drawbacks of these models. A single model will not perform best in all situations, so the chapter also defines the boundaries each model needs to perform best. In the next chapters, we get hands-on experience with a wide array of available foundation models so we can experiment with them. Specifically, we forecast weekly sales of stores, applying zero-shot forecasting and fine-tuning when possible. We also perform anomaly detection on taxi rides to explore this secondary capability of large time models.

## 1.1 Defining a foundation model

Before delving into the subject, it is important to distinguish between the model and the algorithm. The *algorithm* outlines the steps a program must perform to achieve a goal. A *model* is the result of applying an algorithm to a dataset.

Consider a linear regression. The algorithm stays constant in the sense that it always tries to create a straight line that minimizes the sum of the squared distances between all points and the line. But depending on the dataset we fit on, the model can be completely different, as shown in figure 1.1. We see that although both linear models were built with the same algorithm, the results are different because the datasets are different. In the top image, we get a rising line; in the bottom image, we get a falling line.

> **DEFINITION** An *algorithm* outlines the steps to complete to achieve a certain goal. A *model* is the result of applying an algorithm to a particular dataset. Here's one way to look at the difference: the algorithm is the recipe, the dataset is the ingredients, and the model is the cake. The same recipe with different ingredients produces a different cake.

The term *foundation model* was coined by the Stanford Institute of Human-Centered Artificial Intelligence in 2021. It describes a machine learning model that is trained on a large dataset so that it can be applied to a wide variety of tasks [2].

> **DEFINITION** A *foundation model* is a machine learning model trained on large, diverse data that can be used for a wide variety of tasks. A foundation model is often large itself, containing millions of parameters, and can be fine-tuned to a scenario for better results.

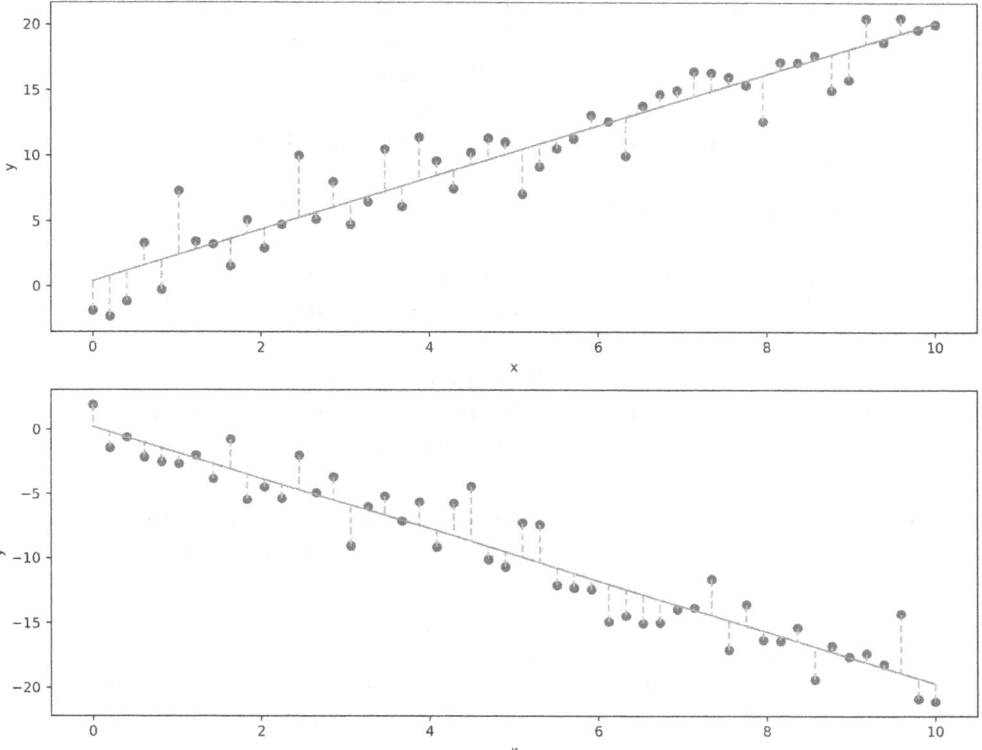


**Figure 1.1 The result of performing linear regression on two different datasets. Although the algorithm used to build the linear model stays the same, the model is different depending on the dataset used.**

A foundation model has four main characteristics:

- The training dataset is large and diverse.
- The model itself is big (has a large number of parameters).
- The model can be used for different tasks.
- The model can be adapted or fine-tuned.

As we will discover in future chapters, foundation forecasting models are trained on large datasets containing billions of data points. This is necessary because for the model to be applied in different scenarios, it must learn dependencies and relationships in a wide variety of situations, which in turn means that the model itself will be large. As we know, models learn by incrementally tweaking their weights, which control the output of the model. If we train the model on a large dataset, the model must also contain a large set of weights, often on the order of millions and billions, and those weights must be saved so the model can access them and make new predictions given new data. Therefore, those models often weigh many gigabytes.

For a model to be considered a foundation model, it must be applicable to many tasks. In time-series forecasting, a single model must be able to predict series with different frequencies, trends, seasonal periods, and so on. The model may not have been trained on data specific to our scenario, but it must have seen time series with similar properties so that it can generate reasonable predictions without specializing in our problem.

Nevertheless, foundation models can be fine-tuned, resulting in better performance. Fine-tuning means training the foundation model on our data before making predictions. We don't train the entire model from scratch, which would take a long time. Instead, we tweak a subset of the model's parameters so that the output is tailored to our use case.

Because neural networks often gain performance as larger datasets are used, foundation models often rely on deep learning architectures. In fact, most foundation models rely on the transformer architecture. Understanding this structure is crucial for several reasons:

- *Most models in this book are derived from the transformer architecture.* By understanding the base architecture, we can spend more time studying the modifications that make each model unique.
- *The architecture allows us to better understand the hyperparameters of large time models, especially when we fine-tune them.* When we fine-tune, we tweak the model at a more granular level. When we understand the architecture and its hyperparameters, we can tune each parameter carefully to achieve the best performance possible.
- *The architecture helps us troubleshoot why a foundation model may not be adapted to our use case.* As we will discover throughout this book, foundation models have (or lack) capabilities that make them less useful for our scenario. Not all models can account for exogenous features or the relationships between multiple target series, for example.

## 1.2 Exploring the transformer architecture

In this section, we study the transformer architecture from a time-series forecasting point of view. The transformer architecture was proposed in 2017 in the seminal paper "Attention Is All You Need" by Google researchers [3]. This architecture revolutionized fields of machine learning such as natural language processing (NLP) and computer vision because it captures complex dependencies in data efficiently.

This architecture is still behind many top-performing models in NLP because it powers large language models (LLMs); it is also the building block of many time-series foundation models. Let's explore its inner workings from a time-series perspective. Figure 1.2 shows a simplified schema of the transformer architecture.

At a high level, the series is sent through an embedding layer, which transforms the input into a format that the model understands. Positional encoding is added to that representation so the model can preserve the order of the time steps, which is crucial in time series.

Then we enter the encoder, where the self-attention mechanism learns different relationships and dependencies in the data. The output of the encoder is sent to the decoder, which is responsible for making predictions.

In the decoder, another attention mechanism generates the predictions. The predictions are generated one at a time, and each one is fed back to the decoder until we obtain a sequence that covers the entire forecast horizon.

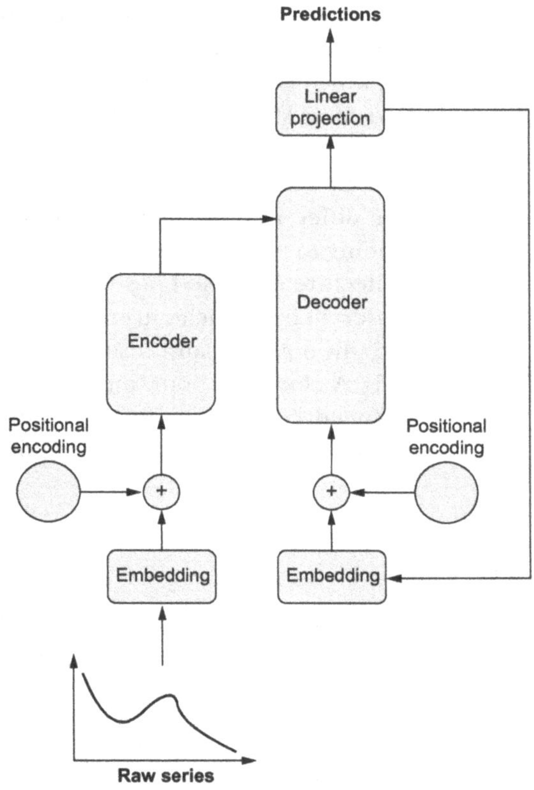


Figure 1.2 Simplified transformer architecture from a time-series perspective. The raw series enters at the bottom-left portion of the figure and flows through an embedding layer and positional encoding before going into the decoder. Then the output comes from the decoder one value at a time until the entire horizon is predicted.

### 1.2.1 Feeding the encoder

The first step, of course, is feeding our raw time series to the transformer. As shown in figure 1.2, the series goes through an embedding layer, which separates the raw series into *tokens*—pieces of information in the time series. A token can be a unique value from the series or a window of values.

Next, the model learns an *embedding*—a deep, abstract representation of the series in the form of a multidimensional numerical vector that encodes its features and that the model understands. Then the embedding can be reused across the model. Figure 1.3 illustrates the output of the embedding layer.

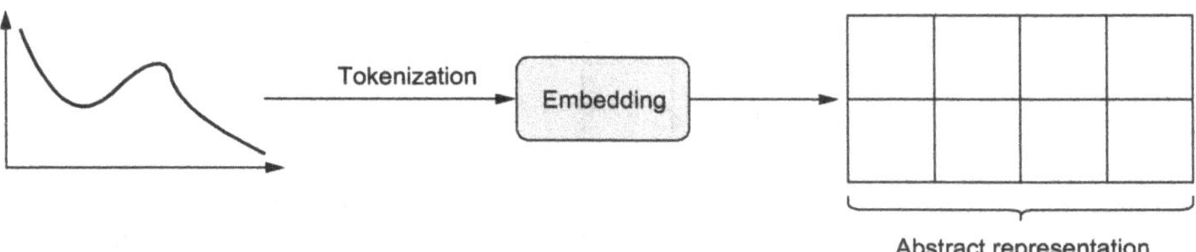


Figure 1.3 Visualizing the result of feeding a time series through an embedding layer. First, the input is tokenized, and an embedding is learned. The result is the abstract representation of the input made by the model.

Next, we add positional encoding to the output of the embedding layer before sending it to the encoder. With positional encoding, the model can account for the order of the data, which is crucial in time series. After all, the model must know that Tuesday always comes after Monday and before Wednesday; otherwise, it might train under conditions in which the future is used to learn the past, which would be a serious mistake.

Another advantage of positional encoding is that our series might have duplicate values at different time steps. To avoid treating these values identically, we use positional encoding to tell the model where these values occur in the sequence. The transformer architecture uses fixed positional encoding for time series, using sinusoidal functions of different frequencies to encode the position of each token. An intuitive way to understand why both sine and cosine functions are used is to think of these functions as clock hands. A clock has hour, minute, and second hands, which complete a cycle at their own speed; combining the information of these hands gives us the precise time.

Positional encoding uses the following equations:

$$PE_{(pos,\ 2i)} = \sin\left(\frac{pos}{10000^{2i/d_{model}}}\right) \tag{1.1}$$

$$PE_{(pos,\ 2i+1)} = \cos\left(\frac{pos}{10000^{2i/d_{model}}}\right) \tag{1.2}$$

In equations 1.1 and 1.2, *pos* is the position of the token; *i* is the index of the positional embedding; and $d_{model}$ is the dimension of the embedding, which can be set by the user.

Using both sine and cosine functions at different frequencies is like having thousands of clock hands that can tell the exact time. Imagine clock hands that show the month, day of the week, hour, minute, second, tenth of a second, and so on. Each hand completes its cycle at its own speed, and combining the information from all hands gives us precise information about time. This result is exactly what positional encoding achieves. Figure 1.4 shows how positional encoding is calculated and added to the input embedding.

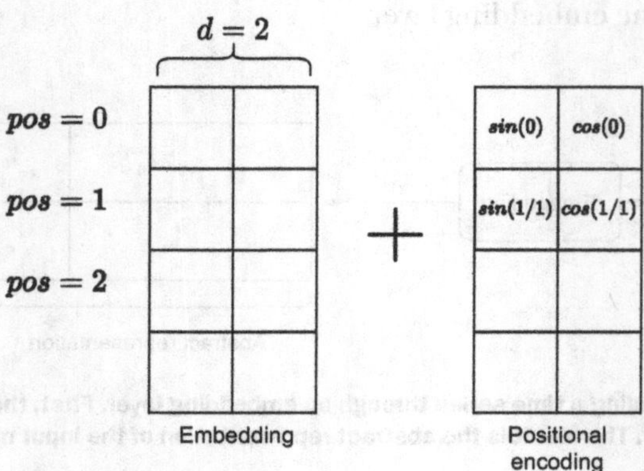


**Figure 1.4 Visualizing positional encoding. The positional encoding matrix must be the same size as the embedding. Also, sine is used in even positions, and cosine is used in odd positions. The length of the input sequence is vertical in this figure.**

In figure 1.4, the positional encoding matrix is added to the embedding matrix, so the matrices must be the same size. Then sine is used in even indices, and cosine is used in odd indices inside the positional encoding matrix.

At this point, we have an embedding of the input series encoding its features, with the addition of positional encoding to identify the order of values in the series. This embedding is fed to the encoder.

### 1.2.2 Inside the encoder

The encoder in the transformer architecture consists of a self-attention mechanism and a simple feed-forward layer. Usually, many of these encoders are stacked as shown in figure 1.5.

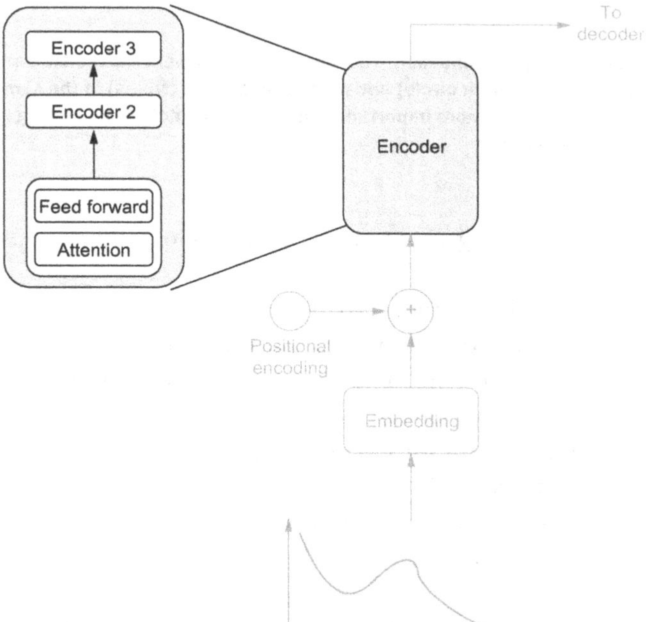


**Figure 1.5 The encoder is made of many encoders that have the same architecture. An encoder is made of a self-attention mechanism and a feed-forward layer.**

Within the self-attention mechanism, the model learns different types of relationships from our series. Although the mathematical details of this mechanism are beyond the scope of this book, this step is where the model learns to associate important tokens together and understand their dependency, as shown in figure 1.6. In other words, the model attends to each past token in a sequence and learns the importance weight of each token for predicting the next value of the series.

We can see that the self-attention mechanism takes the current token and learns its relationships with all other tokens within the same embedding. In this case, this

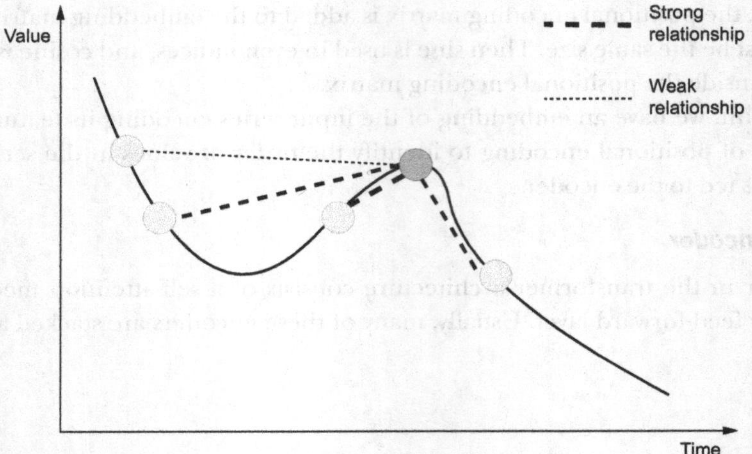


**Figure 1.6 Visualizing the self-attention mechanism. This mechanism is where the model learns relationships between the current token (dark circle) and past tokens (light circles) in the same embedding. In this case, the model assigns more importance (depicted by thicker connecting lines) to closer data points than those farther away.**

attention head seems to be assigning more importance to closer time steps than to those farther in the past.

The transformer architecture is further improved by the use of multiheaded attention. That way, the model can focus on different positions, and each head can learn a different representation of the data. One head can discover trends in time series, for example, while another specializes in identifying seasonal patterns.

As the embeddings are sent through the encoder, which is itself composed of many encoding layers with multiheaded attention, the model learns a deep representation of the data, encoding different properties. Then the encoder output is sent to the decoder.

### 1.2.3 Making predictions

The decoder portion of the transformer architecture is responsible for generating predictions. Fortunately, the decoder is similar to the encoder, as shown in figure 1.7.

We can see that the decoder, like the encoder, is a stack of many decoders. Each decoder is composed of a masked multiheaded attention layer followed by a normalization layer, a multiheaded attention layer, another normalization layer, a feed-forward layer, and a final normalization layer.

The first step is a masked multiheaded attention layer. The mask prevents the model from accessing information from the future, so it can generate predictions only from previous data, which is a crucial condition in time-series forecasting. This layer differs from the encoder, which uses no mask so that the model captures all possible relationships in the known historical data.

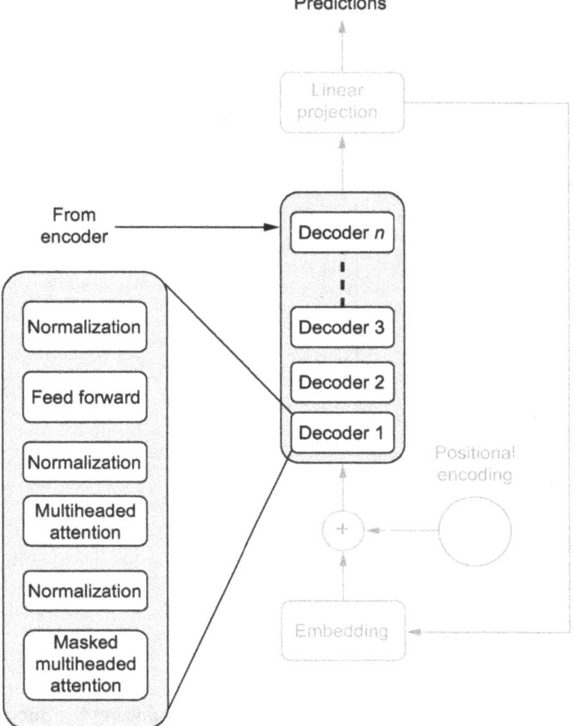


**Figure 1.7 Visualizing the decoder. Like the encoder, the decoder is a stack of many decoders. Multiheaded attention, normalization layers, and a feed-forward layer make up the decoder. The normalization layers keep the model stable during training.**

Next, the second attention mechanism is informed by the output of the encoder, as shown in figure 1.8. The model generates predictions using the deep representation it learned from the encoder.

When the data has flowed through the decoder, the output is sent through a linear projection layer. This step is necessary because the decoder output is a deep representation of the data; the linear projection brings it back to a lower dimension so that we get the predictions of the series. Each prediction is sent back at the bottom of the decoder to repeat the process. Each prediction is used to inform the next prediction, and this cycle continues until the entire horizon is predicted.

To summarize, the transformer architecture has two distinct parts: the encoder and the decoder. The encoder learns relationships in the data, and the decoder generates predictions using information learned in the encoder. Embedding layers represent the data and its features in a format that the model understands. Positional encoding is added to the embedding so that the model knows the order of the data points, which is crucial in time-series forecasting.

As mentioned earlier, the vast majority of foundation models use the transformer architecture. Some models use the full architecture, and others use only the decoder;

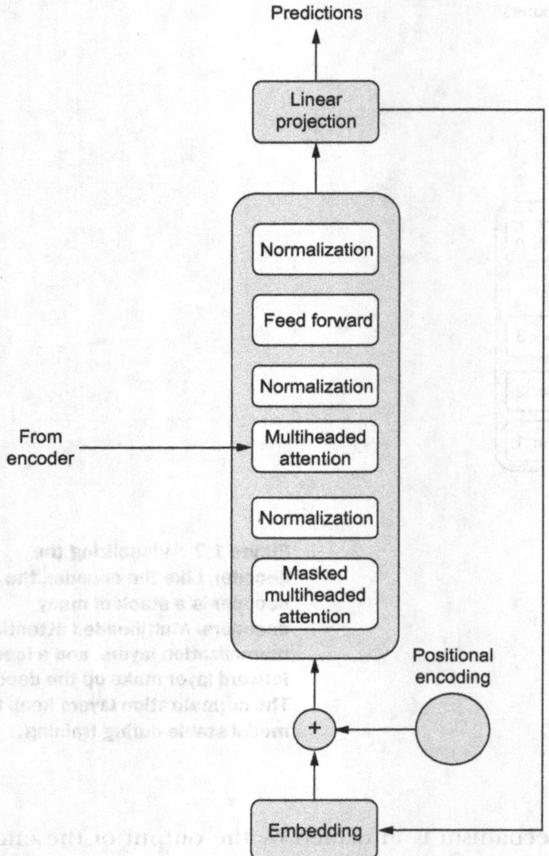


**Figure 1.8 Visualizing the decoder in detail. We see that the output of the encoder is fed to the second attention layer of the decoder; the decoder generates predictions using information learned from the encoder.**

still others tweak the architecture to adapt it further for time-series forecasting. We will address these details when we explore individual models.

## 1.3 Advantages and disadvantages of foundation models

It's important to understand the benefits and drawbacks of using foundation models for time-series forecasting so we can make informed decisions based on each use case. Table 1.1 summarizes these considerations.

**Table 1.1 Advantages and disadvantages of foundation forecasting models**

| Advantages | Disadvantages |
|---|---|
| Use out-of-the-box forecasting pipelines | Privacy concerns |
| Can generate forecasts with few data points | No control of model's capabilities |
| Require less forecasting expertise | May not be optimal for every use case |
| Reusable across tasks | High resource requirements |

### 1.3.1 Benefits of foundation forecasting models

Looking at the advantages first, we see that foundation models can greatly simplify the forecasting pipeline. Instead of training many models, selecting the best-performing one, and designing an entire experiment protocol, using a foundation model typically involves loading it and forecasting immediately. Thus, it requires less expertise to get started with forecasting. With basic programming skills, we can use a foundation model to obtain predictions for a time series.

Time-series forecasting is taught at higher levels of education and can take years to master. Foundation models reduce the barriers to entry in the field and allow programmers from all fields to generate forecasts.

Also, foundation models are great options when we face a situation that involves few data points. Training a model from scratch requires an extensive dataset to ensure that we capture both long-and short-term patterns in our data. When that isn't possible, we can use foundation models to generate predictions because the models were trained on massive amounts of data that we typically cannot access.

Finally, we can reuse the same foundation model across various tasks and datasets. After all, the main objective of a foundation model is to be applicable to many scenarios. This eliminates the need to maintain multiple models; we can focus our efforts on tweaking a single forecasting model.

### 1.3.2 Drawbacks of foundation forecasting models

Foundation models also have disadvantages, such as privacy concerns. Some models are proprietary, meaning that companies maintain and service them. Many companies have mechanisms to capture user data and use it to further train and improve their foundation model, which might raise privacy concerns. Fortunately, these proprietary models often come with self-hosted or private instances so that the data is not shared or accessed by anyone outside the user's organization.

Another drawback is that we lose control of the model's capabilities; we're forced to act within the boundaries of the model we choose. As we will see later, some models cannot exceed a certain forecast horizon; if they do, prediction quality degrades. Also, not all models have the capabilities of data-specific models. Some can't handle multivariate forecasting; others can't consider exogenous features. Some models don't support fine-tuning, so we have to depend on the company or researchers who maintain the model to add features we can use.

Further, although the models are trained on billions of data points, each situation is unique. A foundation model may not be able to handle a specific use case, so a custom solution is required. Although forecasting with foundation models is easier, we must understand how to evaluate these models to design the right solution for our project. Thus, throughout this book, we develop methods to evaluate the performance of foundation models.

Finally, foundation models require many resources. Hosting a foundation model locally takes a lot of storage space, and running inference with it may require a lot of computing power or even a graphics processing unit (GPU) if we want reasonable inference times. Therefore, we may need an expensive infrastructure to host these models. That problem can be circumvented if the model is accessed via API calls; the model is hosted somewhere else, and we simply use function calls to interact with the model, reducing upfront costs and resource requirements.

Ultimately, deciding whether to use a foundation model requires experimentation and a tailored analysis to a particular situation. If a foundation model generates more accurate results than a data-specific model, and the returns outweigh the costs of using this model, using it makes sense. On the other hand, if a foundation model underperforms a data-specific model, and the cost of training a model is smaller than that of using a foundation model, avoid using it. In this book, we gain the knowledge and expertise required to carry out this analysis and recommend the best solution for a project or organization.

## 1.4 Next steps

In the following chapters, we explore and use many foundation forecasting models. We'll start with building our own tiny foundation model to understand the challenges of building foundation forecasting models.

Next, we'll focus on foundation models specifically designed to handle time-series data, including TimeGPT, Lag-Llama, Chronos, Moirai, and TimesFM. We'll explore each model in detail, discover their architectures, use their capabilities, and apply them using real-life data to forecast weekly store sales and assess their performance.

We also use LLMs, including PromptCast and Time-LLM, to see how natural language models can be extended and adapted for time-series data. Although LLMs can handle natural language tasks such as translation, text generation, and question answering, they can't handle time-series data out of the box. These models aim to take available language models and repurpose them for time-series forecasting, which can involve transforming the task of forecasting into a language task or reprogramming the language model for time-series forecasting.

The book concludes with a capstone project that allows us to apply our learnings and compare the performance of foundation models with data-specific statistical methods for predicting daily website traffic.

## Summary

- A foundation model is a large machine learning model trained on massive amounts of data that can be applied to a wide variety of tasks.
- Derivatives of the transformer architecture power most foundation models.
- The advantages of using foundation models include simpler forecasting pipelines, a lower entry barrier to forecasting, and the possibility of forecasting even when few data points are available.

- Drawbacks of using foundation models include privacy concerns and lack of control of the model's capabilities. Also, a foundation model may not be the best solution to our problem.
- Some forecasting foundation models were designed with time series in mind; others repurpose available large language models for time-series tasks.

# Building a foundation model

## 2

### This chapter covers

- Exploring the architecture of N-BEATS
- Pretraining our own model for transfer learning
- Fine-tuning a pretrained model
- Understanding the challenges of building a foundation model

In chapter 1, we defined foundation models, discovered their advantages and drawbacks, and explored the transformer architecture, which powers the vast majority of foundation models that we will encounter throughout this book. Before we delve into those advanced models, let's build our own tiny foundation model to understand the concepts surrounding foundation models and appreciate the challenges researchers overcome to build them.

Although technically, many deep learning models can be pretrained and used for transfer learning, we'll use the N-BEATS model. This lightweight model is fast to train and particularly effective at generalizing to different time series.

In this chapter, we explore basis expansion and the architecture of N-BEATS before training it on a diverse dataset, effectively reproducing the steps for building a foundation model on a much smaller scale. Here, the main goal is to get hands-on experience building a foundation model and to appreciate the difficulty of this task, rather than to build a performant, large time model.

## 2.1 Exploring the architecture of N-BEATS

N-BEATS (which stands for Neural Basis Expansion Analysis for Interpretable Time Series forecasting) was proposed in 2019 [1]. This model represents one of the first pure deep learning approaches to time-series forecasting that does not rely on time-series–specific components such as trend or seasonality. It represents an important innovation because it can learn more complex relationships in the data; it isn't confined to modeling only trend and seasonality, so it can make better predictions. Also, the model was built to be generic, giving it good generalization capabilities, so it's a great candidate for building a small foundation model.

### 2.1.1 Basis expansion

As the name suggests, basis expansion is at the core of this model, so let's explore this concept in detail. *Basis expansion* is a mathematical technique that transforms the original features, enabling models to capture complex nonlinear relationships in the data.

A common basis expansion is the polynomial basis expansion. Suppose that we have a dataset with only two features:

$$\begin{bmatrix} x_1 & x_2 \end{bmatrix} \tag{2.1}$$

Then we can perform a polynomial basis expansion of degree two. This simply means that we add the square of each feature in the set, allowing the model to capture nonlinear patterns in data:

$$\begin{bmatrix} x_1 & x_2 & x_1^2 & x_2^2 \end{bmatrix} \tag{2.2}$$

**DEFINITION** *Basis expansion* is a mathematical operation that maps the original feature space to another feature space, enabling models to learn nonlinear patterns. A polynomial basis expansion of degree two, for example, adds the square of each value of each feature to the dataset so that a model can capture quadratic relationships in the data. Basis expansion can be performed with logarithmic functions, exponential functions, or any arbitrary function.

With a dataset containing squared values, we can fit a second-degree polynomial to our data and model a nonlinear relationship. This is essentially what happens in Microsoft Excel when we fit a line to our data, as shown in figure 2.1.

Figure 2.1 clearly illustrates the effect of basis expansion using Excel. Without basis expansion, we can fit only a linear function to our data, resulting in a poor fit. When we use a second-degree polynomial basis expansion, however, we can fit a quadratic

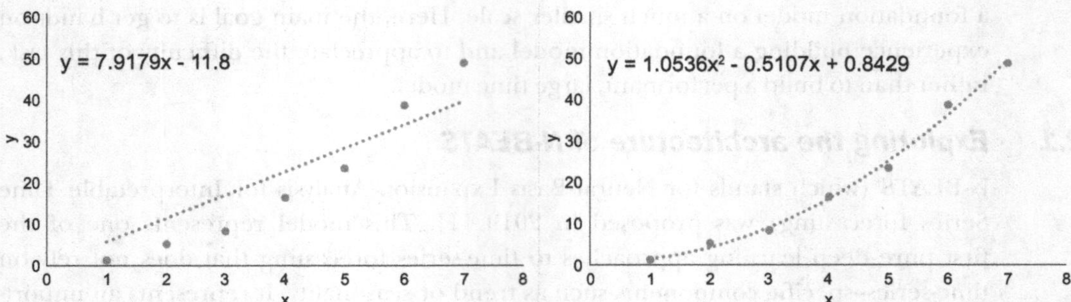


**Figure 2.1 Visualizing the effect of basis expansion. (Left) Without basis expansion, we're stuck using a linear model. (Right) After a second-degree polynomial basis expansion, we can fit a quadratic line, which is a better fit to the data.**

equation. This approach results in a much better fit to our data, and we effectively model nonlinear relationships.

In N-BEATS, the basis expansion is determined by the model—hence the *neural basis* part of the acronym. Based on the data, the model will learn the best coefficients for a generic function to perform basis expansion. With that in mind, let's take a closer look at the architecture.

## 2.2 Architecture of N-BEATS

N-BEATS was designed to be simple and generic without decomposing the series or manipulating the input with transformations, as statistical models often do. Figure 2.2 shows the full architecture of N-BEATS.

N-BEATS consists of stacks of blocks. To understand how N-BEATS works, let's start at the bottom of figure 2.2, at the block level, and make our way to the top.

### 2.2.1 A block in N-BEATS

A *block* is the basic unit of N-BEATS. It's made of fully connected layers—the most basic architecture of deep learning. In figure 2.2, one fully connected layer is responsible for a forecast, and another is responsible for the backcast. Here, the forecast represents the prediction of the block, and the backcast represents the information learned by the block. Each layer is responsible for learning a coefficient $\Theta$, which represents the expansion coefficient. This coefficient is used for basis expansion, represented by the functions $g$. The superscript $f$ indicates a forecast, and the superscript $b$ indicates a backcast. Again, the forecast represents future values of the series as predicted by the model, whereas the backcast is a reconstruction of the input from what the block has learned.

### 2.2.2 A stack in N-BEATS

At the stack level, each stack is composed of many blocks. Each stack has two outputs: a prediction and residuals. The prediction of each block is summed up; it represents a

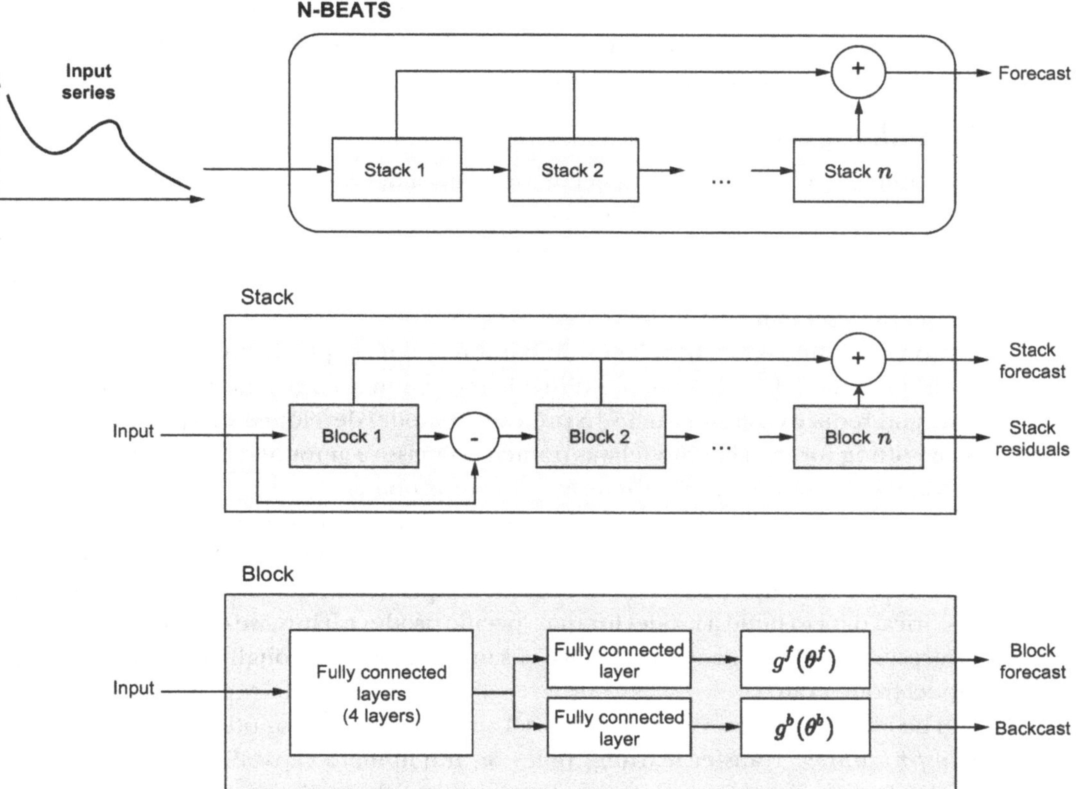


**Figure 2.2 Architecture of N-BEATS. N-BEATS consists of stacks of blocks. Each block outputs a forecast and a backcast.**

partial forecast at the stack level. Then the residuals are calculated using the backcast of the block and a residual connection. In figure 2.2, a residual connection skips block 1, which contains the original information coming from the input. Then the backcast of block 1 is subtracted from the input. The result of that operation is residuals. Remember that the backcast represents information captured by the block. Therefore, as input, block 2 gets the information from the series that block 1 didn't capture. This operation is repeated within a stack, with each block learning information that previous blocks didn't capture.

### 2.2.3 Assembling N-BEATS

Finally, we reach the top level of figure 2.2, where N-BEATS is composed of many stacks. Each stack outputs a partial prediction, and the sum of all results is the final prediction of N-BEATS. Again, residuals are passed from one stack to another, with each stack trying to capture information that the previous one missed.

Thus, we see how N-BEATS learns complex relationships in time series by using only fully connected layers and basis expansion. Each stack treats the input sequentially and tries to model information that previous stacks missed.

## 2.3 Pretraining our model

Pretraining is a fundamental aspect of foundation models. *Pretraining* refers to training a model on a large dataset to learn general patterns and relationships in data. We can pretrain a model on a large monthly time series, for example, to produce monthly forecasts on another series for which we don't have enough data points to make a model from scratch.

Consider the task of translation in natural language processing (NLP). Building a translation model from scratch is difficult and requires large amounts of data. To save time and reduce costs, we can use a pretrained model developed by a team that did the heavy lifting for us. That model was trained on massive amounts of data and specializes in translation, so we can apply it directly to our problem.

The same applies to time-series forecasting. We can face situations in which we don't have enough data to train a model for a specific forecasting task. We may want to forecast the sales of a new product, but because the product is new, we do not have enough historical data to build a model for that specific product. Thus, we can take a pretrained forecasting model to generate predictions until we gather enough data points to train a model from scratch.

The idea of taking a pretrained model and applying it to another problem is called *transfer learning*. Transfer learning relies on the model's capability to generalize and apply what it learned from a previous dataset to another task.

> **DEFINITION** *Transfer learning* refers to applying a pretrained model to a scenario that the model has not seen. We rely on the model's generalization capability to use the knowledge it learned from other datasets.

This is the entire idea behind foundation models: all of them were trained on massive amounts of data, but none have seen the particular problem we want to solve. Hence, we use a models' generalization capability to make predictions in a situation that is unknown to them. As we will see, the models can still perform well and reduce development time and costs.

Let's see this scenario in action by pretraining our own N-BEATS model and using transfer learning to forecast another dataset. That way, we gain firsthand experience in pretraining a model and effectively mimick the development of a foundation model on a much smaller scale.

For this experiment, we pretrain on the M3 dataset, compiled for the M3 forecasting competition by Spyros Makridakis et al. It contains 3,003 series sampled at different frequencies, such as yearly, quarterly, and monthly. For this experiment, we use only the monthly portion of the dataset. The series comes from a wide variety of industries, including marketing, macroeconomics, microeconomics, and demographics, but their particular origins are anonymized. We start by importing the required libraries and loading the dataset, as shown in the following listing.

**Listing 2.1 Importing libraries and loading the dataset**

```
import pandas as pd
import numpy as np
import matplotlib.pyplot as plt

from datasetsforecast.m3 import M3

import warnings
warnings.filterwarnings('ignore')
Y_df, *_ = M3.load(directory='../data/',
    group='Monthly')                          # Loads the monthly series from the M3 dataset only
Y_df['ds'] = pd.to_datetime(Y_df['ds'])

Y_df.head()
```

We have 1,428 unique series in this dataset, all sampled at a monthly rate. We can visualize a portion of the dataset, resulting in figure 2.3. Don't be confused by the label of

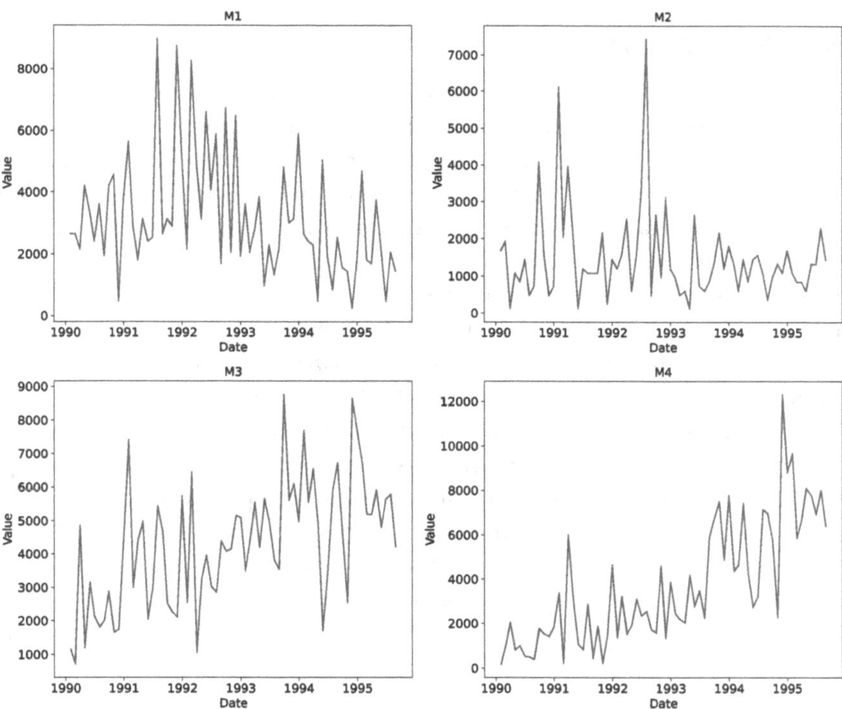


**Figure 2.3 Plotting the first four series of the monthly M3 dataset. The title refers to a label for each series. Each series is part of the M3 dataset.**

each series and the name of the M3 dataset. All series are part of the large M3 dataset. The label `M1` simply means "monthly series 1." When we train on the M3 dataset, we use all series, from `M1` to M1428, as in the following listing.

**Listing 2.2 Plotting the first four series of the dataset**

```
fig, axes = plt.subplots(nrows=2, ncols=2, figsize=(14,12))

for i, ax in enumerate(axes.flatten()):          ◄ Plots only the first four series
    id = f"M{i+1}"
    filtered_df = Y_df[Y_df['unique_id'] == id]

    ax.plot(filtered_df['ds'], filtered_df['y'])
    ax.set_xlabel('Date')
    ax.set_ylabel('Value')
    ax.set_title(f"M{i+1}")

plt.tight_layout()
```

Figure 2.3 shows a small sample of our dataset. The sample shows no clear temporal patterns of seasonality or trend, but that may be due to the sample we chose to plot. We have only an identification code for each series, so we don't know the domain of the series we're plotting.

## 2.4 Pretraining N-BEATS

Now we're ready to pretrain an N-BEATS model on the monthly M3 dataset. One advantage of N-BEATS is that its simple architecture allows it to be trained quickly, even on a CPU. In this section, we use the `neuralforecast` library, an open source Python package that implements deep learning methods for time-series forecasting. It has a simple interface, similar to `scikit-learn`'s, making it faster and easier to use advanced models.

First, we define the horizon, input size, and maximum number of steps to train the model. In this case, we set the horizon to 12, which is equivalent to one year into the future for monthly data. The input size is twice the horizon: our model will learn to take 24 months of input to predict the next 12 months. Finally, we train the model for 1,000 steps.

We define the number of steps but not the number of epochs. A *step* is defined as a gradient update, and an *epoch* is defined as the model processing every sample of the dataset once. The idea behind using steps instead of epochs is that steps are a more consistent, flexible training measurement that can adapt to datasets of different sizes.

Setting the number of steps too small could result in the model not seeing all the data, which is why we use 1,000 steps—generally a good number to use for deep learning models. Let's begin by initializing the N-BEATS model to prepare for pretraining.

**Listing 2.3 Initializing the N-BEATS model**

```
from neuralforecast.core import NeuralForecast
from neuralforecast.models import NBEATS
```

```
horizon = 12

models = [
    NBEATS(
        input_size=2*horizon,
        h=horizon,
        max_steps=1000)
]
```

Input size is 24 months.

Horizon is 12 months.

Trains for 1,000 steps

Next, we create an instance of the `NeuralForecast` object, which creates windows of data, batches the data, and trains the models. Then we use the `fit` method to pretrain N-BEATS, as follows.

**Listing 2.4 Pretraining the model**

```
nf = NeuralForecast(models=models, freq='M')
nf.fit(df=Y_df)
```

Specifies a monthly frequency

When the model is done pretraining, we save it to use for transfer learning later.

**Listing 2.5 Saving the pretrained model**

```
nf.save(path='./model',
        model_index=None,
        overwrite=True,
        save_dataset=False)
```

## 2.5 Transfer learning with our pretrained model

At this point, we have a model pretrained on the monthly M3 dataset. Now let's see whether this model can be applied to a time series it has never seen.

For this experiment, we use a dataset on monthly antidiabetic drug prescriptions in Australia from 1991 to 2008, compiled by Rob J. Hyndman and George Athanasopoulos and released under the GPL-3 license. The dataset is available in this book's repository. The first step is loading our model so that it's ready to be used for forecasting.

**Listing 2.6 Loading the pretrained model**

```
pretrained_model = NeuralForecast.load(path='./model')
```

Next, we can load the data. Here, we'll apply some preprocessing steps because it makes more sense to report the volume of prescriptions at the end of the month than at the beginning. Also, we add a `unique_id` column, required by the `neuralforecast` package. This column identifies a unique time series. Also, `neuralforecast` expects the `date` column to be named `ds` and the column with the actual values of the series to be named `y`.

**Listing 2.7 Loading the dataset**

```
df = pd.read_csv('../data/AusAntidiabeticDrug.csv')
df['ds'] = pd.to_datetime(df['ds'])
df['ds'] = df['ds'] + pd.offsets.MonthEnd(0)    # Rewrites the date as an end-of-month date
df.insert(0, 'unique_id', 1)                     # Adds a unique_id column, expected by neuralforecast

df.head()
```

The dataset is plotted in figure 2.4. The figure shows a clear trend and seasonality in our data, with the volume increasing over time, and a yearly seasonal pattern with peaks often occurring at the beginning of each year.

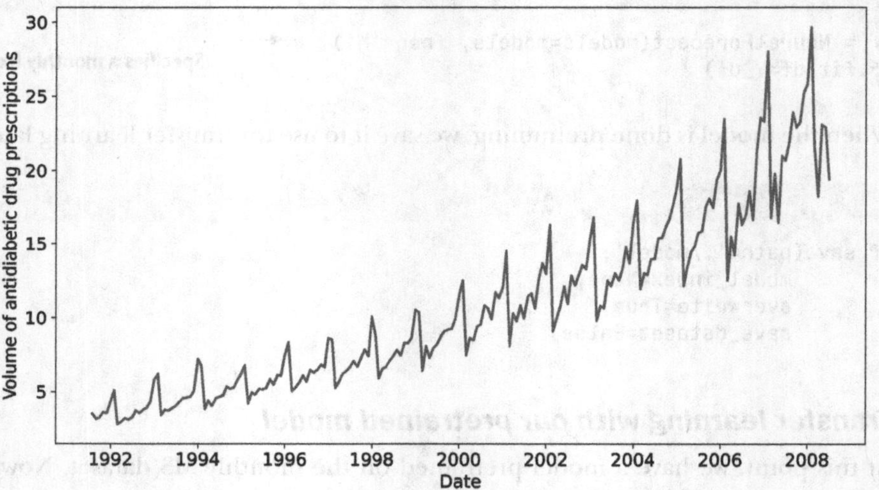


**Figure 2.4 Monthly volume of antidiabetic drug prescription in Australia from 1991 to 2008**

Now let's reserve the last 12 time steps of data as our test set. Our pretrained model was trained with a horizon of 12, meaning that it can predict no more than 12 time steps into the future.

**Listing 2.8 Splitting data**

```
input_df = df[:-12]
test_df = df[-12:]
```

Next, we apply transfer learning. In this case, we perform *zero-shot forecasting*, in which we pass the data and ask the model for predictions without training the model on the data. Here, we call the `predict` method and pass `input_df`; `neuralforecast` does all the heavy lifting for us.

**Listing 2.9 Zero-shot forecasting with our pretrained model**

```
zero_shot_preds = pretrained_model.predict(input_df)
zero_shot_preds.head()
```

That's it! We've successfully pretrained an N-BEATS model and used transfer learning to perform zero-shot forecasting on a dataset it has never seen before.

We can see how fast it is to use our pretrained model. All we had to do was load it and pass the data to generate predictions—much simpler and faster than training a data-specific model for this dataset only.

## 2.6 Fine-tuning our pretrained model

Zero-shot forecasting may not always be the optimal solution, of course. We must always test different approaches to a problem to find the best solution. Let's try fine-tuning our pretrained model and see if it can generate better predictions. *Fine-tuning* is a process in transfer learning that allows the pretrained model to fit on a specific dataset. The objective is to help the model specialize in the current task. Usually, we train only the last layers of a model because training all the layers can be time-consuming and computationally expensive.

There are different levels of fine-tuning. Usually, we train only the last layers of a model on the current dataset so that the layers closest to the output learn to solve a particular problem. We can also train all layers of the model, although this approach can be time-consuming and computationally expensive if we're working with large models. Further, fine-tuning the entire model may cause *overfitting*, where the model loses its generalization capabilities, and forecasting performance degrades. Throughout the book, we'll develop protocols to test fine-tuning and measure its effect on a model's performance.

For this experiment, we'll fine-tune the entire model because it is small and requires few computational steps. In fine-tuning, we generally don't train for many steps, which would be equivalent to training a model from scratch. Therefore, let's set the number of fine-tuning steps to 10. That value is arbitrary; feel free to experiment with different values. The idea is to fine-tune for fewer steps than we used to train the model.

First, we define a function that takes an instance of `NeuralForecast`, which is our loaded pretrained N-BEATS model, and the number of maximum training steps. The function modifies that parameter inside the `NeuralForecast` instance.

**Listing 2.10 Setting the maximum number of fine-tuning steps**

```
def set_max_steps(nf, max_steps):
    trainer_kwargs = {**{"max_steps": max_steps}}    # Defines the number of steps
    nf.models[0].trainer_kwargs = trainer_kwargs     # Sets the number of steps

set_max_steps(pretrained_model, 10)
```

Next, to fine-tune the model, we use the `fit` method:

```
pretrained_model.fit(input_df)
```

Finally, we can generate predictions with our fine-tuned model:

```
finetuned_preds = pretrained_model.predict()
```

Before we evaluate the performance of each method, let's train an N-BEATS model specifically for this dataset. We follow the same steps: we initialize the N-BEATS model, pass it to an instance of `NeuralForecast`, fit the model, and make predictions.

**Listing 2.11 Training a data-specific model and making predictions**

```
models = [NBEATS(input_size=2*horizon, h=horizon, max_steps=100)]

nf = NeuralForecast(models=models, freq='M')
nf.fit(df=input_df)

trained_preds = nf.predict()
```

Take some time to appreciate how easy it is to use N-BEATS and generate predictions with `neuralforecast`. In only four lines of code, we're using one of the major contributions to the field of time-series forecasting without having to implement lengthy code and logic to handle time-series data and deep learning architectures.

## 2.7 Evaluating each approach

At this point, we have predictions from a pretrained model, a fine-tuned model, and a model specifically trained on our dataset. Now we can compare each method's performance to see which performs best in this use case. This step is crucial because a model is good only in relation to other methods. This is why we evaluate three approaches in this experiment.

For this evaluation, we use two metrics: the mean absolute error (MAE) and the symmetric mean absolute percentage error (sMAPE). We use the MAE because it is robust to outliers, easy to interpret, and in the same units as our data, and it penalizes all error sizes equally.

Following is the MAE equation. $H$ represents the forecast horizon, $t$ is considered to be the present time step, and $\hat{y}$ is the prediction by a model:

$$\text{MAE} = \frac{1}{H} \sum_{T=t+1}^{t+H} |y_T - \widehat{y_T}| \tag{2.3}$$

We also use the sMAPE because it is easy to understand, expressed as a percentage. Unlike its mean absolute percentage error (MAPE) counterpart, the sMAPE is equally sensitive to over- and underforecasting. We must avoid using it when values are close or equal to zero, but that is is not the case here. The sMAPE equation follows:

$$\text{sMAPE} = \frac{100}{H} \sum_{T=t+1}^{t+H} \frac{|y_T - \widehat{y_T}|}{|y_T| + |\widehat{y_T}|} \tag{2.4}$$

We use two metrics for a more robust evaluation of the approaches. If a method performs better on more than one metric, we can be more confident in our conclusion that it performed better overall. To simplify the evaluation of each approach, let's combine the predictions of all methods into a single DataFrame that also contains the actual values.

**Listing 2.12 Combining predictions in a single DataFrame**

```
zero_shot_preds = zero_shot_preds.rename(columns={"NBEATS":
➥ "NBEATS_pretrained"})
finetuned_preds = finetuned_preds.rename(columns={"NBEATS":
➥ "NBEATS_finetuned"})
trained_preds = trained_preds.rename(columns={"NBEATS": "NBEATS_trained"})

test_df = pd.merge(test_df, zero_shot_preds,
➥ 'left', 'ds')
test_df = pd.merge(test_df, finetuned_preds, 'left', 'ds')
test_df = pd.merge(test_df, trained_preds, 'left', 'ds')
```

Renames column to label the method that produced the predictions

Merges on the same date

Now we can plot the prediction against the real values, as shown in figure 2.5.

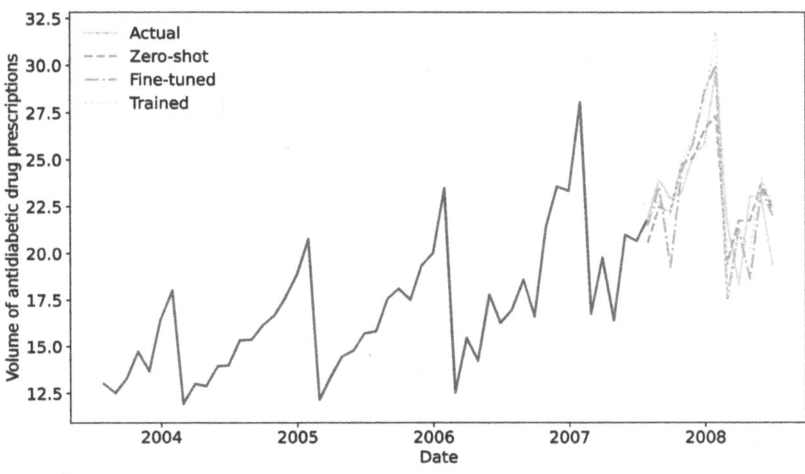


**Figure 2.5 Plotting the predictions against the actual values**

In figure 2.5, the predictions of each method mostly overlap the actual values of the test set, but the predictions of our pretrained model with zero-shot forecasting come closest to the real values. Let's verify by computing the MAE and sMAPE. To do so, we use the `utilsforecast` library. This open source Python package comes with many utility functions for evaluating time-series models; it implements the MAE and sMAPE as well as other functions. The following listing outputs a table that compiles the performance metrics for each method; table 2.1 shows the results.

**Listing 2.13 Evaluating the performance of each method**

```
from utilsforecast.losses import mae, smape
from utilsforecast.evaluation import evaluate

evaluation = evaluate(
    test_df,
    metrics=[mae, smape],                                   # Specifies the metrics to compute
    models=["NBEATS_pretrained", "NBEATS_finetuned",
    ➥ "NBEATS_trained"],                                    # Specifies the columns with predictions
    target_col="y",                                         # Specifies the column with the actual values
)

evaluation = evaluation.drop(['unique_id'], axis=1)
evaluation = evaluation.set_index('metric')
evaluation
```

**Table 2.1 Performance metrics of pretraining, fine-tuning, and training N-BEATS**

| Metric | NBEATS_pretrained | NBEATS_finetuned | NBEATS_trained |
|---|---|---|---|
| MAE | 1.59 | 1.99 | 1.90 |
| sMAPE (%) | 3.56 | 4.63 | 4.23 |

The pretrained N-BEATS model with zero-shot forecasting achieved the lowest MAE at 1.59 and the lowest sMAPE at 3.6%. Thus, we can say that, on average, the pretrained model was off by 1.59 prescriptions, or 3.6% off the actual value.

This result is exciting because it highlights the power of generalization in pretrained models. Although the model had never seen this particular dataset, it was able to produce better predictions. This result can be explained by the fact that the pretrained model was trained on more time steps than were available in this dataset, and deep learning models usually benefit from training on large amounts of data.

## 2.8 Forecasting at another frequency

Now that we've tested our pretrained model on monthly data, let's see how changing the frequency of the data affects the performance of our tiny foundation model. For this experiment, we use our pretrained model to forecast daily data, using a dataset that compiles the minimum daily temperature in a city in Australia during the entire year of 1981.

Keep in mind that our pretrained model was trained only on monthly data. Thus, using it to forecast daily data can lead to poor performance because patterns in time series vary greatly depending on their frequency. Daily data can exhibit more granular changes than monthly data, for example, or it can display weekly seasonality not present in monthly data.

First, we load the dataset and rename the columns as required by the `neuralforecast` library.

**Listing 2.14 Loading daily data**

```
daily_df = pd.read_csv('../data/daily_min_temp.csv')

daily_df = daily_df.rename(
  columns={"Date": "ds", "Temp": "y"})              ← Renames columns
daily_df['ds'] = pd.to_datetime(daily_df['ds'])
daily_df.insert(0, 'unique_id', 1)                  ← Adds a unique_id column
```

Again, we keep the last 12 time steps for the test set. Remember that our pretrained model was trained to predict 12 time steps into the future, so we're limited to that forecast horizon:

```
d_input_df = daily_df[:-12]
d_test_df = daily_df[-12:]
```

Next, we perform zero-shot forecasting using our pretrained model.

**Listing 2.15 Zero-shot forecasting on daily data**

```
pretrained_model = NeuralForecast.load(path='./model')

d_zero_shot_preds = pretrained_model.predict(d_input_df)
```

Now that we have predictions from our pretrained model, let's train an N-BEATS model for this dataset specifically.

**Listing 2.16 Training a data-specific model on the daily data**

```
models = [NBEATS(input_size=2*horizon, h=horizon, max_steps=500)]

nf = NeuralForecast(models=models, freq='D')
nf.fit(df=d_input_df)
d_trained_preds = nf.predict()
```

At this point, we have predictions from the pretrained model and the data-specific model. Again, we combine all predictions in the test DataFrame to plot and evaluate each approach, as shown in the next listing. Figure 2.6 shows the resulting plot.

**Listing 2.17 Combining predictions in a single DataFrame**

```
d_zero_shot_preds = d_zero_shot_preds.rename(columns={"NBEATS":
➥ "NBEATS_zero_shot"})
d_zero_shot_preds = d_zero_shot_preds
➥ .reset_index(drop=True)
d_trained_preds = d_trained_preds.rename(columns={"NBEATS":
➥ "NBEATS_trained"})

d_test_df = pd.merge(d_test_df, d_trained_preds, 'left', 'ds')
d_test_df = pd.concat([d_test_df, d_zero_shot_preds['NBEATS_zero_shot']],
➥ axis=1)
```

**Drops the index for concatenation**

**Uses concatenation instead of merging because the dates are at a monthly frequency, but we have daily data**

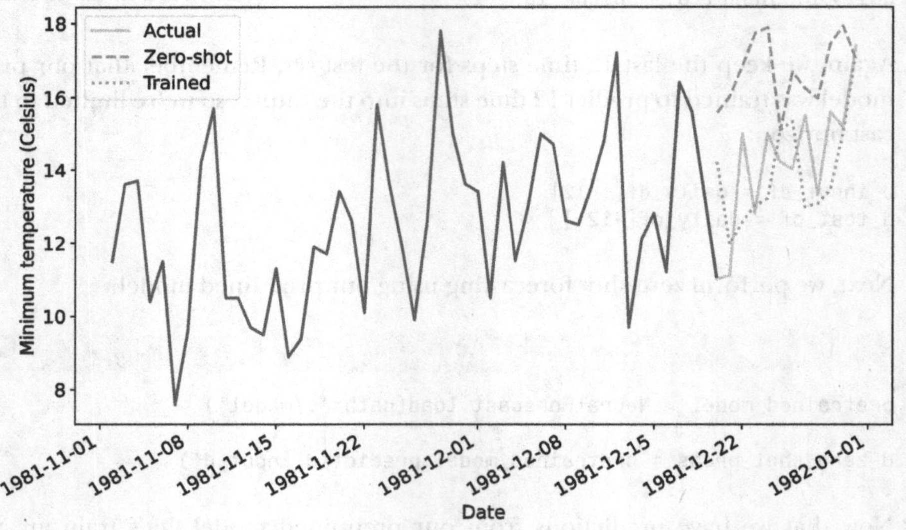


**Figure 2.6 Predictions on daily data using the pretrained model and a data-specific model. The pretrained model fails to make accurate predictions because the dashed line (zero-shot forecasts) never overlaps the solid line (actual values). The forecasts from the trained model (dotted lines), however, are closer to the actual values.**

We can see that the pretrained model fails to make accurate predictions on daily data because the zero-shot forecasts don't overlap the actual values. This result is expected; the model was trained on monthly data only, so it has trouble forecasting the more granular variations observed in daily data. Now the data-specific model generates better forecasts than the pretrained model, an outcome that we can further support by measuring the MAE and sMAPE. Table 2.2 shows the results.

**Listing 2.18 Evaluating each method**

```
d_evaluation = evaluate(
    d_test_df,
    metrics=[mae, smape],
    models=["NBEATS_zero_shot", "NBEATS_trained"],
    target_col="y",
)

d_evaluation = d_evaluation.drop(['unique_id'], axis=1)
d_evaluation = d_evaluation.set_index('metric')
d_evaluation
```

**Table 2.2 Performance metrics of pretraining N-BEATS and training N-BEATS to forecast a daily dataset**

| Metric | NBEATS_zero_shot | NBEATS_trained |
|---|---|---|
| MAE | 2.59 | 1.34 |
| sMAPE (%) | 8.69 | 4.87 |

Here, we see that the pretrained model achieves an MAE of 2.59, and the data-specific model achieves 1.34. Similarly, the pretrained model achieves a sMAPE of 8.7% versus 4.9% for the data-specific N-BEATS. Hence, our trained model represents a 50% improvement on both metrics.

This small experiment shows us that the frequency of the data greatly affects the performance of pretrained forecasting models due to the different patterns that arise when data is recorded at different frequencies. Different patterns also exist depending on the domain of the series, of course. Weather data may display a clear seasonal behavior, for example, whereas financial data is more erratic, with sudden changes in trend.

## 2.9 Understanding the challenges of building a foundation model

So far in this chapter, we've developed a tiny foundation model and explored the fundamental concepts of pretraining and fine-tuning. Although the pretrained model delivered exciting results on monthly data, its performance degraded on daily data.

This result is one of the many challenges involved in building a robust foundation forecasting model. Models trained on a particular frequency usually fail to adapt to data at another frequency. Therefore, the foundation models we explore in this book had to be trained on varied datasets at different frequencies so they could be used in a wide array of use cases.

In our case, our model was limited to predicting a maximum of 12 time steps into the future—another challenge to overcome with foundation models, especially when we're dealing with different frequencies. Suppose that we want to forecast the next week of data. At a daily frequency, the forecast represents 7 time steps, but at an hourly frequency, we need to predict 168 time steps. We can solve this problem by using generative models, which we explore further in chapter 3.

Also, we pretrained and stored a fairly small model using only a CPU and a few minutes of training. Unlike our toy model, foundation models are typically trained for hours or even days, using GPUs and massive amounts of data. These resources are not available to everyone, which is why so few teams are capable of developing foundation models.

Finally, as mentioned earlier, building foundation models requires extensive amounts of data, and in the time-series field, open source data is particularly scarce. This explains in part why we saw foundation models in NLP before seeing them for time-series forecasting: natural language data is more readily available. This makes sense. Humans communicate using natural language instead of numbers, so the amount of textual data vastly exceeds the amount of time series data. Beyond data scarcity, aggregating time-series data from different sources is a colossal task, and foundation forecasting models are better when they train on data from various industries and sources.

## 2.10 Next steps

Our goal in this chapter was to experience the fundamental concepts that power foundation models. At its base, a foundation model is a pretrained model that can perform zero-shot forecasting or be fine-tuned, and we got to experiment with those concepts by building a tiny foundation model.

We also experienced some of the challenges of building large foundation models, but on a smaller scale. We saw the need for training on large datasets with varying frequencies to build a robust model. Although we were able to do this on relatively small computing resources, we can appreciate the fact that aggregating massive amounts of data and training huge models require resources that are not available to most practitioners.

In chapter 3, we discover the first foundation model of this book and one of the earliest models to appear: TimeGPT.

## Summary

- A pretrained model is trained on large amounts of data so that it can be used in another scenario.
- Transfer learning involves using a pretrained model on a dataset that the model has not seen.
- Pretrained models can generate zero-shot predictions or be fine-tuned. With zero-shot predictions, the model never trains on the new dataset. Fine-tuning allows the model to specialize in the task at hand by training for a few steps.
- We can easily build a pretrained model, but it won't perform well on other frequencies, and it has a limited forecast horizon.
- Building foundation models is hard. These models require massive amounts of data and expensive resources that are not available to the vast majority of practitioners.

# Part 2

# Foundation models developed for forecasting

Now that we understand the fundamental concepts of foundation forecasting models, we can start our exploration of the major contributions. Specifically, we start with the models built exclusively for forecasting.

In chapter 3, we start with TimeGPT, which is one of the first foundation models proposed. We learn to forecast, fine-tune it, work with exogenous features, and even perform anomaly detection.

In chapter 4, we move on to Lag-Llama, which is especially suited to research purposes. We discover its architecture and pretraining protocol and learn to use it for zero-shot inference. We also study how its parameters affect its performance and how to fine-tune it.

Chapter 5 explores Chronos, a framework that adapts large language models (LLMs) to time-series forecasting. We use this univariate model for forecasting and anomaly detection, and we also fine-tune it.

In chapter 6, we study Moirai, which released one of the largest publicly available time-series datasets to further the research in the field. We learn to use Moirai with exogenous features and for anomaly detection.

This part concludes with chapter 7, where we discover TimesFM. This model is a deterministic model, which is ideal for achieving reproducible results at all times.

# 3 Forecasting with TimeGPT

**_This chapter covers_**

- Defining generative models
- Exploring the architecture and inner workings of TimeGPT
- Forecasting with TimeGPT
- Detecting anomalies with TimeGPT

In chapter 2, we built our own tiny foundation forecasting model and survived the challenges of building such models. Because we trained only on monthly data, for example, the model struggled to make accurate predictions on daily data. Thus, unless we're willing to spend months collecting varied data and pretraining large models, we should use existing large time models.

In this chapter and the next six chapters, we'll use a dataset that tracks the weekly sales of many Walmart stores from February 5, 2010 to October 26, 2012 as the forecasting scenario for the foundation models we explore in this book. This dataset is released under the Creative Commons 0 license. Although the original dataset tracked thousands of stores, we'll use a subset of only four stores. The dataset also includes exogenous variables such as a holiday indicator, average temperature, average fuel price, average consumer price index (CPI), and average unemployment rate for each store location. We'll use this dataset to compare the performance of different approaches throughout the book. The dataset was specifically selected for the presence of different types of external variables, allowing us to highlight different capabilities for each method because some models cannot handle exogenous features.

Our exploration of large time models starts with TimeGPT, the first foundation model for time-series forecasting [1]. This model marked an important paradigm shift in the field of forecasting because most practitioners were building and tweaking a single model per scenario. With TimeGPT, a single model can forecast a wide range of time-series data and even perform anomaly detection.

> **DEFINITION** A *generative pretrained transformer* (GPT) uses the transformer architecture and is pretrained on a vast amount of data. The model is generative because it can use an input sequence to generate another sequence. The output sequence is produced autoregressively, meaning that each element in the sequence depends on the previous element, allowing the model to generate an output sequence of arbitrary length.

First, we'll define a generative model and explore the inner workings of TimeGPT. Then we'll get hands-on experience performing forecasting and anomaly detection with TimeGPT.

> **NOTE** TimeGPT is not an open source model but a proprietary solution developed and owned by Nixtla. Some details of the model are not publicly disclosed.

## 3.1 Defining generative pretrained transformers

From its name, we know that TimeGPT uses the transformer architecture and is pretrained. At this point, we're comfortable with both of these concepts; we explored the transformer architecture in detail in chapter 1 and got experience pretraining a model in chapter 2. But how is the architecture generative? A *generative model* is a machine learning model that can generate new data instances: a new image, new text, or (in time-series forecasting) a new sequence of numbers.

The transformer architecture, shown in figure 3.1, is especially suitable for generative modeling for two key reasons:

- It can map an input sequence to an output sequence,
- The model is autoregressive. In other words, future values depend on past values.

The input data is a sequence from our time series, and the encoder learns relationships from the input sequence. Then the decoder is responsible for making predictions. Using information learned by the encoder, the decoder generates a prediction, which is fed back to the decoder as an input. Thus, the next element in the sequence is based on the model's previous prediction. This process is repeated until the sequence reaches the forecast horizon.

Hence, we realize that the transformer architecture can take a sequence of data and generate another sequence. More important, it generates the output sequence in an autoregressive manner. *Autoregression* is defined as a regression against past values. In other words, future values depend on past values. In this case, each element in the output sequence depends on its previous element as they are being fed back to the decoder. This is how the model can generate an output sequence of arbitrary length.

To summarize, a GPT model is a transformer that is pretrained on large amounts of data. The model is generative because it is trained to take an input sequence and generate an output sequence using autoregression. This allows the model to generate any output length. By contrast, the foundation model we built in chapter 2 was stuck predicting at most 12 time steps into the future.

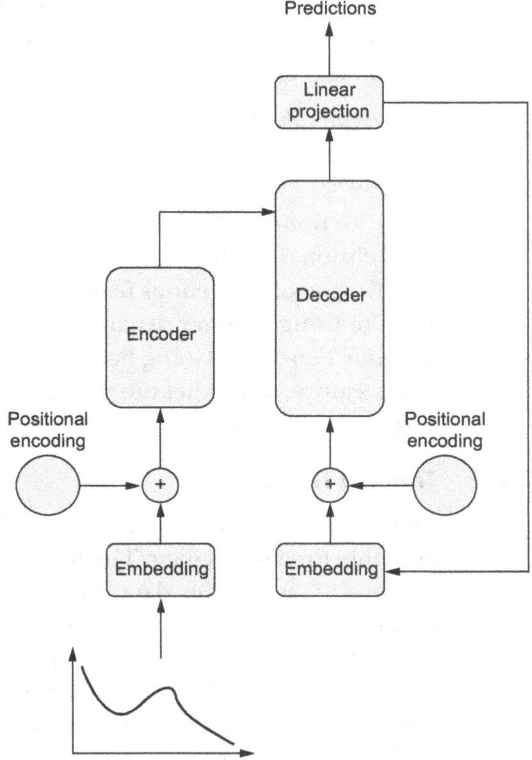


**Figure 3.1 Overall architecture of the transformer model. Notice that the output of the decoder is sent back as an input to continue generating the output sequence.**

## 3.2 Exploring TimeGPT

At its core, TimeGPT is a full encoder–decoder transformer pretrained on time-series data. TimeGPT was trained to handle exogenous features as well as past values of the series. Including exogenous features is crucial because time-series data is often influenced by external variables. Electricity demand, for example, often depends on temperature. Colder weather requires more heating, and hotter weather requires more air conditioning, but during milder days, demand may be lower.

The objective of TimeGPT is to estimate the conditional distribution:

$$P\left(y_{[t+1:t+h]} \middle| y_{[0:t]},\ x_{[0:t+h]}\right) = f_\theta\left(y_{[0:t]},\ x_{[0:t+h]}\right) \tag{3.1}$$

You'll see that $y_{[t+1:t+h]}$ designates the future values of the series over the forecast horizon $h$. Then $y_{[0:t]}$ represents the current and past values of the series. Also, $x_{[0:t+h]}$ represents both past and future values of the exogenous features. Exogenous features can include other series or punctual events, such as holidays. Finally, $f_\theta$ designates the function that TimeGPT is trying to estimate from the training data, where θ is the symbol of the parameters of that function. Therefore, we can read equation 3.1 as follows:

> *The probability of future values of the series, given the past values of the series and the past and future values of exogenous features, is determined as a function of past values of the series and past and future values of the features.*

Thus, we notice that TimeGPT is a probabilistic model because it was trained to output a conditional probability of a future sequence from an input sequence. Also notice that the use of exogenous features requires both past and future values of the features. If we're using another dynamic series as a feature, we must predict its future values to use it in TimeGPT. Going back to the example of electricity demand being affected by temperature, to predict the next 24 hours of electricity demand, we also need the next 24 hours of temperature. In section 3.5, we'll see what that process entails.

### 3.2.1 Training TimeGPT

One challenge of building a foundation model is overcoming the scarcity of publicly available time-series data. The team behind TimeGPT compiled one of the largest collections of time-series data, totaling 100 billion data points, to train TimeGPT. The dataset comes from a wide array of domains, such as finance, demographics, health care, and energy. (The authors do not disclose the specific sources of the data.) This vital aspect of training foundation models increases the models' generalization capabilities and their performance in unseen scenarios.

Figure 3.2 shows different temporal patterns that result from different domains. We can see that data from diverse domains allows the model to learn many temporal

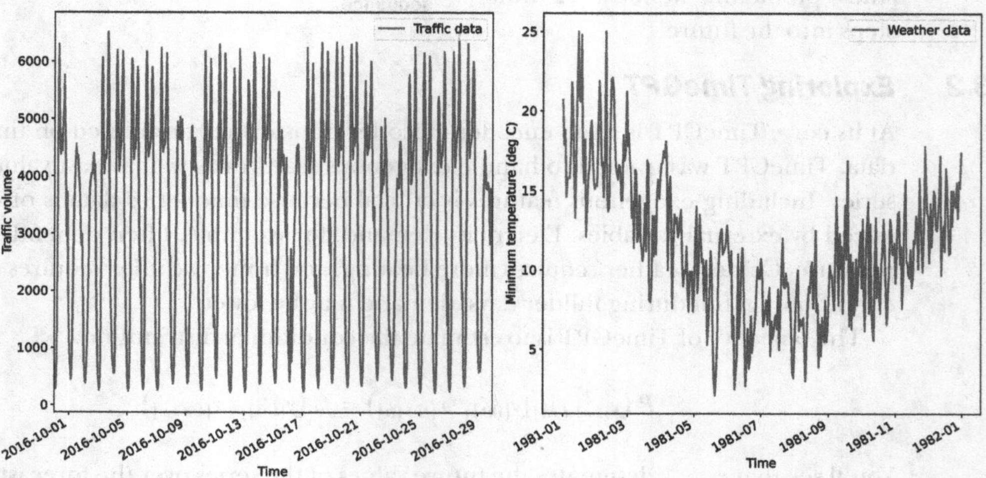


**Figure 3.2 Different temporal patterns appear with different domains. (Left) Hourly traffic data shows a daily and weekly seasonality. (Right) Daily temperature data exhibits a yearly seasonality.**

patterns, with different seasonal lengths and types of trends. On the left, hourly traffic data exhibits a daily seasonality (more cars on the road during the day than at night) and a weekly seasonality (more cars during weekdays than on weekends). On the right, daily weather data shows a yearly seasonality due to the change in seasons.

Furthermore, the training dataset was kept in its raw form. Only interpolation was done for missing values, although the specific technique used for interpolation was not specified. This means that TimeGPT has seen data with noise and outliers on different scales. The idea is to increase the robustness of the model while minimizing preprocessing steps at the time of inference.

Finally, training TimeGPT required multiple days on a cluster of graphics processing units (GPUs). Although the specific number of days and GPUs was not specified, this training reminds us that building a foundation model is an expensive endeavor; using powerful computing power over many days comes at a hefty price.

### 3.2.2 Quantifying uncertainty in TimeGPT

Forecasts from a model inherently have some error margin. The challenge is quantifying that interval. With accurate prediction intervals, we can better assess the risk of the forecast and make informed decisions.

In TimeGPT, prediction intervals are generated using conformal predictions. The subject of conformal predictions deserves an entire book. Nonetheless, we'll cover the fundamental principles of conformal predictions here to show how they generate intervals around predictions, which will help us use TimeGPT more effectively.

*Conformal prediction* is a nonparametric framework for quantifying uncertainty. It's a model-agnostic approach that doesn't rely on any fixed statistical distribution. The only input required for conformal predictions is a confidence level.

To better understand this concept, suppose that we must forecast daily visits to a website and that the point forecast is 300 visits. An 80% prediction interval could be between 200 and 400 visits, but a 90% prediction interval could be between 100 and 500 visits. Usually, a higher level translates to a wider range.

In the context of conformal prediction, the confidence level determines how many times the actual value falls inside the interval. Thus, with a 90% confidence level, we are technically guaranteed to have the actual values fall inside the interval 90% of the time. Thus, 10% of the time, the actual value might fall outside the interval. In other words, the prediction region contains the true value 90% of the time.

Applying conformal prediction assumes the exchangeability of the data. *Exchangeability* means that for a given collection of values in a certain order, we can reorder the values, and the new sequence will be equally likely, as illustrated in figure 3.3.

In figure 3.3, the exchangeability assumption is valid. Suppose that we roll the die four times and get the numbers 5, 3, 4, and 1. Under the exchangeability assumption, we can say that it is equally likely that we could have rolled 4, 5, 1, and 3. The assumption holds true for this example because there are equal chances of rolling any number

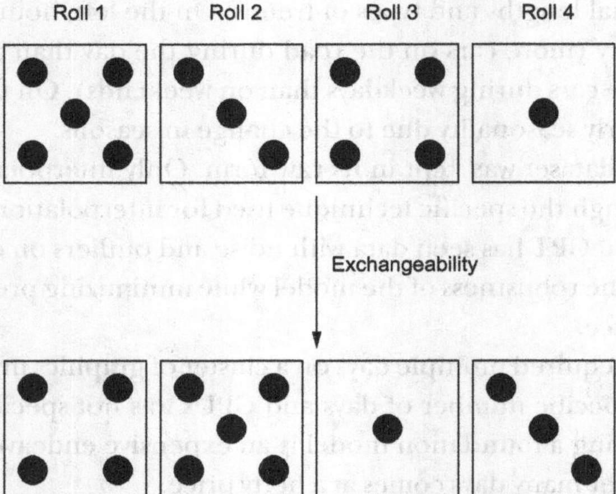


**Figure 3.3 Rolling a die is an example of exchangeability. Here, the die is rolled four times. Rearranging the obtained values gives a sequence that is as likely as the original one.**

in any order, but it doesn't hold true for time-series data. In a time series, future data points often depend on past data points, and theoretically, rearranging time-series data is flawed. Data observed on Wednesday must always come after Tuesday and before Thursday because time series have an inherent order that cannot be modified. Therefore, applying conformal prediction requires an adapted method, shown in figure 3.4.

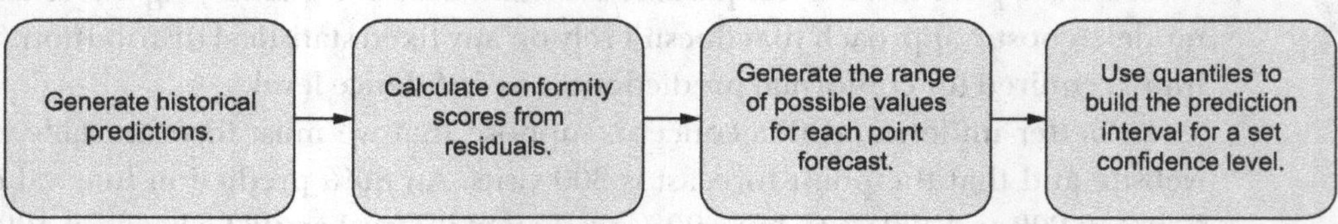


**Figure 3.4 Overview of conformal prediction for time-series data. Historical predictions are used to calculate conformity scores, which are used to generate a range of possible values for each point forecast. From that range of possible values, we calculate the quantiles corresponding to a user-specified confidence level.**

In the first step, we generate predictions on historical data, for which we know the actual values. This step is important because we need to know the actual values to calculate the residuals in the next step. Usually, those predictions are done using cross-validation (described in detail in section 3.3.3).

In short, *cross-validation* is a process in which we predict many fixed horizons within our training set. After every prediction window, the input set is updated to include the actual values from the preceding window, which are used to forecast the values in the next window.

Let's use figure 3.5 as a guiding example as we walk through the process of building conformal prediction intervals. Here, we'll suppose that we're running cross-validation over two windows, with a forecast horizon of three time steps. For each window, we have the actual values. The forecasts represent predicted values, which we do not know. The goal is to build the prediction intervals for the forecasts shown in figure 3.5.

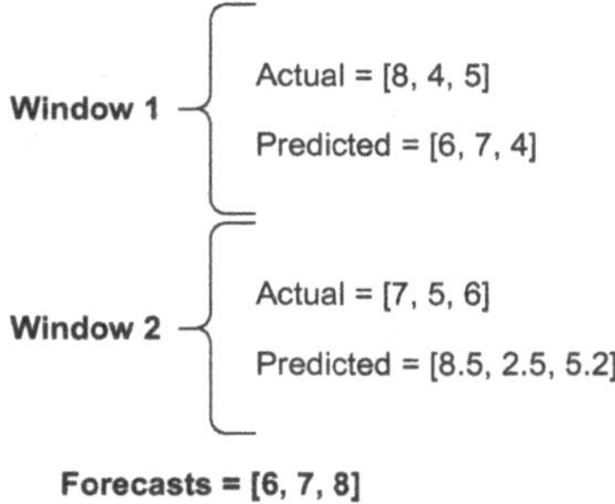


**Figure 3.5 Guiding example to build conformal prediction intervals. Here, we're supposing that we're running cross-validation using two windows and a horizon of three time steps. For each window, we have the actual and predicted values. The forecasts represent predictions; we don't know the actual values. The goal is to build the conformal prediction interval for each point forecast.**

When we have our predicted and actual values from cross-validation, we can calculate the *conformity score*—the absolute value of the residuals, which is the difference between actual and predicted values. Although there are other ways to calculate conformity scores, TimeGPT uses this method.

Let's update figure 3.5 with the conformity scores for each window by taking the absolute difference between actual and predicted values. Figure 3.6 shows the result.

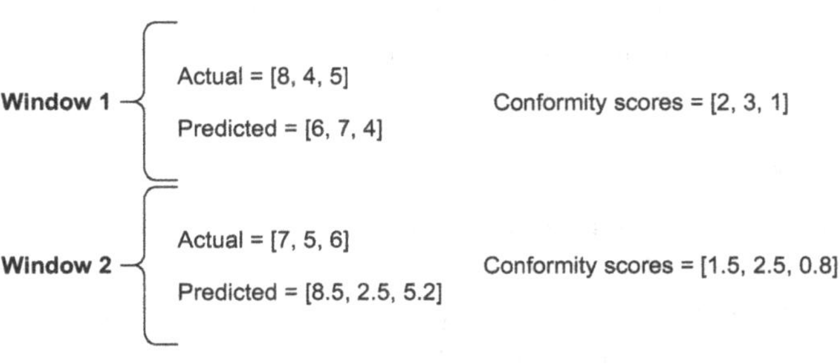


**Figure 3.6 Adding conformity scores for each window. Here, the conformity score is calculated as the absolute difference between the actual and predicted value.**

When the conformity scores are calculated, we generate the range of possible values for each forecast step by adding and subtracting each conformity score. Thus, for the forecast value of 6 in figure 3.6, we build the range of possible values by adding and subtracting 2, 3, 1, 1.5, 2.5, and 0.8, which correspond to the conformity scores calculated from the two cross-validation windows. Figure 3.7 shows the result of that operation.

In figure 3.7, we see that the range for a forecast step is calculated by adding and subtracting the conformity scores. The operation is repeated for each forecast step.

From there, we can build the prediction interval according to a user-specified confidence level. If we specify an 80% prediction interval, the lower bound corresponds to

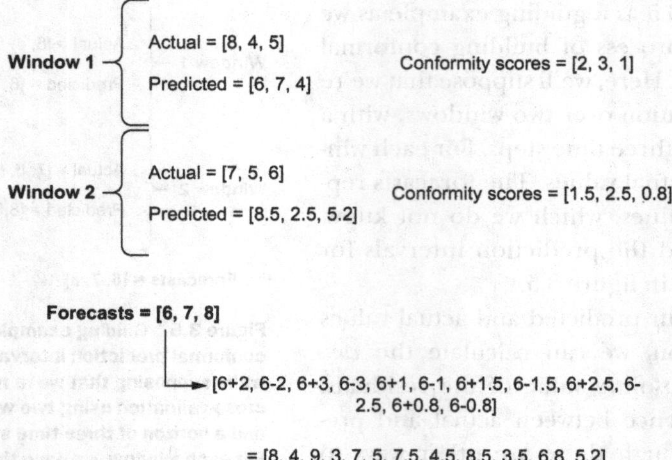


**Figure 3.7 Calculating the range of possible values for the first point forecast. Notice that we add and subtract all conformity scores from the forecast to get its range of possible values. We repeat this step for each point forecast.**

the 10th percentile of the calculated distribution, and the upper bound corresponds to the 90th percentile. For the range of values calculated in figure 3.7, the 10th percentile is 3.55, and the 90th percentile is 8.45. Thus, the conformal prediction interval with a confidence level of 80, for the point forecast value of 6, is between 3.55 and 8.45. The same process is repeated for the following forecast steps.

This example, in essence, is how conformal prediction is applied to time-series data. In TimeGPT, the details are not disclosed, but the general principles are largely the same.

## 3.3 Forecasting with TimeGPT

Because TimeGPT is a proprietary model, it can't be downloaded and used locally. The simplest way to access TimeGPT is to use its API, which requires an access token that anyone can generate. TimeGPT can also be used through self-hosted versions and through Microsoft Azure AI, but those solutions are geared toward enterprises, requiring cloud subscriptions or on-premises hosting machines. Although this approach offloads the need for local computation resources, it also means that we rely on network stability and the reliability of external servers, so there may be some latency between sending data and receiving the predictions.

At the time of this writing, users access the API with the Python package `nixtla` or the R package `nixtlar`. Otherwise, requests can be made to the different API endpoints using `curl`, Node.js, Ruby, PHP, and Python.

The fact that the model is accessed by API means that it is hosted on a remote server maintained by Nixtla, so we don't need expensive computing resources to run TimeGPT. A simple internet connection is enough; all the computation is done on a remote server. That arrangement, however, means that we may fall victim to latency or a server outage beyond our control.

You can get an API key at https://dashboard.nixtla.io. Sign in with your Google or GitHub account to generate the API key. At this writing, Nixtla offers a 30-day free trial period for TimeGPT, allowing users to experiment with the model. Users are automatically assigned to the free plan, which allows up to 50 API calls per month. You don't need to enter payment details to activate your trial, so you won't be charged if you exceed the usage limit. Figure 3.8 shows the general workflow of TimeGPT.

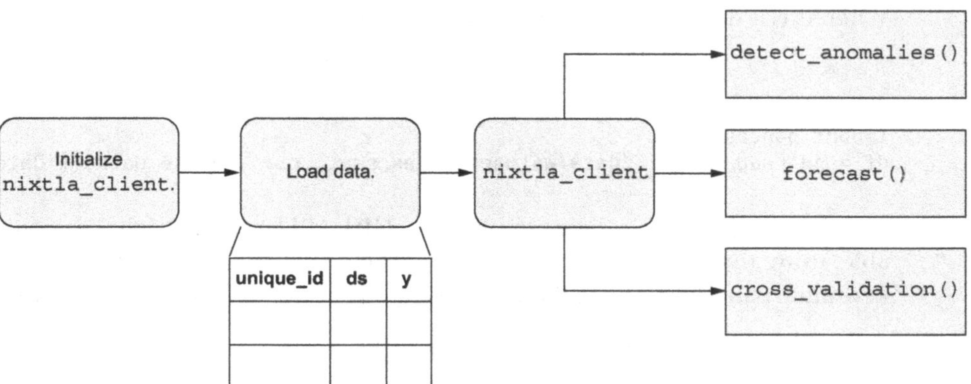


**Figure 3.8 General workflow of TimeGPT. After initializing the client and loading the data, we use the client for anomaly detection, forecasting, and cross-validation.**

First, we initialize `nixtla_client`, the Python object that accesses TimeGPT; then we load our data. In figure 3.8, TimeGPT expects at least three columns: `unique_id`, `ds`, and `y`. The `unique_id` object assigns a label to a time series. If the dataset contains a single series, that column holds a constant value. Otherwise, we can assign different values to differentiate each series in the dataset. The `ds` column contains the timestamp, which TimeGPT uses to infer the frequency of the data. Finally, the `y` column holds the actual value of the series.

> **NOTE** The dataset doesn't have to follow this naming convention, but it must follow the same structure.

When the data is loaded, we can use `nixtla_client` to perform anomaly detection, forecasting, and cross-validation. The dataset is available in this book's GitHub repository, specified by the path in listing 3.1.

### 3.3.1 Initial setup

Before we start using TimeGPT, I highly recommend that we store our API key in a `.env` file at the root of our project so we don't have to write the key inside the code or set an environment variable manually:

```
project_folder/
├── .env
└── my_file.py
```

The `.env` file looks like this.

```
NIXTLA_API_KEY=API_KEY_FROM_DASHBOARD
```

**Replace API_KEY_FROM_DASHBOARD with the actual value provided there.**

When this is done, we can get started and load the dataset.

**Listing 3.1 Loading the dataset**

```
import pandas as pd
df = pd.read_csv('../data/walmart_sales_small.csv', parse_dates=['Date'])
```

Next, we programmatically assign the TimeGPT API key to the right environment variable, using the `dotenv` library, as shown in the next listing. This Python package reads key–value pairs from a `.env` file and sets them as environment variables automatically.

**Listing 3.2 Setting environment variables**

```
from dotenv import load_dotenv

load_dotenv()
```

Then we create an instance of `NixtlaClient`.

**Listing 3.3 Initializing `NixtlaClient`**

```
from nixtla import NixtlaClient

nixtla_client = NixtlaClient()
```

At this point, we're ready to use the capabilities of TimeGPT and its Python client. The latter conveniently comes with plotting capabilities, so let's plot the data to visualize the weekly sales at the different stores.

**Listing 3.4 Plotting data**

```
nixtla_client.plot(
    df,
    time_col='Date',
    id_col='Store',
    target_col='Weekly_Sales'
)
```

**Passes the entire dataset**

**Specifies the name of the column containing the date**

**Specifies the name of the column identifying each series**

**Specifies the column with the target values of the series**

In listing 3.4, we notice that although our dataset doesn't follow the default naming convention that TimeGPT expects, we can still use it as long as we specify the right column names. In this case, the column with the timestamp is called `Date`, the identification column is `Store`, and the column with the target values is `Weekly_Sales`. If no values are specified, TimeGPT looks for `ds`, `unique_id`, and `y`.

**NOTE** For clarity and for more control of the plots, all figures in this chapter are generated using `matplotlib`, but we show the equivalent code snippet that uses `nixtla_client`.

Figure 3.9 shows the weekly sales of four stores tracked by our dataset. Although each store has a general pattern in its weekly sales, with evident peaks occurring toward the end of the year, the more granular behavior is unique to each series.

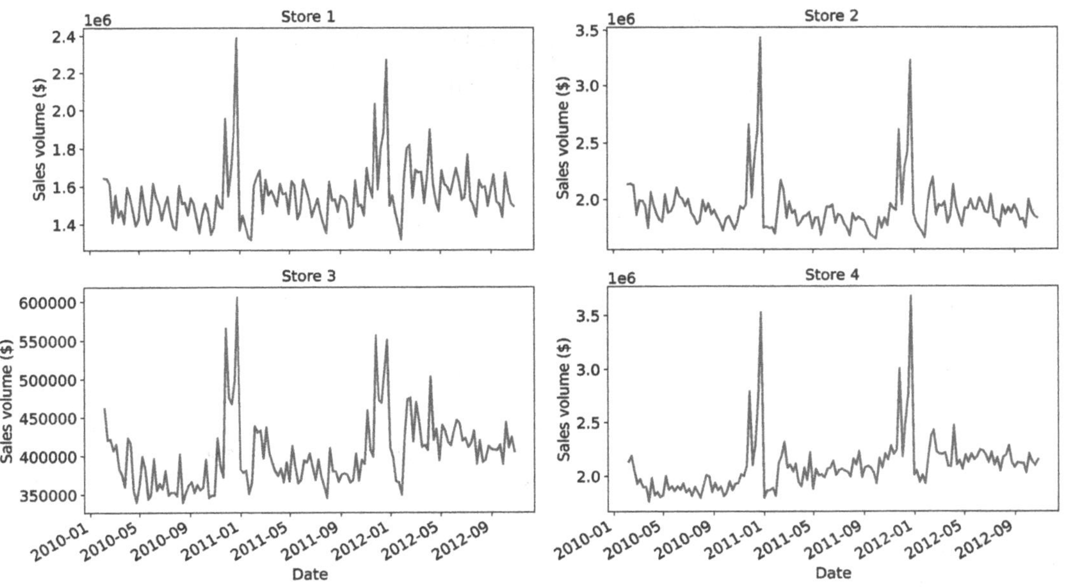


**Figure 3.9 Plotting the weekly sales of four Walmart stores**

## 3.3.2 *Zero-shot forecasting*

Now we can predict each series with a single function call by specifying the forecast horizon and prediction interval. Let's use a horizon of eight weeks and a prediction interval of 80%, as shown in the following listing.

**Listing 3.5 Zero-shot forecasting with TimeGPT**

```
preds_df = nixtla_client.forecast(
    df,
```

```
    h=8,                              ◄── Specifies the forecast horizon
    level=[80],                       ◄── Specifies the prediction interval. Many
    time_col='Date',                      values can be used in a single list.
    id_col='Store',
    target_col='Weekly_Sales'
)
```

That's it! By calling the `forecast` method, we generate predictions for the next eight weeks of sales for each store. Then we can use the client again to plot the predictions, as in the next listing. Figure 3.10 shows the predictions TimeGPT made for each series.

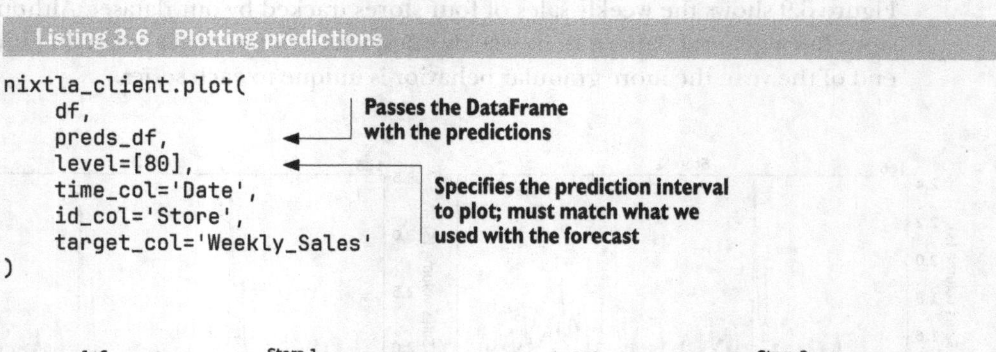

**Listing 3.6 Plotting predictions**

```
nixtla_client.plot(
    df,
    preds_df,                         ◄── Passes the DataFrame
                                          with the predictions
    level=[80],                       ◄── Specifies the prediction interval
    time_col='Date',                      to plot; must match what we
    id_col='Store',                       used with the forecast
    target_col='Weekly_Sales'
)
```

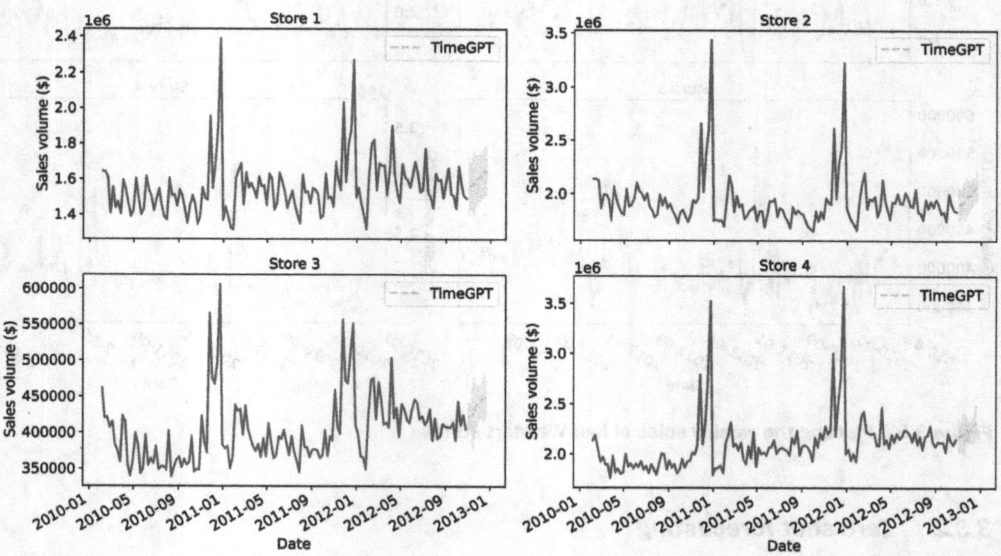


**Figure 3.10 Plotting the predictions obtained with TimeGPT. Notice that the prediction intervals are different for each series.**

TimeGPT automatically inferred the frequency from the timestamp of the data and concurrently generated the predictions for each series. But it didn't perform multivariate forecasting in the sense that it didn't use data from store 1 to predict store 2.

Instead, it predicted each series in parallel. Thus, it may have missed potential interdependencies that could enhance the accuracy of the predictions. In section 3.5, we'll see how to use exogenous variables with TimeGPT.

### 3.3.3 Performance evaluation

Generating predictions with TimeGPT was easy, but we have no way of evaluating the model because the predictions are for future time steps, and we don't have actual values. Therefore, let's split the dataset into an input set and a test set so we can evaluate TimeGPT's performance.

**Listing 3.7 Splitting and forecasting over the test set**

```
test_df = df.groupby('Store').tail(8)
input_df = df.drop(test_df.index)
    .reset_index(drop=True)

preds = nixtla_client.forecast(
    input_df,
    h=8,
    level=[80],
    time_col='Date',
    id_col='Store',
    target_col='Weekly_Sales'
)
```

- The last eight time steps for each store are kept as a test set.
- Removes the test set from the dataset to get the input set

Now that we have predictions over the test set, we can evaluate the model. We use the mean absolute error (MAE) and symmetric mean absolute percentage error (sMAPE) with the `utilsforecast` library, as shown in the next listing. Table 3.1 reports the results.

**Listing 3.8 Evaluating performance**

```
from utilsforecast.losses import mae, smape
from utilsforecast.evaluation import evaluate

eval_df = test_df.copy()

preds['Date'] = pd.to_datetime(preds['Date'])

eval_df = pd.merge(eval_df, preds, 'left',
    ['Store', 'Date'])

evaluation = evaluate(
    eval_df,
    metrics=[mae, smape],
    models=['TimeGPT'],
    target_col='Weekly_Sales',
    id_col='Store'
)

avg_metrics = evaluation.groupby('metric')['TimeGPT']
    .mean()
```

- Converts column to datetime for merging
- Merges predictions with the test set
- Averages the metrics across all stores

Table 3.1 Average performance of TimeGPT in forecasting the past eight weeks of sales across all stores

| Metric | TimeGPT |
|---|---|
| MAE | 54047 |
| sMAPE (%) | 1.76 |

Here, TimeGPT achieves an MAE of about 54047$ and a sMAPE of 1.76%. The MAE seems large because the data is in the scale of millions, so the sMAPE is easier to interpret in this case. This metric is averaged across all stores. Thus, TimeGPT is off by 1.76% on average when forecasting the next eight weeks of sales across all four stores. This performance is achieved with a basic use of TimeGPT, meaning that we didn't perform fine-tuning or use exogenous variables.

## 3.4 Fine-tuning with TimeGPT

In this section, let's use the same dataset but focus on a single store for a simpler scenario. Previously, we generated predictions with TimeGPT. Those predictions were zero-shot because the model was never trained on that particular dataset. One characteristic of foundation models is that they usually can be fine-tuned, meaning that we allow them to train on our data for a few steps to specialize them on the task at hand. In TimeGPT, we can fine-tune by specifying two parameters in the `forecast` method.

### 3.4.1 Fine-tuning TimeGPT

First, let's select data for Store 1 only to simplify our experiment and focus on fine-tuning and its effect on performance. Then we'll create our input and test sets using the same forecast horizon of eight weeks.

**Listing 3.9 Getting a subset of the dataset**

```
sub_df = df[df['Store'] == 1]        ◄── Selects data for Store 1 only

test_df = sub_df.tail(8)
input_df = sub_df.drop(test_df.index).reset_index(drop=True)
```

Next, we get zero-shot forecasts from TimeGPT to act as a baseline, which helps us measure the change in performance when using fine-tuning.

**Listing 3.10 Zero-shot forecasting as baseline**

```
preds = nixtla_client.forecast(
    df=input_df,
    h=8,
    time_col='Date',
    id_col='Store',
    target_col='Weekly_Sales'
)
```

Now that we have our baseline zero-shot predictions, let's apply fine-tuning. To do so, we specify the `finetune_steps` parameter, which takes an integer representing the number of steps to train TimeGPT. Again, a step is an update to the model's parameters after a batch of data is processed.

In practice, fine-tuning often results in better performance, but not always. If we set a large number of fine-tuning steps, the model may overfit and lose its generalization capabilities, resulting in poor forecasts. Also, fine-tuning for more steps means that generating predictions takes more time. A good starting point is setting `finetune_steps` to `10` and gradually increasing that number to see how it affects performance on a validation set. For now, we'll stick to 10 steps of fine-tuning.

Along with setting the number of steps for fine-tuning, we can specify the loss function to use through the `finetune_loss` parameter, which takes any values in `['mae', 'mse', 'rmse', 'mape', 'smape']`. The loss function directs the training of the model during fine-tuning, so setting it ensures that the model is trained to minimize the selected metric. For a quick overview of each loss function and its characteristics, see table 3.2.

**Table 3.2 Characteristics of loss functions supported for fine-tuning TimeGPT**

| Loss function | Characteristics |
|---|---|
| Mean absolute error (`mae`) | Robust to outliers<br>Penalizes all errors equally<br>Same units as data |
| Mean squared error (`mse`) | Heavier penalty for large errors<br>Sensitive to outliers<br>Not the same units as data |
| Root mean squared error (`rmse`) | Same units as data<br>Heavier penalty for large errors |
| Mean absolute percentage error (`mape`) | Expressed as a percentage<br>Heavier penalty on positive errors<br>Avoid if data points are close or equal to `0`. |
| Symmetric mean absolute percentage error (`smape`) | Expressed as a percentage<br>Equal penalty for positive and negative errors<br>Avoid if data points are close or equal to `0`. |

Now let's apply 10 steps of fine-tuning and use the MAE as the loss function, as shown in the next listing.

**Listing 3.11 Fine-tuning TimeGPT**

```
finetune_preds = nixtla_client.forecast(
    df=input_df,
    h=8,
    finetune_steps=10,
```

Sets the number of steps for fine-tuning

```
    finetune_loss='mae',          ◄── (Optional) Sets the loss function
    time_col='Date',                  to be used during fine-tuning
    id_col='Store',
    target_col='Weekly_Sales'
)
```

### 3.4.2 Evaluating the fine-tuned model

At this point, we have zero-shot predictions and predictions from a fine-tuned model. Let's evaluate the performance of both methods to see which produces fewer errors. Table 3.3 reports the metrics.

**Listing 3.12 Merging predictions in a single DataFrame**

```
eval_df = test_df.copy()

preds['Date'] = pd.to_datetime(finetune_preds['Date'])

finetune_preds['Date'] = pd.to_datetime(finetune_preds['Date'])
finetune_preds.rename(columns={"TimeGPT": "TimeGPT-finetuned"},
➥inplace=True)                                          ◄──

eval_df = pd.merge(eval_df, finetune_preds, 'left', ['Store', 'Date'])
eval_df = pd.merge(eval_df, preds, 'left', ['Store', 'Date'])

evaluation = evaluate(                   Renames column to differentiate
    eval_df,                                  between zero-shot and
    metrics=[mae, smape],                       few-shot predictions
    models=['TimeGPT', 'TimeGPT-finetuned'],
    target_col='Weekly_Sales',
    id_col='Store'
)
```

**Table 3.3 Performance metrics when fine-tuning TimeGPT**

| Metric | TimeGPT | TimeGPT-finetuned |
|---|---|---|
| MAE | 75237 | 70822 |
| sMAPE (%) | 2.41 | 2.28 |

In the evaluation table, we see that TimeGPT without fine-tuning achieves an MAE of 75237$ and a sMAPE of 2.41%. On the other hand, TimeGPT with fine-tuning achieves an MAE of 70822$ and a sMAPE of 2.28%. Therefore, fine-tuning resulted in better performances, lowering the MAE by 5.9% and the sMAPE by 5.4%.

### 3.4.3 Controlling the depth of fine-tuning

Besides specifying the number of steps for fine-tuning and the loss metric to use, we can control the number of parameters that are fine-tuned using the `finetune_depth` argument. The argument takes integer values from `1` to `5`, where `1` means that few parameters are tuned and `5` means that all parameters of the model are fine-tuned. Unfortunately, the exact number of parameters being fine-tuned for each value of `finetune_depth` is not disclosed in the official documentation.

Again, increasing this parameter results in more time required to generate predictions because more parameters are being tuned to a specific dataset. It may also result in overfitting if both `finetune_steps` and `finetune_depth` are set to large values. Although increasing both parameters can result in better forecasts, especially when we're dealing with large datasets, I recommend gradually increasing `finetune_depth` and monitoring the model's performance on a validation set.

Therefore, let's increase the `finetune_depth` slightly to `2` to see how it affects the performance of the forecasts. We'll add the performance metrics in table 3.4.

**Listing 3.13 Fine-tuning TimeGPT with `finetune_depth`**

```
finetune_depth_preds = nixtla_client.forecast(
    df=input_df,
    h=8,
    finetune_steps=10,
    finetune_depth=2,              <-- Sets finetune_depth to any integer value from 1 to 5
    finetune_loss='mae',
    time_col='Date',
    id_col='Store',
    target_col='Weekly_Sales'
)

finetune_depth_preds.rename(columns={"TimeGPT": "TimeGPT-finetuned-depth"},
➥ inplace=True)
eval_df = pd.merge(eval_df, finetune_depth_preds, 'left', ['Store', 'Date'])

evaluation = evaluate(
    eval_df,
    metrics=[mae, smape],
    models=['TimeGPT', 'TimeGPT-finetuned', 'TimeGPT-finetuned-depth'],
    target_col='Weekly_Sales',
    id_col='Store'
)
```

**Table 3.4 Performance of tuning more parameters in TimeGPT**

| Metric | TimeGPT | TimeGPT-finetuned | TimeGPT-finetuned-depth |
|---|---|---|---|
| MAE | 75237 | 70822 | 63544 |
| sMAPE (%) | 2.41 | 2.28 | 2.04 |

From listing 3.13, we should see that increasing the number of parameters being fine-tuned results in an MAE of 63544$ and a sMAPE of 2.04%, meaning that we've further increased the accuracy of the predictions. Thus, by setting these three parameters, we can fine-tune TimeGPT, which in this case resulted in better forecasts.

## 3.5 Forecasting with exogenous variables

Up to now, we've used only the time series to make predictions even though exogenous variables are available. In this section, let's use these exogenous variables to generate predictions with TimeGPT.

Our dataset contains exogenous variables including a holiday indicator, average temperature, price of fuel, CPI, and unemployment rate. These variables can affect the weekly sales of stores, so including them during the forecast process may result in better performance.

The tricky part of forecasting with exogenous variables is having to provide their future values over the forecast horizon. Some variables are easier to predict than others. Predicting the next holiday, for example, is easy because holidays occur at fixed dates that we know in advance with total certainty. But other dynamic variables, such as temperature and fuel price, can't be known in advance with perfect certainty, so we must also predict these variables and use the predictions to generate forecasts for our target. If we make poor predictions for the exogenous variables, the predictions of our target will suffer.

### 3.5.1 Preparing the exogenous features

To use exogenous variables with TimeGPT, we must create a DataFrame that contains the future values of our exogenous variables over the forecast horizon. For this example, let's use the holiday indicator, CPI, and fuel price as exogenous variables.

Because holidays occur on fixed dates that we know in advance, we can take the `Holiday_Flag` column from the test set to start creating a DataFrame of future values:

```
future_exog = test_df[['Store', 'Date', 'Holiday_Flag']]
```

The CPI and fuel price can't reasonably be known in advance, so let's use TimeGPT's zero-shot forecasting capability to predict both features. Then we'll add those predictions to the `future_exog` DataFrame, as shown in the following listing.

**Listing 3.14 Forecasting exogenous features**

```
fuel_preds = nixtla_client.forecast(          ◄── Forecasts fuel price
    df=input_df,
    h=8,
    time_col='Date',
    id_col='Store',
    target_col='Fuel_Price'
)
fuel_preds.rename(columns={"TimeGPT": "Fuel_Price"}, inplace=True)

cpi_preds = nixtla_client.forecast(          ◄── Forecasts CPI
    df=input_df,
    h=8,
    time_col='Date',
    id_col='Store',
```

```
    target_col='CPI'
)
cpi_preds.rename(columns={"TimeGPT": "CPI"}, inplace=True)

fuel_preds['Date'] = pd.to_datetime(finetune_preds['Date'])
cpi_preds['Date'] = pd.to_datetime(finetune_preds['Date'])

future_exog = pd.merge(future_exog, fuel_preds, 'left',
    ['Store', 'Date'])                                    # Adds fuel price predictions to the DataFrame
future_exog = pd.merge(future_exog, cpi_preds, 'left',
    ['Store', 'Date'])                                    # Adds the CPI predictions to the DataFrame
```

### 3.5.2 Forecasting with exogenous variables

At this point, we have a DataFrame containing the future values of our features over the forecast horizon. To signal TimeGPT to use these values as exogenous variables, we pass the DataFrame in the `X_df` argument. This tells TimeGPT that we want to use those three variables as features for our target.

**Listing 3.15 Forecasting with exogenous features**

```
preds_exog = nixtla_client.forecast(
    df=input_df,
    X_df=future_exog,          # Passes DataFrame with future values of exogenous variables
    h=8,
    finetune_steps=10,
    finetune_loss='mae',
    time_col='Date',
    id_col='Store',
    target_col='Weekly_Sales',
    feature_contributions=True          # Returns the Shapley values for model explainability
)
```

### 3.5.3 Explaining the effect of exogenous features with Shapley values

When we're working with features, we can use `nixtla_client` to extract their Shapley values to understand and visualize their effect on the final forecast. *Shapley values* enable us to explain a particular model that relies on game theory. In this case, they can help us quantify the contributions of exogenous features to the final forecast. At a high level, Shapley values are computed from the output of the model when no exogenous features are known and from the output when exogenous variables are known. The difference comes from the inclusion of the features.

By setting `feature_contributions` to `True`, as shown in the following listing, we can access them using the `feature_contributions` attribute of `nixtla_client`. This method is possible only when exogenous features are used.

**Listing 3.16 Accessing Shapley values in TimeGPT**

```
exog_shap = nixtla_client.feature_contributions
```

Then, using the `shap` Python package, we generate plots to explain how the features affect our model. We'll start by plotting their average values across the entire horizon in a bar plot, as shown in figure 3.11.

**Listing 3.17 Plotting the Shapley values of the exogenous features**

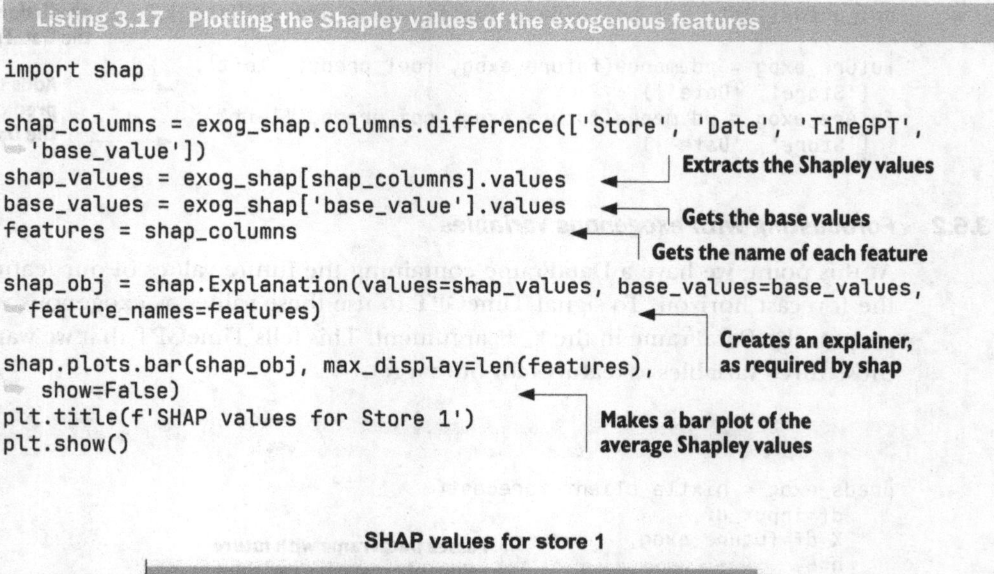

```
import shap

shap_columns = exog_shap.columns.difference(['Store', 'Date', 'TimeGPT',
➥ 'base_value'])
shap_values = exog_shap[shap_columns].values
base_values = exog_shap['base_value'].values
features = shap_columns

shap_obj = shap.Explanation(values=shap_values, base_values=base_values,
➥ feature_names=features)

shap.plots.bar(shap_obj, max_display=len(features),
➥  show=False)
plt.title(f'SHAP values for Store 1')
plt.show()
```



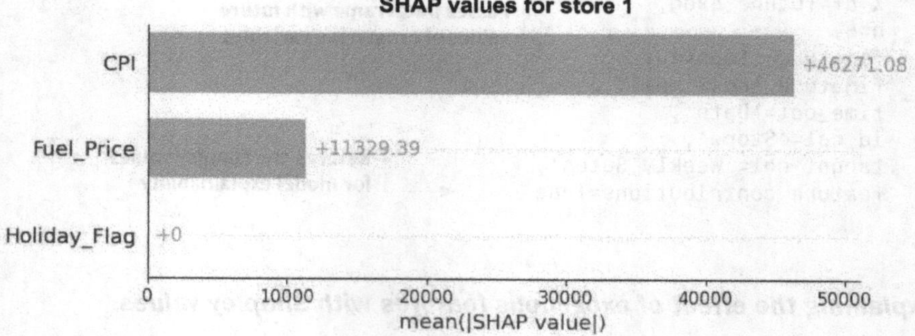


**Figure 3.11 Average Shapley values of exogenous variables for predicting the weekly sales of a Walmart store. On average, the CPI feature increases the base forecast by 46271, and the fuel price feature increases it by 11329 on average. Holidays have no effect on the final value.**

Figure 3.11 shows that CPI and fuel price are the most influential factors in predicting the weekly sales of a store and that the effect of holidays is null. The values represent how each feature affects the base value of the model, which is the value when the model is not using features. In this case, CPI increases the final forecast by 46271 on average, and fuel price increases it by 11329 on average.

One key property of Shapley values is additivity. If we sum the base value with the Shapley values, we should arrive at the final forecast. We can easily depict this forecast in a waterfall plot, as shown in the next listing and figure 3.12.

**Listing 3.18 Waterfall plot of a single prediction**

```
selected_ds = '2012-09-07'

filtered_df = exog_shap[exog_shap['Date'] == selected_ds]

shap_values = filtered_df[shap_columns].values.flatten()
base_value = filtered_df['base_value'].values[0]
features = shap_columns

shap_obj = shap.Explanation(values=shap_values, base_values=base_value,
➥ feature_names=features)

shap.plots.waterfall(shap_obj, show=False)
plt.title(f'Waterfall Plot: Store 1, date: {selected_ds}')
plt.show()
```

Selects a particular date. Waterfall plots visualize only one prediction.

Creates the waterfall plot

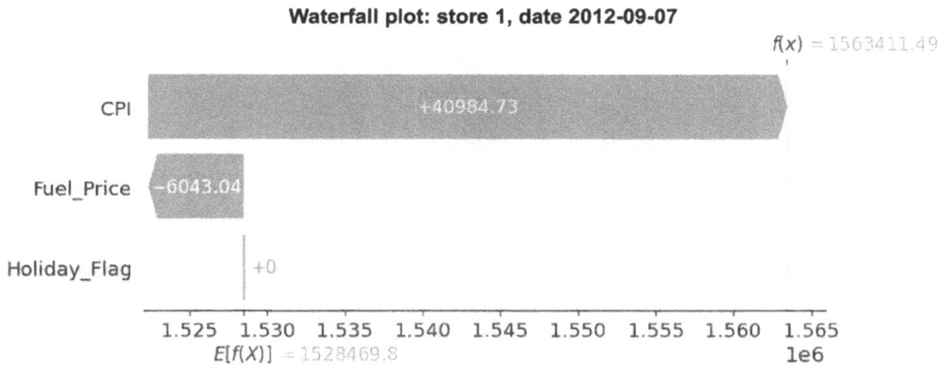

**Figure 3.12 Waterfall plot for the prediction on 2012-09-07. The base value of 1528469.8 is the forecast if no exogenous features were used. Then the fuel price value at that date decreases the prediction by 6043.04. The value of CPI increases it by 40984.73, which results in a final prediction of 1563411.49.**

Figure 3.12 enables us to analyze a single prediction in more detail. We start with the base value—the prediction of the model when no features are used. This value is represented by *E[f(x)]* and equals 1528469.8. Next, we see that the fuel price reduced the forecast by 6043.04 and is shown on the plot as a negative value. CPI, however, pushes the prediction up by 40984.73. Thus, if we perform 1528469.8 – 6043.04 + 40984.73, we obtain the final forecast denoted by *f(x)*, which is equal to 1563411.49.

Thus, we see the additive property of Shapley values in action. The fuel price alone would cause the predicted sales to be lower than the base value. The CPI pushes the forecast sales upward, however. Knowing whether there is a holiday has no effect in this case.

### 3.5.4 Evaluating forecasts with exogenous features

Now we can evaluate the performance of TimeGPT when using exogenous features and fine-tuning. See the following listing and figure 3.13.

**Listing 3.19 Evaluating the performance of each method**

```
preds_exog.rename(columns={"TimeGPT": "TimeGPT-exog"}, inplace=True)
eval_df = pd.merge(eval_df, preds_exog, 'left', ['Store', 'Date'])

evaluation = evaluate(
        eval_df,
        metrics=[mae, smape],
        target_col='Weekly_Sales',
        id_col='Store',
        time_col='Date'
)
```

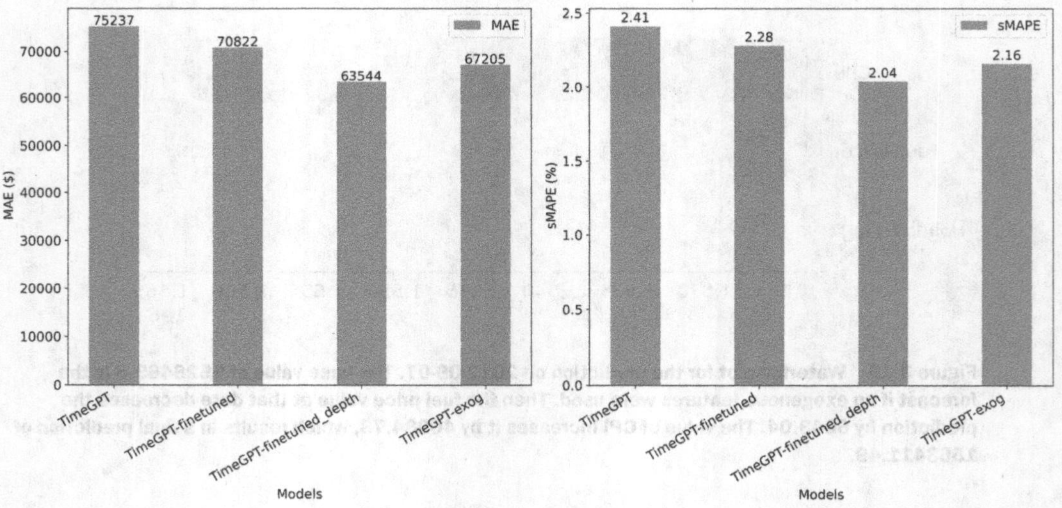


**Figure 3.13 Plotting the performance of zero-shot forecasting, fine-tuning, and fine-tuning with exogenous variables. The lowest values indicate the best performance. Here, fine-tuning more parameters without using features results in the best performance.**

Figure 3.13 shows that using fine-tuning with a `finetune_depth` of 2 produces the best results: MAE of 63544$ and sMAPE of 2.04%. Compared with the zero-shot-forecasting baseline, this result represents an improvement of 15% for both MAE and sMAPE.

Here, using features did not produce the best performance. This is likely due to the fact that we forecast exogenous features, so any error in those predictions is magnified when they are themselves used to inform other forecasts. Also, we used the features in combination with `finetune_depth`, which may have resulted in slight overfitting; feel free to experiment with removing `finetune_depth` to see whether accuracy improves. Even though we used TimeGPT to forecast our features, ignoring them ultimately resulted in the best performance across all methods.

## 3.6 Cross-validating with TimeGPT

We've been evaluating the performance of TimeGPT over a horizon of only eight steps, which represents a small test set, so the reported metrics are not very reliable. Ideally, we test on at least 30 data points to approximate the true performance of a model. To solve this problem, we can use cross-validation, which is implemented for us in the `nixtla_client`.

*Cross-validation* is a process in which we predict many fixed horizons within our training set. After every prediction, the input set is updated to mimic the real-life situation in which we make forecasts, wait to collect new actual data, and produce new forecasts based on the new data. Cross-validation also allows us to evaluate on many windows, creating a more robust estimate of a model's performance. By using cross-validation, we can evaluate TimeGPT's capability to forecast the next eight weeks of sales over multiple test periods, as shown in figure 3.14.

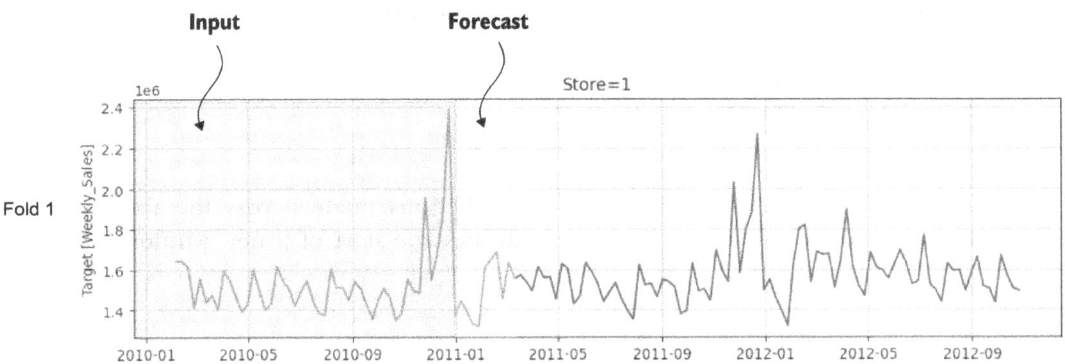


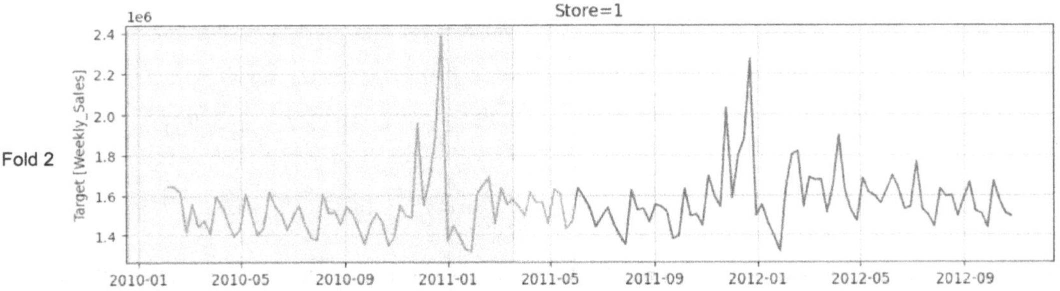


**Figure 3.14 Illustrating the behavior of cross-validation with TimeGPT. A fold designates one round of cross-validation. By default, nonoverlapping windows are used.**

TimeGPT uses nonoverlapping windows during cross-validation, which means that it uses an initial input set and makes predictions for the set horizon. Then the input set is updated with the actual data of the forecast horizon, and the next horizon is predicted. In our case, this translates to forecasting eight weeks of sales and then updating the input set with the next eight data points before forecasting another eight weeks of sales. That way, we can evaluate the model over more testing periods while keeping the forecast horizon constant.

To apply cross-validation, we use the `cross_validation` method implemented for us in the client and then specify the number of windows or folds. This setting determines the number of test periods to be used. Because the windows are nonoverlapping, we can't set a large number of windows; TimeGPT needs an input set to make predictions. The client issues a warning if the number of windows is too large for the dataset. In this case, let's use four windows, which brings the total number of test data points to 32.

**Listing 3.20 Cross-validating with TimeGPT**

```
cv_df = nixtla_client.cross_validation(
    df=sub_df,
    h=8,                          # Sets the forecast horizon
    n_windows=4,                  # Sets the number of windows, which means
    finetune_steps=10,            # we have four windows of eight data points
    finetune_depth=2,
    finetune_loss='mae',
    time_col='Date',
    id_col='Store',
    target_col='Weekly_Sales'
)
```

In figure 3.15, we can plot different predictions made across the four windows of cross-validation. Each vertical line indicates the start of a new window. The four

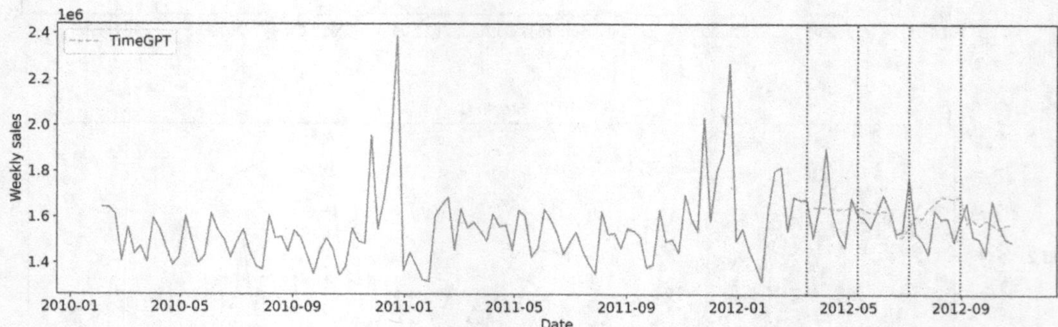


**Figure 3.15 Visualizing cross-validation in TimeGPT. Each vertical line indicates the start of a cross-validation window or fold. There are four folds, which correspond to windows set in listing 3.19. Between vertical lines, we see the predictions made at each fold. The prediction line (dashed) is hard to see because it mostly overlaps the actual data.**

vertical lines correspond to the number of windows set in listing 3.20. Also, folds (vertical lines) are separated by the horizon length, which is eight time steps. Any predicted values past a vertical line use all values that precede it as input.

Next, we can evaluate the performance of the model, as shown in the following listing, and report the metrics in table 3.5.

**Listing 3.21 Evaluating the cross-validation method**

```
evaluation = evaluate(
    cv_df,                          # Uses the cross-validation DataFrame
    metrics=[mae, smape],
    models=['TimeGPT'],
    target_col='Weekly_Sales',
    id_col='Store'
)
```

**Table 3.5 Performance metrics for cross-validation using four windows of eight weeks**

| Metric | TimeGPT |
|---|---|
| MAE | 75179 |
| sMAPE (%) | 2.35 |

Here, we get an MAE of 75179$ and a sMAPE of 2.35%. These metrics are more reliable and representative of the true performance of the model in forecasting weekly sales because we evaluated the predictions over multiple windows instead of a single window of eight weeks, as in section 3.3.2.

> **TIP** Again, if the dataset is large enough, I recommend using cross-validation. It reduces the risk of getting good results by chance, and it represents a more robust evaluation of performance.

We can also use all the fine-tuning parameters with the `cross_validation` method of TimeGPT, such as `finetune_steps`, `finetune_depth`, and `finetune_loss`. The fine-tuning process is done only once on the data that precedes the first cutoff date. Afterward, the model is fixed.

## 3.7 Forecasting on a long horizon with TimeGPT

We've been using TimeGPT for a rather short forecast horizon. TimeGPT can also handle long-horizon forecasting, which we explore in this section. A *long horizon* is longer than a seasonal period. If we have hourly data with a daily seasonality, for example, a long horizon would forecast more than 24 hours into the future.

In the current scenario of forecasting weekly sales, it seems that we have a yearly seasonality, meaning that our seasonal period is 52 because there are 52 weeks in a year. A longer horizon poses unique challenges, of course, because past events may not have a great effect on predicting a far future, and events can arise that affect our series and throw off our initial predictions.

To overcome these challenges, we can use a model specifically designed for long-horizon forecasting: `timegpt-1-long-horizon`. This model has the same architecture that we explored at the beginning of this chapter, but it was pretrained using a longer forecast horizon, so it's trained to learn past information that can help it make predictions over longer periods of time.

To use `timegpt-1-long-horizon`, we pass it to the `model` parameter of the client. First, though, let's create the input and test sets. In this case, we use a horizon of 52 time steps, which corresponds to an entire year:

```
test_df = sub_df.tail(52)
input_df = sub_df.drop(test_df.index).reset_index(drop=True)
```

Then let's make predictions using the base model and the model specifically built for long-horizon forecasting, as shown in the next listing.

**Listing 3.22 Long-horizon vs. short-horizon forecasting**

```
long_preds = nixtla_client.forecast(
    df=input_df,
    h=52,
    model='timegpt-1-long-horizon',     ◄── Specifies the model for
    time_col='Date',                         long-horizon forecasting
    id_col='Store',
    target_col='Weekly_Sales'
)
long_preds.rename(columns={"TimeGPT": "TimeGPT-long"}, inplace=True)

short_preds = nixtla_client.forecast(
    df=input_df,
    h=52,
    time_col='Date',
    id_col='Store',
    target_col='Weekly_Sales'
)
short_preds.rename(columns={"TimeGPT": "TimeGPT-short"}, inplace=True)
```

Finally, we evaluate both models and compare their performance. See the following listing and figure 3.16.

**Listing 3.23 Evaluating both approaches**

```
eval_df = test_df[['Store', 'Date', 'Weekly_Sales']]

eval_df = pd.merge(eval_df, long_preds, 'left', ['Store', 'Date'])
eval_df = pd.merge(eval_df, short_preds, 'left', ['Store', 'Date'])

evaluation = evaluate(
```

```
    eval_df,
    metrics=[mae, smape],
    models=['TimeGPT-long', 'TimeGPT-short'],
    target_col='Weekly_Sales',
    id_col='Store'
)
```

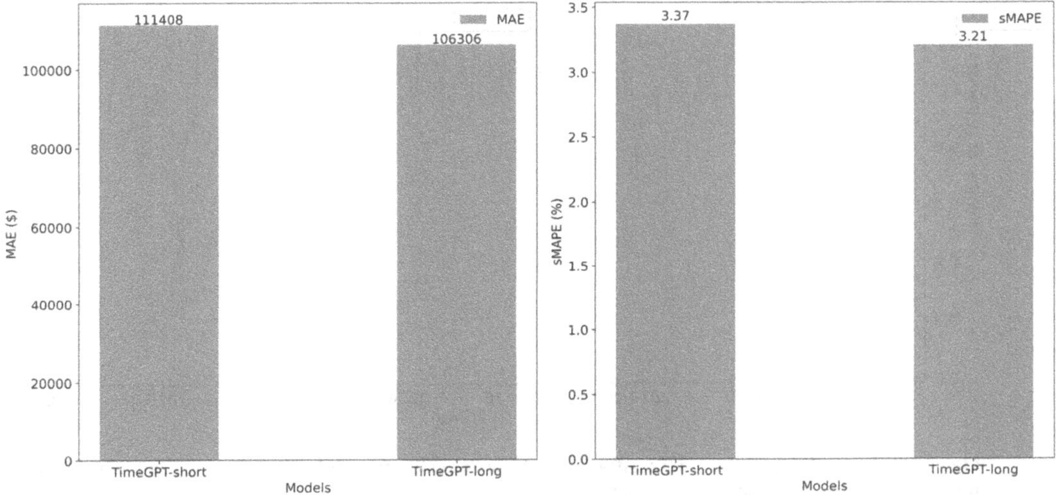


**Figure 3.16 Comparing the performance of the base model and `timegpt-1-long-horizon`. Lower values are better. Here, because we're forecasting on a long horizon, using the adapted model generated better results.**

In figure 3.16, we see that using `timegpt-1-long-horizon` produced better results than the base model. This makes sense because `timegpt-1-long-horizon` was built to handle long forecast horizons. Here, it reduced the MAE by 4.6% and lowered the sMAPE by 4.7%.

## 3.8 Detecting anomalies with TimeGPT

TimeGPT is also able to detect anomalies within time series. It doesn't implement techniques specific to anomaly detection; instead, it generates historical forecast with a 99% prediction interval. If a point falls outside the prediction interval, it is labeled an anomaly. Therefore, it repurposes its forecasting capability for anomaly detection.

The main limitation of this method is that it can't detect anomalies that occur at the beginning of the dataset. This limitation is due to the method's use of historical forecasts. Early time steps are used as an initial input to the model to make predictions, so detection can't be done on the initial input sequence.

To test this functionality, we'll use a dataset of the daily number of taxi customers in New York City from July 2014 to the end of January 2015. The dataset is labeled with the actual anomalies, which are represented by dots in figure 3.17. Let's see whether TimeGPT can detect those anomalies.

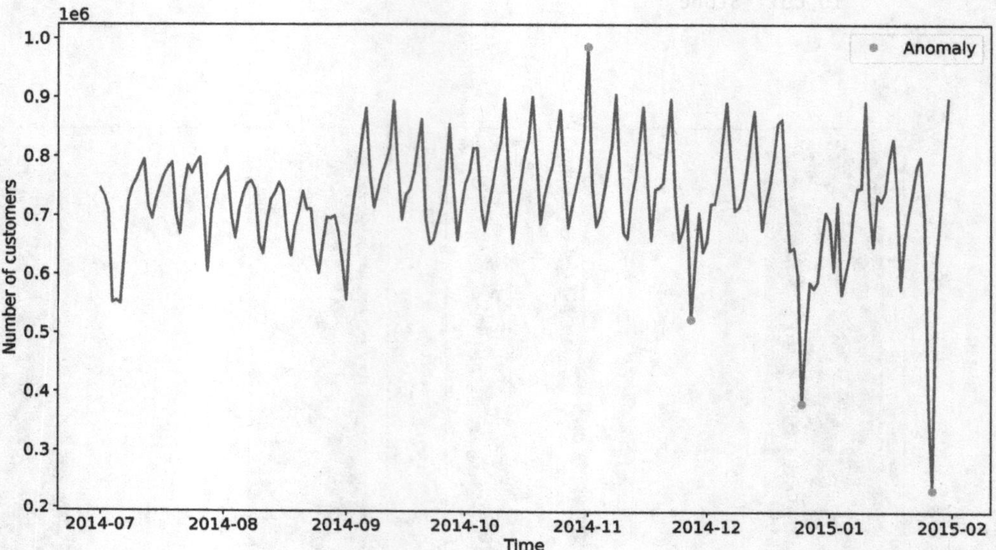


**Figure 3.17 Daily number of taxi customers in New York City from July 2014 through January 2015. The four dots represent the anomalous points.**

### 3.8.1 Detecting anomalies

To detect anomalies, we use the `detect_anomalies` method, shown in the following listing.

**Listing 3.24 Detecting anomalies with TimeGPT**

```
anomalies_df = nixtla_client.detect_anomalies(
    df[['timestamp', 'value']],        # Removes the target column. Otherwise, the column will be used as a feature for anomaly detection.
    time_col='timestamp',
    target_col='value',
)
anomalies_df['anomaly'] = anomalies_df['anomaly']
➥ .astype(int)        # Casts boolean as an integer for easier evaluation
```

The resulting DataFrame contains the predictions from TimeGPT, the boundaries for the 99% prediction interval, and a label that indicates an anomaly. Remember that TimeGPT assigns an anomaly label if the true value falls outside the 99% prediction interval. Using the `plot` method, we can see which points were labeled anomalous; see the following listing and figure 3.18.

**Listing 3.25 Plotting the detected anomalies**

```
nixtla_client.plot(
    df,
    anomalies_df,
    level=[99],
    time_col='timestamp',
    target_col='value'
)
```

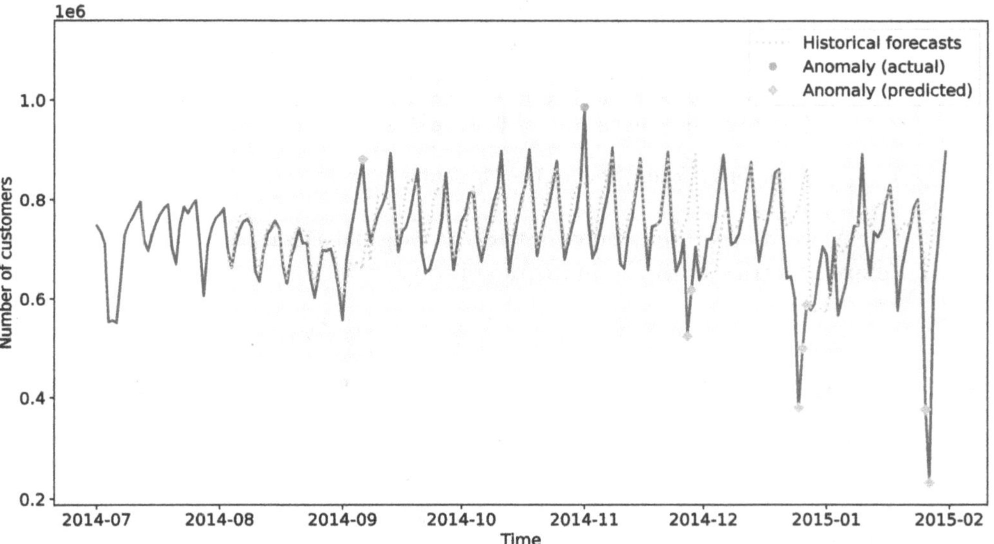


**Figure 3.18 Plotting the anomalies detected by TimeGPT. The dotted line shows the historical forecasts. The shaded area represents the 99% prediction interval. If a point falls outside the interval, it is labeled an anomaly. Diamonds indicate predicted anomalies, and dots represent the actual anomalies not detected by TimeGPT. If a detected anomaly and an actual anomaly coincide, meaning that the model identified the anomaly correctly, only a diamond is shown.**

In figure 3.16, eight points are labeled anomalous, whereas only four points are actually anomalies. In this case, a single anomaly was not detected because we see only one dot in figure 3.16.

Also, notice that we don't have predictions for the entire dataset. This result is normal because the model requires some input to make historical predictions. Therefore, if an anomaly is at the beginning of the dataset, TimeGPT won't detect it.

### 3.8.2 Evaluating anomaly detection

To better assess the performance of anomaly detection, let's define a function to measure the precision, recall, and F1 Score.

**Listing 3.26 Function to evaluate anomaly detection**

```
def evaluate_anomaly_detection(df, preds_col, actual_col):
    tp = ((df[preds_col] == 1) & (df[actual_col] == 1)).sum()

    tn = ((df[preds_col] == 0) & (df[actual_col] == 0)).sum()

    fp = ((df[preds_col] == 1) & (df[actual_col] == 0)).sum()

    fn = ((df[preds_col] == 0) & (df[actual_col] == 1)).sum()

    precision = tp / (tp + fp) if (tp + fp) != 0 else 0

    recall = tp / (tp + fn) if (tp + fn) != 0 else 0

    f1_score = 2 * (precision * recall) / (precision + recall) if
    ➥ (precision + recall) != 0 else 0

    return precision, recall, f1_score
```

Next, we merge the predictions to the original DataFrame and measure the performance metrics, as shown in the next listing.

**Listing 3.27 Evaluating anomaly detection**

```
anomaly_eval_df = pd.merge(anomalies_df, df, 'left', ['timestamp'])

precision, recall, f1_score = evaluate_anomaly_detection(anomaly_eval_df,
➥ 'anomaly', 'is_anomaly')

print(f"Precision: {round(precision,2)}")
print(f"Recall: {round(recall,2)}")
print(f"F1-Score: {round(f1_score,2)}")
```

This code gives a precision of 0.38, a recall of 0.75, and an F1 Score of 0.5. TimeGPT detected 75% of the true anomalies (three of four), but of all the anomalies it detected, only 38% were correct.

It's possible to change the prediction interval to detect more anomalies. When we reduce the prediction interval, more points fall outside it, so more points will be labeled as anomalies. In other words, reducing the prediction interval usually increases the recall but lowers the precision, so many false positives will appear.

Let's test it by setting the `level` to `90`. This parameter can take any value between `0` and `100`, including decimal numbers.

**Listing 3.28 Evaluating anomaly detection with a different prediction interval**

```
anomalies_df_90 = nixtla_client.detect_anomalies(
    df,
    level=90,                    ◄── Sets the prediction interval.
    time_col='timestamp',            The default value is 99.
```

```
    target_col='value',
)

anomalies_df_90['timestamp'] = pd.to_datetime(anomalies_df_90['timestamp'])

anomaly_eval_df = pd.merge(anomalies_df_90, df, 'left', ['timestamp'])

precision, recall, f1_score = evaluate_anomaly_detection(anomaly_eval_df,
    'anomaly', 'is_anomaly')

print(f"Precision: {round(precision,2)}")
print(f"Recall: {round(recall,2)}")
print(f"F1-Score: {round(f1_score,2)}")
```

Figure 3.19 shows that using a smaller interval decreased the precision to 0.20 while leaving the recall constant. TimeGPT detected more anomalies but still missed one, and the detected anomalies are less accurate because only 20% of the anomalies detected were actually anomalies.

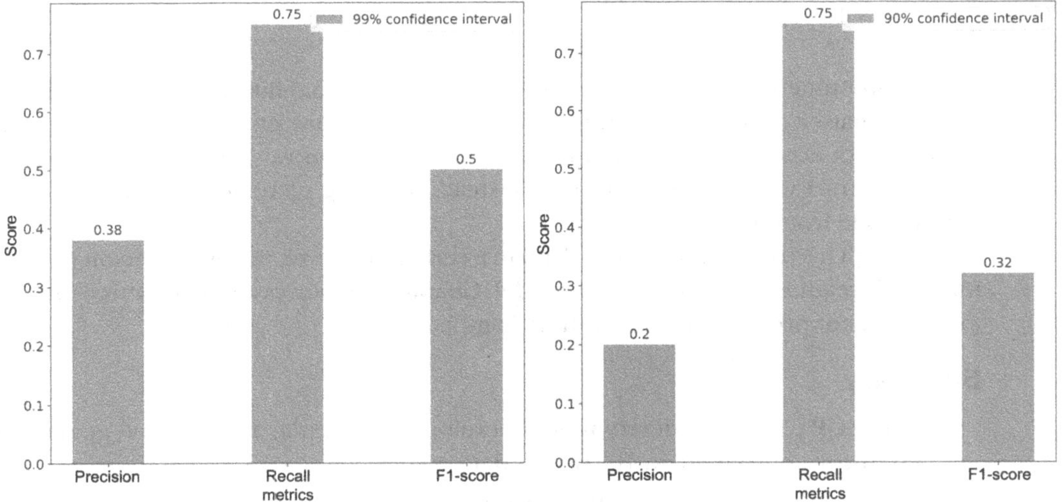


**Figure 3.19 Comparing the performance of anomaly detection using different prediction intervals. Higher values are better. The 99% prediction interval results in more balanced results because the F1 Score is higher than when we reduce the prediction interval.**

This is expected because a smaller interval results in more points falling outside it and being labeled anomalies. The result is an increase in recall and a decrease in precision. Depending on the situation, one metric can be prioritized over the other. If capturing all anomalies is more important, even if it means having false positives, recall is prioritized, and we should use a smaller prediction interval. If we must avoid false positives, precision is more important, and a larger prediction interval is better.

## 3.9 Next steps

In this chapter, we discovered TimeGPT, one of the first foundation models for time-series forecasting. We experimented with many of its functionalities, including zero-shot forecasting, multiple-series forecasting, fine-tuning, long-horizon forecasting, and anomaly detection.

Throughout the book, we will discover many foundation forecasting models, each with its own advantages and disadvantages. Table 3.6 keeps track of the models and their key characteristics.

**Table 3.6 Pros and cons of foundation forecasting models**

| Model | Pros | Cons | When to use |
|---|---|---|---|
| TimeGPT | Easy and fast to use<br>Comes with many native functions<br>Works on any device, regardless of hardware<br>Free plan | Paid product for a certain use<br>May not be available if the server is down | Forecasting on long and short horizons with exogenous features<br>Fine-tuning without local resources |

Take some time to realize how easy it was to use the capabilities of TimeGPT. It was mostly a matter of using the right method or setting a few parameters, which is one advantage of accessing the model through an API. When we have our access token, we can interact with the model quickly instead of setting up a local environment and writing code from scratch.

Although it's free to test TimeGPT up to a certain use level, not every person or organization is ready to start paying for a model. Chapter 4 explores an open source foundation model for probabilistic forecasting: Lag-Llama.

## Summary

- TimeGPT is a proprietary model developed by Nixtla, a pretrained generative transformer trained on 100 billion data points.
- TimeGPT can be accessed via API and requires an access token.
- With TimeGPT, we can perform zero-shot forecasting, forecast multiple series concurrently, fine-tune the model, include exogenous variables, perform cross-validation, and detect anomalies.
- When fine-tuning, we can specify the number of steps and the loss function to be used.
- When forecasting on a long horizon, remember to use the `timegpt-1-long -horizo` model.
- When doing anomaly detection, a smaller level or a smaller prediction interval results in detection of more anomalies, so recall increases and precision decreases. The opposite is true when the prediction interval is large.

# Zero-shot probabilistic forecasting with Lag-Llama

**This chapter covers**

- Exploring the architecture of Lag-Llama
- Forecasting with Lag-Llama
- Fine-tuning Lag-Llama

In chapter 3, we explored TimeGPT, a proprietary foundation model developed by Nixtla. Although it comes with an API that is easy and intuitive to use, it will eventually be a paid solution, which may deter some practitioners from using it.

Thus, this chapter explores Lag-Llama, an open source foundation model published around the time TimeGPT was released. On top of being an open source model, it has key differences from TimeGPT:

- At this time of writing, using Lag-Llama requires cloning the code base, so it's used mostly for quick proof-of-concept or research projects. No Python package or API is available for interacting with the model.
- Lag-Llama supports only univariate forecasting, so only one series at a time can be predicted, and no exogenous features can be included. Although technically, anomaly detection can be done with Lag-Llama, I don't cover it here because this model is not meant to be used in production.

Now that we have a general idea of what Lag-Llama can do, let's explore it in detail and discover its architecture. This step is crucial because if we understand a model's architecture, we can understand its hyperparameters and tune them for our scenario, leading to better results.

## 4.1 Exploring Lag-Llama

Lag-Llama is a probabilistic forecasting model. Instead of outputting point forecasts, it outputs a distribution of possible future values [1].

**Probabilistic vs. deterministic forecasting**

A *probabilistic* forecasting model outputs the conditional distribution of future values given an input sequence. Therefore, the model returns a range of possible future values. A *deterministic* model, on the other hand, predicts single values over the forecast horizon.

This distinction is important because the model is trained to answer the following question:

> *What is the distribution of possible future values over the forecast horizon, given the input sequence?*

By contrast, the output in more traditional deterministic models is a single prediction. Thus, in Lag-Llama, the prediction interval is inherent within the output because we obtain a distribution of possible future values. Then we can select the range of values based on a specific interval set by the user, as we will do later in this chapter.

### 4.1.1 Viewing the architecture of Lag-Llama

The Lag-Llama architecture is based on the decoder-only large language model (LLM) LLaMA proposed by Meta and uses lagged values of the series to create features, which is why it's named *Lag-Llama.* Figure 4.1 shows the overall architecture.

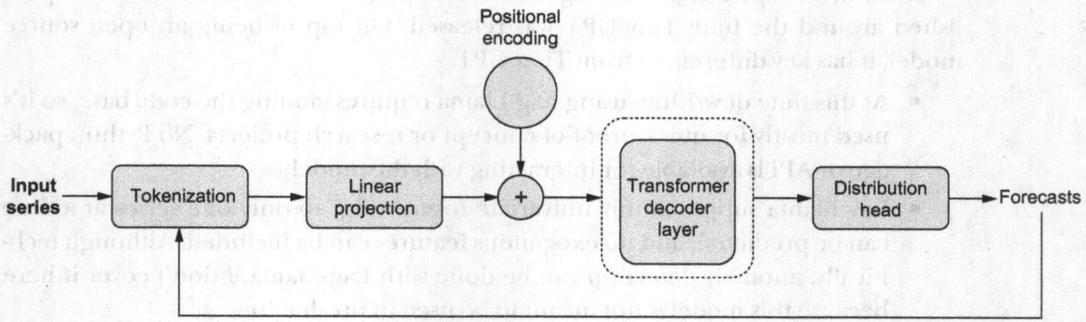


**Figure 4.1 General architecture of Lag-Llama. It features only the decoder portion of the transformer architecture; the distribution head is responsible for generating the distribution of future values.**

First, the input series is sent through a tokenization process. Then the tokens are sent to a linear projection step that maps the input tokens to the hidden dimensions of the attention module in the decoder. Again, positional encoding is used to track the positions of the tokens in the sequence.

Next, the tokens are sent through many decoder layers, where the multihead attention mechanism learns information from the input. Finally, the output of the decoder is sent to a distribution head that outputs the distribution of possible values for the next step. The sequence of possible future values is generated autoregressively by feeding the output back to the start of the model.

We have two main concepts to explore in the Lag-Llama architecture: tokenization and the distribution head. The following sections discuss them in detail.

#### UNDERSTANDING TOKENIZATION IN LAG-LLAMA

Tokenization is a key step in Lag-Llama. In addition to taking the input series, it constructs lagged features, as shown in figure 4.2.

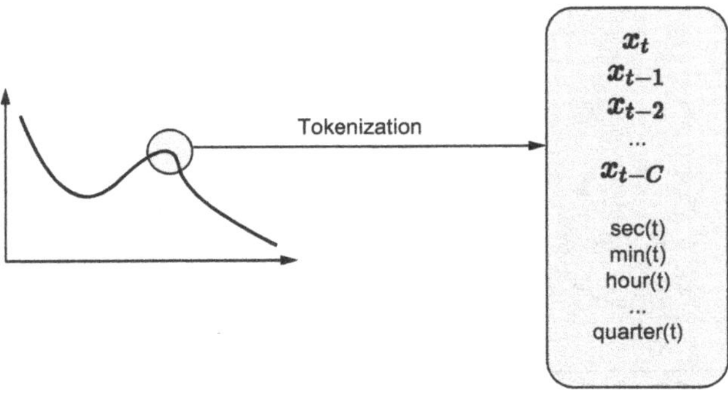


**Figure 4.2 Tokenization process in Lag-Llama. Here, the token of the current time step includes lagged values of the series over a certain context length, as well as date-time features.**

A single token includes past time steps over fixed context length *C*, as well as date-time features at all frequencies, such as second-of-minute, minute-of-hour, hour-of-day, and so on up to quarter-of-year. This technique allows the model to learn the frequency of the time series implicitly because all date-time features but one are constant from one time step to the next.

If we have hourly data, for example, only hour-of-day changes from one point to the next. Day-of-week and day-of-month also change, but only once every 24 steps. This is how the model can deduce that hourly data is being processed.

Although this technique provides many features to help the model learn the structure of the series to make predictions, it involves a fairly large context window because it includes both the previous values of the series and all possible date-time features. This results in longer inference time because more data needs to be processed.

#### EXPLORING THE DISTRIBUTION HEAD IN LAG-LLAMA

Because Lag-Llama is a probabilistic model, the distribution head plays a crucial role during inference: it's responsible for outputting the distribution of the future values. In figure 4.3, researchers used the Student's t-distribution. They chose this distribution function for its simplicity. They acknowledged that more expressive distributions would enhance the model, but those distributions would make training and optimizing the model more difficult. Therefore, they used Student's t-distribution.

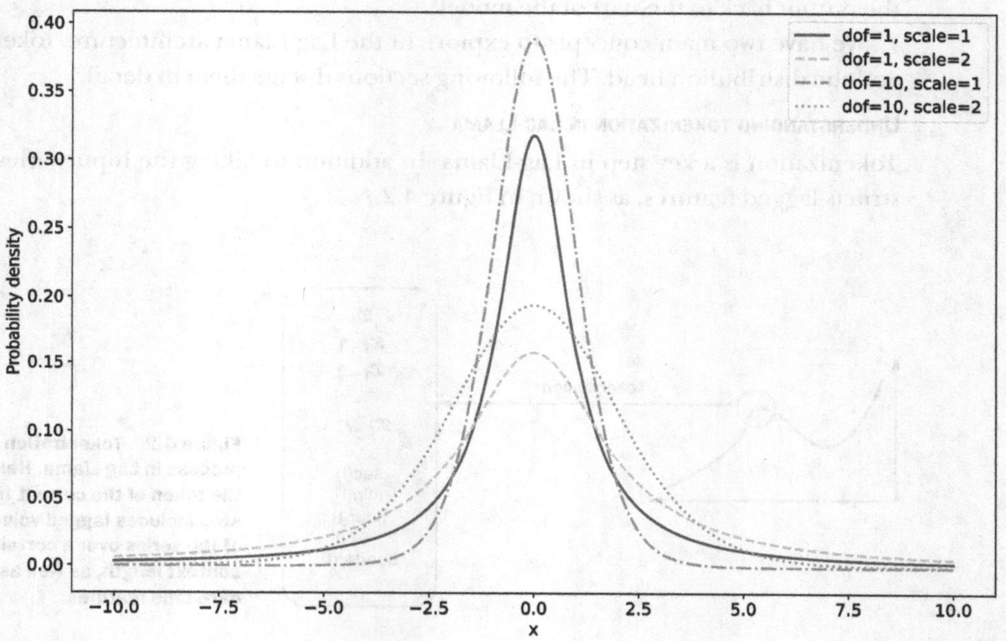


**Figure 4.3 Student's t-distribution with varying scales and degrees of freedom. More degrees of freedom result in a lower peak, while the scale (also called the *standard deviation*) widens the peak and increases its value.**

Figure 4.3 shows a general form of the standard normal distribution, centered around zero. We recognize the bell shape of the normal distribution. Although the figure shows two parameters varying, the distribution is influenced by three parameters: degrees of freedom, scale, and mean. In the figure, the mean is kept at a constant value of 0, but varying the mean will cause the distribution to shift right (if the mean is positive) or left (if the mean is negative). When degrees of freedom increase, the probability of extreme values decreases, and it becomes more similar to a standard normal distribution.

Thus, the distribution head in Lag-Llama outputs the parameters degrees of freedom, mean, and scale to construct the probability distribution of future values. This allows us to generate prediction intervals right away, quantifying the uncertainty of the predictions.

### 4.1.2 Pretraining Lag-Llama

Before we start using Lag-Llama, it's important to know how the model was pretrained and on which dataset, which heavily influences the performance of the model. As we have found, having a large corpus of varied time series is essential for a performant foundation forecasting model.

Here, Lag-Llama was pretrained on 20 datasets in the domains of energy, transportation, nature, economics, air quality, and cloud operations. The prediction length ranged between 24 and 60 time steps into the future. It's important to note that the frequencies of the datasets used were daily, hourly, every 15 minutes, and every minute. Thus, Lag-Llama has not seen weekly, monthly or quarterly data.

Again, this information is crucial because the pretraining protocol heavily influences the model's generalization capabilities. In this case, because the model has never seen weekly, monthly or quarterly data, it's reasonable to expect its zero-shot forecasting performance to be underwhelming at those frequencies, as we saw in our experiment in chapter 2. As a result, fine-tuning Lag-Llama at those frequencies is highly recommended.

Also, because the model was trained with prediction lengths ranging from 24 to 60, the model normally performs best in those horizon lengths. If a particular use case requires a forecast horizon larger than 60 time steps, the quality of the predictions may suffer.

> **Lag-Llama**
>
> Lag-Llama is a zero-shot probabilistic forecasting model. This means that it outputs the distribution of future values. It uses a decoder-only architecture assuming a Student's t-distribution of the predictions to generate prediction intervals.
>
> During tokenization, it uses past values of the series as well as date-time features to inform the predictions.
>
> The model was pretrained on frequencies of every day, hour, 15 minutes, and minute, and on forecast horizons ranging from 24 to 60 time steps.

## 4.2 Forecasting with Lag-Llama

As mentioned at the beginning of this chapter, Lag-Llama is not available through a Python package, so we have to clone the repository and work inside it to use Lag-Llama for predictions. Furthermore, Lag-Llama requires GluonTS, an open source Python package developed by Amazon for time-series analysis and forecasting. In this exercise, Lag-Llama uses GluonTS as an interface for inference, so it expects the input data to be in a format compatible with GluonTS. Note, however, that downloading GluonTS doesn't give us access to Lag-Llama. This foundation model is not straightforward, so getting the setup right takes a bit of fiddling.

### 4.2.1 Setting up Lag-Llama

The first step is cloning the repository to access the model. The following code was run in a notebook:

```
!git clone https://github.com/time-series-foundation-models/lag-llama/
```

Inside the notebook, change the directory to the `lag-llama` folder:

```
!cd lag-llama
```

Then we can use `pip install` to install the requirements:

```
!pip install -r requirements.txt
```

**TIP** I recommend working within a virtual environment to avoid incompatibility with the many dependencies' versions.

Finally, we can download the weights of the model using the `huggingface-cli`, making sure to download the weights in the current directory using ./:

```
!huggingface-cli download time-series-foundation-models/Lag-Llama lag-
➥llama.ckpt --local-dir ./
```

### 4.2.2 Zero-shot forecasting with Lag-Llama

At this point, Lag-Llama is set up locally, and we can perform zero-shot forecasting. We start by importing the required packages. Most important, we have to import `PandasDataset` from GluonTS because Lag-Llama expects this format. We also have to import `LagLlamaEstimator` from the repository.

**Listing 4.1 Importing libraries**

```
import torch
import pandas as pd

from gluonts.dataset.pandas import PandasDataset

from lag_llama.gluon.estimator import LagLlamaEstimator
```

Next, we define a function to perform zero-shot forecasting and return the forecasts. Note that this function is heavily influenced by the notebook shared by the authors of Lag-Llama [2]. In the original notebook, however, the authors used GluonTS's `make_evaluation_predictions` method, which returns only in-sample forecasts. In this case, we modify the function to generate out-of-sample forecasts so we can use it to predict future time steps.

**Listing 4.2 Defining a function to get predictions from Lag-Llama**

```
def get_lag_llama_predictions(dataset,
                              prediction_length,
                              device,
                              context_length=32,
                              num_samples=100):

    ckpt = torch.load("lag-llama.ckpt",
    ➥ map_location=device)                          ◄── Loads the weights of the model that we previously downloaded
    estimator_args = ckpt["hyper_parameters"]["model_kwargs"]

    estimator = LagLlamaEstimator(
        ckpt_path="lag-llama.ckpt",
        prediction_length=prediction_length,
        context_length=context_length,
        input_size=estimator_args["input_size"],     ◄── Assigns the parameters to Lag-Llama
        n_layer=estimator_args["n_layer"],
        n_embd_per_head=estimator_args["n_embd_per_head"],
        n_head=estimator_args["n_head"],
        scaling=estimator_args["scaling"],
        time_feat=estimator_args["time_feat"],
        batch_size=1,
        num_parallel_samples=num_samples,
        device=device,
    )

    lightning_module =
    ➥ estimator.create_lightning_module()          ◄── Pytorch Lightning is used for inference.
    transformation =
    ➥ estimator.create_transformation()            ◄── A transformation is required because the model uses scaling.
    predictor = estimator.create_predictor(
    ➥ transformation, lightning_module)            ◄── The predictor is finally created from the PyTorch Lightning and transformation instances.

    forecasts = predictor.predict(                 ◄── Gets predictions and returns an iterator object
        dataset=dataset,
    )

    forecasts = list(forecasts)                    ◄── Creates a list from the iterator object to get all the predictions

    return forecasts
```

Let's break down the `get_lag_llama_predictions` function to understand each step:

1. We set five inputs for the function:
   a. The dataset containing the data we want to predict
   b. The length of the forecast horizon
   c. The device (which we can set if a graphics processing unit [GPU] or CPU is available)

- **d** The context length. We set this to 32, which is the size of the input window that Lag-Llama will consider. (By default, Lag-Llama was trained on a context window of 32 time steps, but users can change that value.)
- **e** The number of samples to be used to generate the output distribution. A setting of 100 usually is a good starting point. Increasing the number of samples will generate a more precise distribution.

**2** Inside the function, we extract the model weights and parameters, which are assigned inside `LagLlamaEstimator`. These parameters were optimized during Lag-Llama's pretraining of Lag-Llama, so we don't modify them; we assign them when initializing `estimator`.

**3** We use PyTorch Lightning to create the estimator. PyTorch Lightning is an open source deep learning framework that simplifies putting deep learning models in production. Here, we use it to create an instance of an estimator followed by a transformation because Lag-Llama uses scaling.

**4** We create an instance of a predictor. Note that decoupling the estimator and predictor is logic from GluonTS; the estimator can be trained once, and the predictor can be used multiple times afterward.

**5** To obtain the forecasts, we use the `predict` method from the predictor instance and pass the dataset. Here, in accordance with GluonTS, this method returns an iterator. We have to transform this iterator into a list to get all the predictions over the horizon.

#### READING THE DATA

With the `get_lag_llama_predictions` function ready, using Lag-Llama for forecasting will be easier. Let's load the dataset containing the weekly sales data for Walmart stores, which we used in chapter 3. We'll use this same dataset all the way to chapter 9 to ensure comparable performances by all the methods we'll explore in this book.

**Listing 4.3 Reading the dataset**

```
df = pd.read_csv('../../data/walmart_sales_small.csv', parse_dates=['Date'])
```

Lag-Llama expects the input to be in a format compatible with GluonTS, and the values must be encoded as 32-bit floating numbers, as shown in the following listing.

**Listing 4.4 Formatting input for Lag-Llama**

```
df['Weekly_Sales'] = df['Weekly_Sales']
➥.astype('float32')                          ◄── Ensures that the type is float32
dataset = PandasDataset.from_long_dataframe(df, target="Weekly_Sales",
➥item_id="Store")                ◄── Loads the dataset in a format
                                      compatible with GluonTS
```

Now we must define our forecasting horizon. To stay consistent with chapter 3, let's use a horizon of eight time steps. Furthermore, we must specify the device on which to run the model. Here, we run it on the CPU. (If you have a GPU, you can change the value to `cuda:0`. The number specifies which GPU to use in case many GPUs are available.)

**Listing 4.5 Defining the horizon and device for inference**

```
prediction_length = 8
device = torch.device("cpu")        ◄── Use torch.device("cuda:0") if you have a GPU.
```

#### ZERO-SHOT FORECASTING

Everything is set to get the predictions for the next eight weeks.

**Listing 4.6 Zero-shot forecasting with Lag-Llama**

```
forecasts = get_lag_llama_predictions(dataset, prediction_length, device)
```

Remember that Lag-Llama is a probabilistic model, so it outputs a distribution of future values. Here, if we study the shape of the forecasts for the first store using `forecasts[0].samples.shape`, we get a 2D array of shape (100, 8). This array indicates that we have 100 samples from the distribution of the future values for the next eight time steps.

Let's write a function that extracts the median and the upper and lower bounds of the distribution according to an interval set by the user. We also construct the timestamp for the future values and return a DataFrame.

**Listing 4.7 Function to format the output as a DataFrame**

```
import numpy as np

def get_median_and_ci(data,
                      start_date,
                      horizon,
                      freq,
                      id,
                      confidence=0.95):

    n_samples, n_timesteps = data.shape

    medians = np.median(data, axis=0)        ◄── Gets the median value of the distribution

    lower_percentile = (1 - confidence) / 2 * 100    ◄── Calculates the percentiles
    upper_percentile = (1 + confidence) / 2 * 100        according to the set confidence level


    lower_bounds =
    ➥ np.percentile(data, lower_percentile,
    ➥  axis=0)                              ◄── Gets the lower and upper bounds
    upper_bounds = np.percentile(data, upper_percentile, axis=0)
```

```
    pred_dates = pd.date_range(start=start_date, periods=horizon,
    ➥ freq=freq)
    formatted_dates = pred_dates.strftime('%m-%d-%Y').tolist()

    df = pd.DataFrame({
        'Date': formatted_dates,
        'Store': id,
        'Lag-Llama': medians,
        f'Lag-Llama-lo-{int(confidence*100)}': lower_bounds,
        f'Lag-Llama-hi-{int(confidence*100)}': upper_bounds
    })

    return df
```

Generates the list of future timestamps for the forecasts

In the get_median_and_ci function, we pass the forecasts from Lag-Llama, along with the start date of the first forecast, the length of the horizon, the frequency of our data, the identifier of the predicted series, and the confidence level (set to 95% by default).

The function calculates the median value of the distribution of future values, which we consider the point prediction of Lag-Llama. We use the median instead of the mean to prevent being influenced by extreme values in the output. Then we get the upper and lower bounds of the interval set by the confidence level and return everything nicely formatted in a DataFrame. Next, let's use this function to extract the predictions for each store.

**Listing 4.8 Formatting predictions**

```
preds = [
    get_median_and_ci(
        data=forecasts[i].samples,
        start_date='11-02-2012',
        horizon=8,
        freq='W-FRI',
        id=i+1
    )
    for i in range(4)
]

preds_df = pd.concat(preds, axis=0, ignore_index=True)
preds_df['Date'] = pd.to_datetime(preds_df['Date'])
```

We can plot the forecasts that Lag-Llama generates as shown in figure 4.4.

In the figure, the dashed line represents the median of the distribution, which can be considered the point forecast. The shaded area represents the 95% prediction interval.

> **NOTE** These predictions are out of sample, so we can't compare them with actual values to measure the performance of Lag-Llama.

As we have found, forecasting with Lag-Llama is a bit convoluted. We had to clone the repository, work inside it, and define many functions manually to abstract many steps required to obtain the final results.

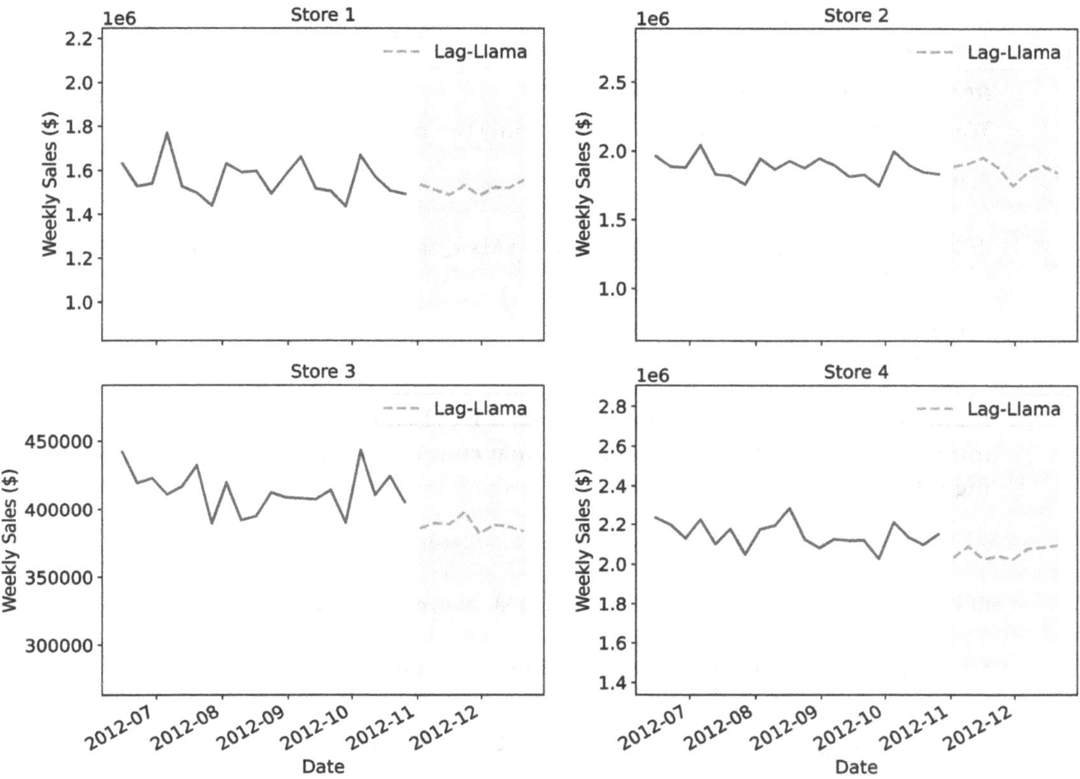


**Figure 4.4 Zero-shot predictions from Lag-Llama for the next eight weeks of sales at four Walmart stores. The shaded area represents the 95% prediction interval.**

### 4.2.3 Changing the context length in Lag-Llama

Lag-Llama's performance is also influenced by context length, which represents the length of the input sequence. In this section, we explore how changing the context length affects performance in Lag-Llama.

The context length defines the length of the input window. Usually, it's a good idea to tune this parameter because depending on the dataset, a longer or shorter input window will affect the model's performance. If our historical data shows a clear pattern with no sudden disturbances, for example, using a longer context length can improve the model's performance. On the other hand, if a recent anomaly occurred in our dataset, it may be a good idea to shorten the input sequence. Ultimately, there's no hard rule about selecting input length, so let's set up an experiment to find the right length for a particular scenario.

In the following experiment, we'll restrict our dataset to one store. Also, we'll run cross-validation with Lag-Llama on four windows of eight weeks so that we reproduce the conditions used in TimeGPT in chapter 3. That way, we can get comparable performances among models.

#### READING THE DATA FOR ONE STORE ONLY

We read the data again, but restrict it to only the first store of the dataset.

**Listing 4.9 Reading and splitting the data**

```
df = pd.read_csv('../../data/walmart_sales_small.csv', parse_dates=['Date'])
df = df[df['Store'] == 1]

input_df = df[:-32]
test_df = df[-32:]
```

Before making predictions, remember that Lag-Llama requires data as 32-bit floating numbers, and that data must be in a format compatible with GluonTS as shown in listing 4.10.

**Listing 4.10 Formatting the input**

```
df['Weekly_Sales'] = df['Weekly_Sales'].astype('float32')
```

We keep the forecast horizon to eight, and again, we use the CPU:

```
prediction_length = 8
device = torch.device("cpu")     ◄── Change to "cuda :0" if a GPU is available.
```

#### CROSS-VALIDATING WITH LAG-LLAMA

Now let's define a function to perform cross-validation. This function uses nonoverlapping cross-validation windows, as in TimeGPT, so we'll get comparable results. It also reuses the `get_lag_llama_predictions` and `get_median_and_ci` functions.

**Listing 4.11 Cross-validating**

```
def cross_validation_lagllama(df, h, n_windows, device, context_length,
    confidence=0.95):
                                         Initializes a list to store all
    all_forecasts = []              ◄── forecasts across all windows

    for i in range(n_windows, 0, -1):     ◄── Loops through all windows
        input_ds = PandasDataset
          .from_long_dataframe(      ◄── Gets the input for a particular window
            df[:-(h * i)],
            target="Weekly_Sales",
            item_id="Store"
        )
                                                          Makes predictions
                                                          for that window
        forecasts = get_lag_llama_predictions(input_ds, h, device,
          context_length)                             ◄──
```

```
        start_date = df.iloc[-(h * i)]['Date']          # Gets the cutoff date for that window

        forecast_df = get_median_and_ci(               # Extracts the median and prediction intervals bounds
            data=forecasts[0].samples,
            start_date=start_date,
            horizon=h,
            freq='W-FRI',
            id=1,
            confidence=confidence
        )
        all_forecasts.append(forecast_df)              # Appends the forecasts to the list

    final_df = pd.concat(all_forecasts, axis=0,
    ➥ ignore_index=True)                               # Creates a DataFrame with all forecasts
    final_df = final_df.sort_values('Date')            # Sorts by date to put everything in chronological order

    return final_df
```

We can use the cross-validation function defined in listing 4.11 to predict over four windows of eight weeks as we did in chapter 3. Here, we also vary `context_length` to see how it affects the model's performance.

**Listing 4.12 Making predictions with different context lengths**

```
fcsts_16 = cross_validation_lagllama(
    df=df,
    h=8,
    n_windows=4,
    device=device,
    context_length=16
)

fcsts_32 = cross_validation_lagllama(
    df=df,
    h=8,
    n_windows=4,
    device=device,
    context_length=32
)

fcsts_64 = cross_validation_lagllama(
    df=df,
    h=8,
    n_windows=4,
    device=device,
    context_length=64
)
```

#### Evaluating performance

At this point, we have predictions for each context length, obtained through cross-validation, using four windows and a horizon of eight weeks. Now we can evaluate the model's performance.

**Listing 4.13 Evaluating the performance of Lag-Llama for each context length**

```
from utilsforecast.losses import mae, smape
from utilsforecast.evaluation import evaluate

eval_df = test_df[['Date', 'Store', 'Weekly_Sales']].copy()

eval_df.loc[:, 'Lag-Llama(16)'] = fcsts_16['Lag-Llama'].values
eval_df.loc[:, 'Lag-Llama(32)'] = fcsts_32['Lag-Llama'].values
eval_df.loc[:, 'Lag-Llama(64)'] = fcsts_64['Lag-Llama'].values

evaluation = evaluate(
    eval_df,
    metrics=[mae, smape],
    target_col='Weekly_Sales',
    id_col='Store',
    time_col='Date'
)
```

Figure 4.5 shows Lag-Llama's performance with each context length. In this case, a context length of 64 results in the best performance because it achieves the lowest metrics in cross-validation.

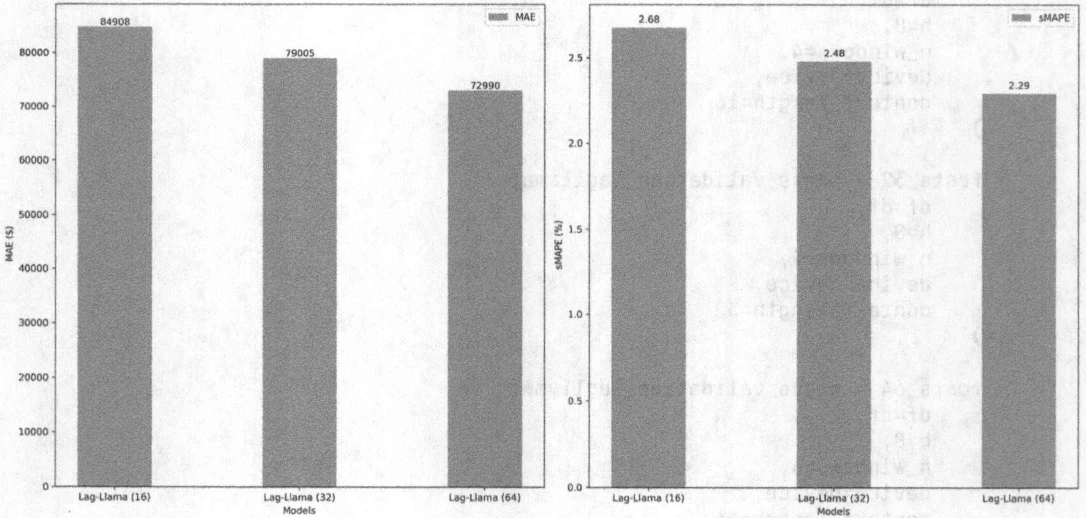


**Figure 4.5 Mean absolute error (MAE) and symmetric mean absolute percentage error (sMAPE) for each context length. Lower values are better. Here, a context length of 64 time steps generated the best results.**

Optionally, we can plot the best forecasts obtained using a context length of 64, as shown in figure 4.6.

**Listing 4.14 Evaluating the model for each context length**

```
from utilsforecast.losses import mae, smape
from utilsforecast.evaluation import evaluate

eval_df = test_df[['Date', 'Store', 'Weekly_Sales']].copy()

eval_df.loc[:, 'Lag-Llama(16)'] = preds_16['Lag-Llama'].values
eval_df.loc[:, 'Lag-Llama(32)'] = preds_32['Lag-Llama'].values
eval_df.loc[:, 'Lag-Llama(64)'] = preds_64['Lag-Llama'].values

evaluation = evaluate(
    eval_df,
    metrics=[mae, smape],
    target_col='Weekly_Sales',
    id_col='Store',
    time_col='Date'
)
```

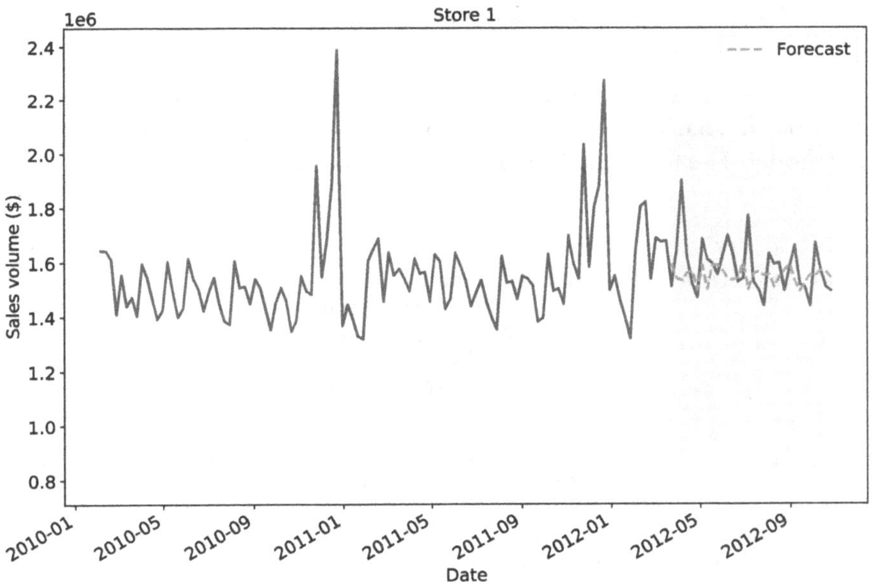


**Figure 4.6 Plotting the best-performing forecasts from Lag-Llama using a context length of 64**

Figure 4.6 shows that the forecasts obtained using a context window of 64 time steps mostly overlap the true values of the series. The prediction intervals are large, however, which is one of the downsides of assuming a Student's t-distribution.

## 4.3 Fine-tuning Lag-Llama

A common way to improve the performance of a foundation model is to fine-tune it. This process trains the model for a few steps on a specific dataset, generally resulting in more accurate forecasts.

Because we're working with the model locally, fine-tuning it requires a fair amount of computing power. To ensure that everyone can reproduce the following experiment, we use Google Colab, which gives us access to a free instance with a T4 GPU. That way, we can perform fine-tuning for free and in a fraction of the time it would take on a CPU.

### 4.3.1 Handling initial setup

Because we're working in Colab, we need to redo the steps to set up Lag-Llama, including the following:

- Cloning the repository
- Installing the dependencies
- Downloading the model's weights and parameters
- Including the `get_lag_llama_prediction`, `get_median_and_ci`, and `calculate_mae_smape` functions

Note that we slightly modify the `get_lag_llama_prediction` function to specify a predictor object. That way, we can reuse this function to get predictions from the fine-tuned model. The following listing shows the modified function.

**Listing 4.15 Function to get predictions from the fine-tuned model**

```
def get_lag_llama_predictions(dataset,
                              prediction_length,
                              context_length=64,
                              device="cuda",
                              num_samples=100,
                              predictor=None):

    ckpt = torch.load("lag-llama.ckpt", map_location=device)
    estimator_args = ckpt["hyper_parameters"]["model_kwargs"]

    estimator = LagLlamaEstimator(
        ckpt_path="lag-llama.ckpt",
        prediction_length=prediction_length,
        context_length=context_length,
        input_size=estimator_args["input_size"],
        n_layer=estimator_args["n_layer"],
        n_embd_per_head=estimator_args["n_embd_per_head"],
        n_head=estimator_args["n_head"],
        scaling=estimator_args["scaling"],
        time_feat=estimator_args["time_feat"],
        num_parallel_samples=num_samples,
    )

    if predictor is None:
```

```
        lightning_module = estimator.create_lightning_module()
        transformation = estimator.create_transformation()
        predictor = estimator.create_predictor(transformation,
    lightning_module)

    forecasts = predictor.predict(
        dataset=dataset
    )

    forecasts = list(forecasts)

    return forecasts
```

When these steps are complete, we can move on to fine-tune Lag-Llama. Because a context length of 64 resulted in the best performance, let's use that value for fine-tuning as well. Also, we'll train for only 50 epochs because fine-tuning shouldn't require many epochs.

> **NOTE** Unlike `neuralforecast` and TimeGPT, this model uses epochs instead of steps. Whereas a *step* processes a single batch of data, an *epoch* processes all batches of available data.

Also, we use the learning rate, denoted as `lr` in the code, suggested by the authors of Lag-Llama. This value can be tweaked, but that requires more experimentation. If the learning rate is too large, the model may diverge and fail to learn effectively. On the other hand, a small learning rate might require significantly more epochs for the model to converge, increasing the time required for the fine-tuning process.

**Listing 4.16 Initializing Lag-Llama for fine-tuning**

```
device = 'cuda'                     ◄── Uses the GPU for fine-tuning
prediction_length = 8
context_length = 64

ckpt = torch.load("lag-llama.ckpt", map_location=device)
estimator_args = ckpt["hyper_parameters"]["model_kwargs"]

estimator = LagLlamaEstimator(
        ckpt_path="lag-llama.ckpt",
        prediction_length=prediction_length,
        context_length=context_length,

        input_size=estimator_args["input_size"],
        n_layer=estimator_args["n_layer"],
        n_embd_per_head=estimator_args["n_embd_per_head"],
        n_head=estimator_args["n_head"],
        time_feat=estimator_args["time_feat"],

        # Fine-tuning arguments
        nonnegative_pred_samples=True,
        aug_prob=0,
```

```
        lr=5e-4,                              ◄── Sets the learning rate, using the same
        batch_size=64,                            value recommended by the authors
        num_parallel_samples=20,
        trainer_kwargs = {"max_epochs": 50,}  ◄── Sets the number of
    )                                             epochs for training
```

### 4.3.2 Reading and splitting the data in Colab

Next, we read the data. Again, we keep the last eight time steps for the test set and ensure that the data is a 32-bit floating-point type parsed in a format compatible with GluonTS.

**Listing 4.17 Reading data and formatting input**

```
url =
➥ 'https://raw.githubusercontent.com/marcopeix/FoundationModelsForTimeSer
➥ iesForecasting/main/data/walmart_sales_small.csv'

df = pd.read_csv(url)
df = df[df['Store'] == 1]

input_df = df[:-32]
test_df = df[-32:]

input_df['Weekly_Sales'] = input_df['Weekly_Sales'].astype('float32')
df['Weekly_Sales'] = df['Weekly_Sales'].astype('float32')
```

### 4.3.3 Launching the fine-tuning procedure

Now we can launch the fine-tuning procedure, which took approximately 5 minutes to complete in a Colab instance with a free T4 GPU.

**Listing 4.18 Fine-tuning Lag-Llama**

```
predictor = estimator.train(input_ds, cache_data=True,
➥ shuffle_buffer_length=1000)
```

### 4.3.4 Forecasting with a fine-tuned model

At this point, the model is fine-tuned and can be used to generate predictions. Let's use cross-validation again so we can compare the performances of zero-shot forecasting and fine-tuning.

**Listing 4.19 Forecasting with the fine-tuned model**

```
def cross_validation_lagllama(df, h, n_windows, device, context_length,
➥ confidence=0.95):

    all_forecasts = []
```

```
    for i in range(n_windows, 0, -1):
        input_ds = PandasDataset.from_long_dataframe(
            df[:-(h * i)],
            target="Weekly_Sales",
            item_id="Store"
        )

        forecasts = get_lag_llama_predictions(input_ds, h,
          predictor=predictor)                          # Passes the fine-tuned model as the predictor

        start_date = df.iloc[-(h * i)]['Date']

        forecast_df = get_median_and_ci(
            data=forecasts[0].samples,
            start_date=start_date,
            horizon=h,
            freq='W-FRI',
            id=1,
            confidence=confidence
        )
        all_forecasts.append(forecast_df)

    final_df = pd.concat(all_forecasts, axis=0, ignore_index=True)
    final_df = final_df.sort_values('Date')

    return final_df

finetune_preds = cross_validation_lagllama(
    df=df,
    h=8,
    n_windows=4,
    device=device,
    context_length=64
)
```

### 4.3.5 Evaluating the fine-tuned model

Finally, we evaluate the model's performance and report the MAE and sMAPE in table 4.1. We add the performance of TimeGPT under the same conditions, as covered in chapter 3.

**Listing 4.20 Evaluating the fine-tuned model**

```
def calculate_mae_smape(pred_df, test_df, target_col, pred_col):

    y_true = test_df[target_col].values
    y_pred = pred_df[pred_col].values

    mae = int(np.mean(np.abs(y_true - y_pred)))

    denominator = np.abs(y_true) + np.abs(y_pred)
    smape = round(np.mean(2.0 * np.abs(y_true - y_pred) / denominator) * 100,2)/2

    return mae, smape
```

```
mae_finetuned, smape_finetuned = calculate_mae_smape(finetune_preds,
➥ test_df,'Weekly_Sales', 'Lag-Llama')
```

**Table 4.1 Performance metrics of TimeGPT and Lag-Llama in cross-validation over four windows of eight weeks**

| Metric | TimeGPT (best) | Lag-Llama (zero-shot) | Lag-Llama (fine-tuned) |
|---|---|---|---|
| MAE | 63544 | 72990 | 68468 |
| sMAPE (%) | 2.04 | 2.29 | 2.15 |

Table 4.1 shows that fine-tuning returns an MAE of 68468$ and a sMAPE of 2.15%. This performance is slightly better than zero-shot forecasts. We could test fine-tuning for more epochs to see whether they further improve performance. Notice that TimeGPT still performs better than Lag-Llama when it's fine-tuned under the same conditions for cross-validation. We'll perform a more comprehensive experiment in chapter 10, comparing all foundation models covered in this book in another forecasting scenario.

## 4.4 Model comparison table

Table 4.2 updates the table from chapter 3 to include the key characteristics of Lag-Llama.

**Table 4.2 Pros and cons of each foundation forecasting model**

| Model | Pros | Cons | When to use |
|---|---|---|---|
| TimeGPT | Easy and fast to use<br>Comes with many native functions<br>Works on any device, regardless of hardware<br>Free plan | Paid product for a certain usage<br>Model may not be available if the server is down. | Forecasting on long and short horizons with exogenous features<br>You need to fine-tune but do not have the local resources. |
| Lag-Llama | Open source model<br>Free to use | Awkward to use because we must clone the repository<br>Speed of inference depends on our hardware. | Quick proof of concept<br>Ideal for research-oriented projects |

Although the model is free to use, cloning the repository and working inside it are not intuitive and hinder the user experience. It also requires some manual work to extract the predictions, which adds an extra layer of complexity to the model.

## 4.5 Next steps

In chapter 5, we explore Chronos, a foundation model developed by Amazon. Unlike Lag-Llama, Chronos comes as a package, meaning that we can install it and work with it in a more natural, efficient way.

## Summary

- Lag-Llama is an open source probabilistic foundation model that uses a decoder-only architecture. It constructs features using past values and date-time features.
- Lag-Llama was pretrained on frequencies of every day, hour, 15 minutes, and 1 minute, and on forecast horizons ranging from 24 to 60 time steps.
- Because the model must be downloaded locally, using a GPU results in faster inference and fine-tuning.

# 5 Learning the language of time with Chronos

**This chapter covers**

- Exploring the Chronos framework
- Forecasting with Chronos
- Fine-tuning Chronos
- Detecting anomalies with Chronos

In chapters 3 and 4, we explored TimeGPT and Lag-Llama, which are pretrained foundation models for time-series forecasting. After the release of these two models, researchers from Amazon released Chronos. Chronos, however, is technically not a model but a framework for pretrained probabilistic forecasting models [1]. This means Chronos is a process in which time-series data is scaled and quantized into a fixed vocabulary so it can be used to adapt existing language models, such as T5 and GPT-2, for time-series-forecasting tasks.

The researchers had already pretrained forecasting models based on the T5 family, and those models are loosely referred to as *Chronos*. Those models tend to perform best with series that have no strong trends. Unlike Lag-Llama, Chronos models can be used through a Python package, making it more suitable for production-ready environments.

## 5.1 Discovering the T5 family

Understanding the T5 family of models is important because these models are behind Chronos. We'll keep this exploration to a minimum, however, so we can focus on time-series forecasting. If you're already familiar with T5, feel free to jump to section 5.2.

T5 (Text-to-Text Transfer Transformer) represents a group of language models developed by Google Research [2]. It's a language model that uses the full encoder–decoder architecture. Its main innovation is that each task is converted to text-to-text format, so we can prefix the input sequence with the corresponding task. Figure 5.1 is a simplified illustration of how T5 performs various tasks using only text. In this example, the input sequence is prefixed with the task "translate to French," and the T5 model outputs the translated sentence.

**Figure 5.1 How T5 performs various NLP tasks. Here, the model performs translation because this task is specified in the input sequence on the left.**

The T5 models were trained using the *teacher forcing* method, in which every input sequence has its corresponding output sequence. This method resembles what we do in time-series forecasting, where models learn to predict a sequence of numbers based on another input sequence. Thus, it makes sense to apply a language model for time-series forecasting because the tasks are similar, mapping an input sequence to an output sequence.

A language model, however, is built to process words from a fixed vocabulary, whereas time series are numbers from an infinite set. Therefore, the language model must be adapted to time-series tasks, which is where the Chronos framework comes into play.

## 5.2 Exploring Chronos

Using the Chronos framework, we can adapt off-the-shelf language models to time-series tasks. After all, a language model is fundamentally trained to learn the structure of sequential data, like a sentence, and output another sequence of data. Time-series forecasting is essentially the same task, although words come from a fixed vocabulary, whereas values of a time series come from an unbounded and continuous domain. To bridge the gap between time-series and language tasks, Chronos suggests a series of steps that adapt any language model to probabilistic time-series forecasting.

Figure 5.2 is an overview of the Chronos framework. It essentially transforms time-series data to a format that a language model can understand natively. Specifically, the time series is tokenized, a process that consists of two steps: mean scaling and quantization. The output is a finite set of tokens, which we can dub "the language of time." This data can then be used to train a language model to generate an output sequence of tokens given an input sequence.

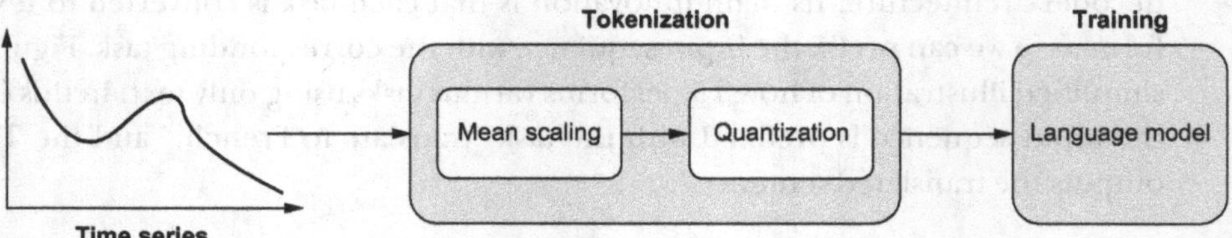


**Figure 5.2 Overview of the Chronos framework, which adapts a language model for time-series forecasting. First, the time series is tokenized, which involves mean scaling and quantization. Then the output can be used to train the language model.**

At prediction time, of course, the model outputs tokens, so the tokenization process must be reversed. The output is dequantized and unscaled to obtain the prediction of the series.

## 5.3 Using tokenization in Chronos

The tokenization step in Chronos is arguably the most important one because it transforms a real-valued time series to a set of tokens of a finite vocabulary, allowing us to use existing language models and their training procedure.

The first step in tokenizing the data is scaling the data. Different time series from various domains vary in scale, which poses a challenge for pretraining deep learning models.

Recall from chapters 3 and 4 that our scenario of weekly store sales reports data on the order of millions of dollars. By comparison, tracking daily traffic on a single road in a single city would record data on the order of hundreds or thousands of vehicles because millions of vehicles would never travel in a specific location in just a day. Therefore, the data must be scaled so that it's in a reasonable range to be quantized. The researchers behind Chronos opted to use *mean scaling*, a scaling strategy that divides each data point by the mean of the absolute values of all points. This method is commonly used in deep learning. It keeps the overall shape of the data and zero values in datasets, which can represent meaningful information, such as a day without sales.

Not everyone may agree with this choice, however. Ideally, mean scaling should be used only on stationary data, in which the mean and variance do not change over time. Otherwise, the mean is affected by the trend in the data, so we lose local patterns during scaling. The creators of Chronos acknowledge that different scalers can be used with minimal changes, but in this iteration of the model, mean scaling was chosen.

**Mean scaling**

*Mean scaling* is a method of scaling individual points in a dataset. It divides each point by the mean of the absolute values, as shown in the following equation:

$$\tilde{x} = \frac{x}{\frac{\sum|x|}{n}}$$

In figure 5.3, we see the effect of scaling the data. The pattern of the series remains unchanged. Now the values vary within a smaller range, from millions to between 0 and 1.5.

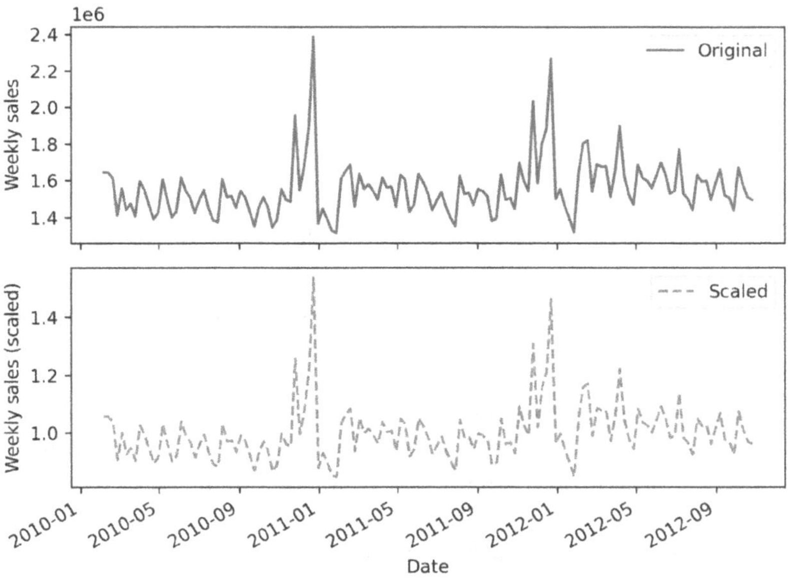


**Figure 5.3 Example of mean scaling. The data at the top is in its original scale, and the data at the bottom was mean-scaled. Notice that the general pattern stays the same. The difference lies in the range of values.**

The second and final step in tokenization is quantization. *Quantization* is a process that maps real values to a set of discrete finite values. Therefore, it's an approximation of real values. Assigning values from a series to their corresponding percentile, for example, is a quantization technique.

Here, quantization is critical because it maps the real values of the series to a set of discrete finite values. The final result resembles the vocabulary of a language.

Figure 5.4 shows the result of quantization on scaled data. Now the continuous real values of the series are assigned to a discrete bin. Although the quantized data retains most of the general shape of the scaled series, we inherently lose some precision.

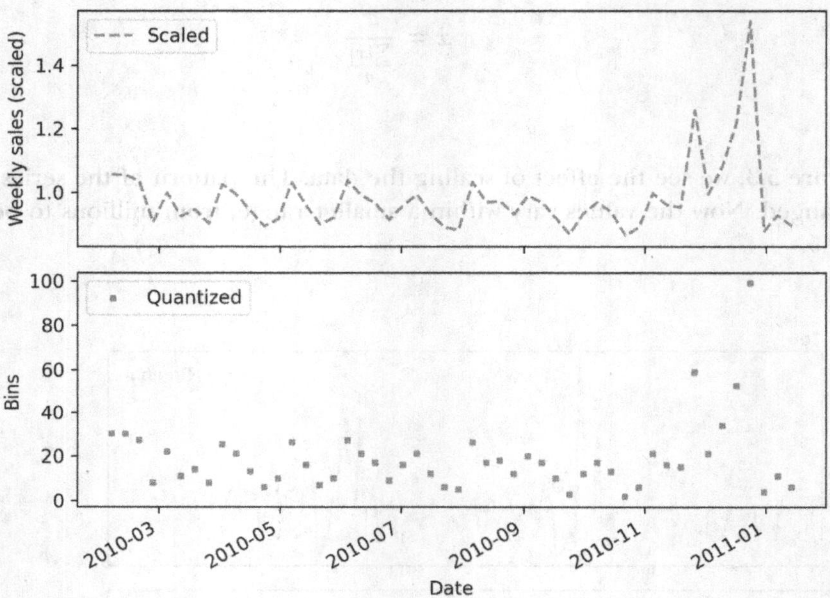


**Figure 5.4 The result of quantization using 100 bins. Here, only the first 50 weeks of data are shown.**

Notice in figure 5.4 that the first two points in the bottom figure are equal. However, that is not the case in the scaled series. This is to be expected, as a bin will contain a range of values. Although the values aren't exactly the same, they're assigned to the same bin, and the language model cannot distinguish them.

Chronos uses uniform binning. A fixed number of equally spaced bins is set, and each point is assigned to its corresponding bin. Specifically, the researchers decided to use 4,094 bins and clip the values of the series between -15 and 15 after scaling. The choice to clip values to the range of -15 to 15 is not explained in the research paper.

Figure 5.5 shows an extreme case of using too few bins to quantize the data. At the top of the figure, we use 100 bins, and at the bottom, we use 5 bins. With 5 bins, we lose a lot of precision. Using this setting is like trying to summarize an entire time series in five words.

It's important to note that because the data is binned, Chronos cannot forecast time series with strong trends. This makes sense because the model will have seen the bin for

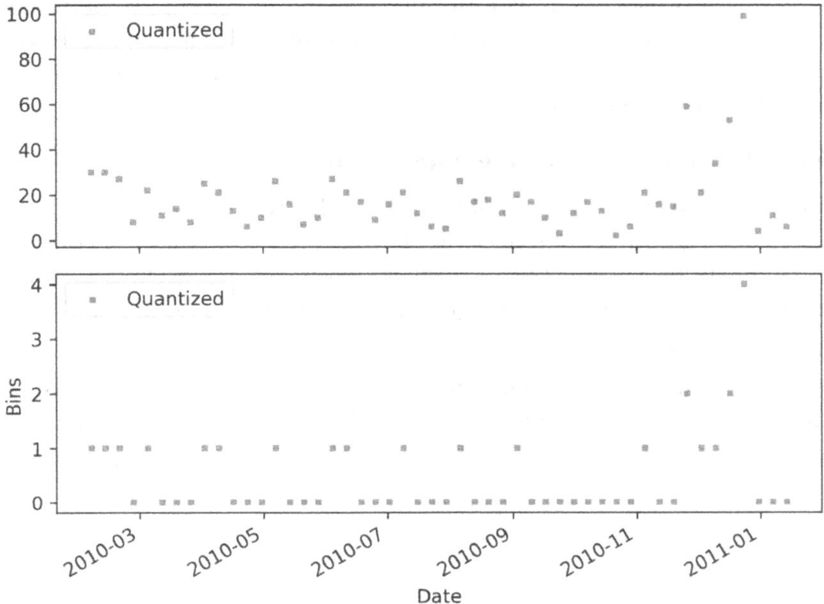


**Figure 5.5 Effect of the number of bins on the resulting tokens. In the top plot, we have a vocabulary of 100 possible bins, and in the bottom plot, we use only 5 bins. With 5 bins, we lose too much precision.**

the largest values, but it can't make up new tokens for new larger values. Therefore, the forecast will tend to plateau, especially when the input sequence is short.

This completes the tokenization process. To summarize, Chronos first applies mean scaling to the series. Then, it forces all values to be between -15 and 15. As such, if a value after scaling is smaller than -15 or larger than 15, it gets assigned to the value of -15 or 15 respectively. Then, each point is quantized into 4094 uniform bins. At this point, the time series data is scaled and assigned to bins, which represent discrete tokens of the series. This type of that can now be used to train a language model.

## 5.4 Training a model with Chronos

Because our time series is tokenized, going from continuous real values to discrete finite tokens, a model can't use distance-based metrics, such as the mean absolute error (MAE) or mean squared error (MSE). Instead, it tries to minimize cross-entropy. Cross-entropy measures the difference between the discovered probability distribution of a classification model and the true distribution. It can take values between 0 and 1, where 0 translates to a perfect classifier and 1 is the worst score.

Language models trained with the Chronos framework perform regression via classification. Technically, the models perform classification because they're trained to take an input sequence of tokens and output the right sequence of future tokens.

At first, this approach seems counterintuitive, but it comes with the massive advantage that the language model doesn't have to be modified. The architecture and training objective of language models are built for classification, so we can apply them directly with the Chronos framework.

### 5.4.1 Tackling data scarcity with augmentation techniques

As mentioned in chapter 1, one challenge in building forecasting foundational models is accessing large quantities of time-series data. There is less time-series data than in the natural language processing (NLP) domain. Thus, the researchers behind Chronos devised two methods to supplement their training dataset: TSMixup and KernelSynth.

#### TSMIXUP

TSMixup is a technique that generates convex combinations of random time-series sequences. It samples random sequences of existing time-series data, scales the sequences, and combines them to create a new series, as shown in figure 5.6.

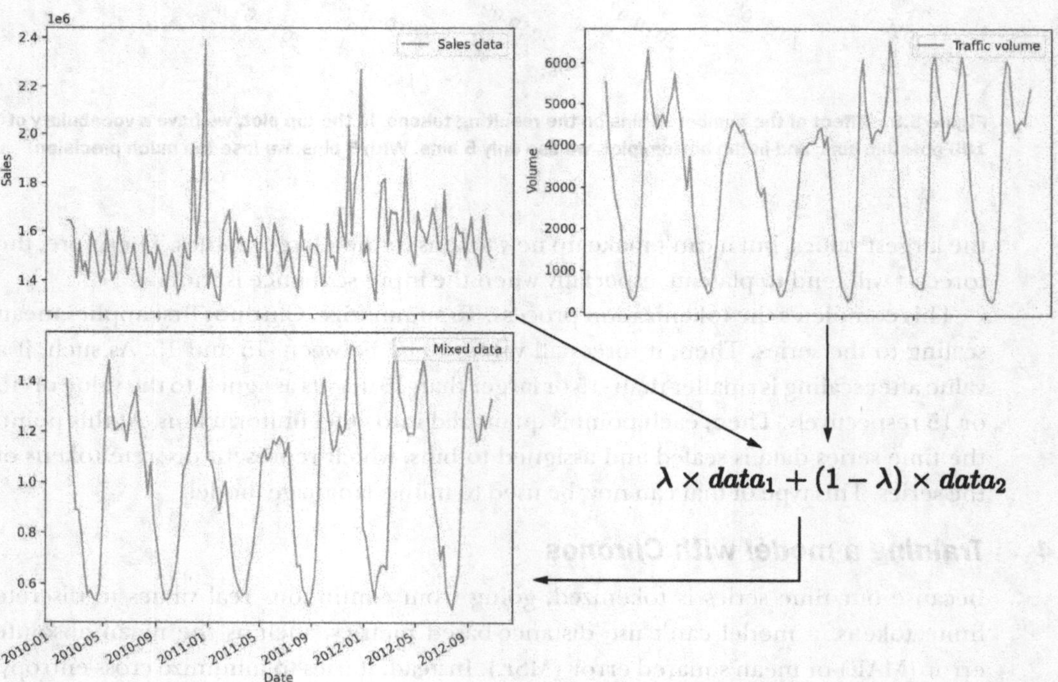


**Figure 5.6 Illustrating TSMixup. At top left, we have our weekly sales data. At top right, we have daily traffic volume data. Both series are scaled and combined to generate a new series, shown at bottom left.**

The figure shows TSMixup using two time series: the weekly sales data that we have been working with (top left) and daily traffic-volume data (top right). Both series are scaled, and we apply the formula shown at bottom right. Here, $\lambda$ takes a value between 0 and 1. The result of that combination is shown at bottom left. Notice that the bottom-left plot has the general structure of the top-right series, but its peaks display patterns from the top-left plot.

This figure shows an example with two series, but the same thing can be done with many series. Also, by sampling different sequences at random from many series from various domains, we can generate large quantities of new time-series data with more varied patterns.

#### KERNELSYNTH

The second technique is KernelSynth. Whereas TSMixup uses only existing data, KernelSynth aims to create synthetic data to supplement the dataset.

The researchers built a bank of functions called *kernels*, which represent fundamental patterns in time series. A linear kernel represents trend, for example, and a sinusoidal kernel represents seasonality in time series. These kernels are randomly sampled and combined by addition or multiplication.

Figure 5.7 is a simplified illustration of KernelSynth. At top left, we have a linear kernel, and at top right, we have a sinusoidal kernel. The kernels are combined using addition, which results in the synthetic series at the bottom.

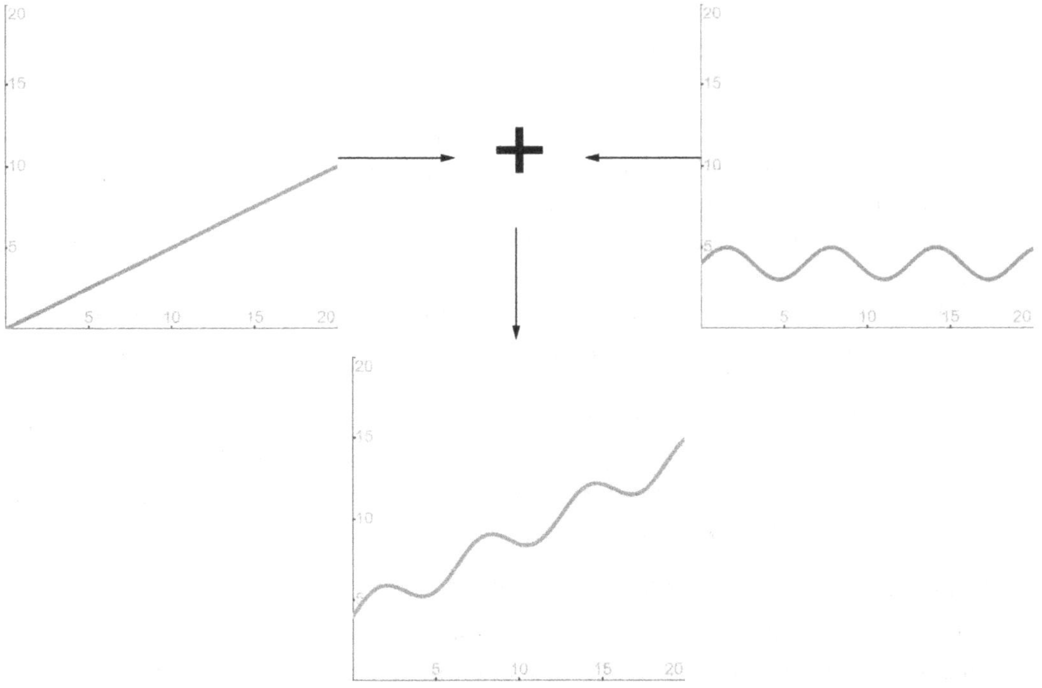


**Figure 5.7 Illustrating KernelSynth. Top left is a linear kernel, and top right is a sinusoidal kernel. The kernels are combined using addition, resulting in the synthetic series at the bottom.**

In practice, KernelSynth contains many more kernels, and random variations have been introduced in them. Also, more than two kernels are combined, resulting in greater variety and more complex synthetic series. For clarity, I kept the figure simple to illustrate the process.

### 5.4.2 Examining the pretrained Chronos models

As mentioned at the beginning of this chapter, Chronos is technically a framework, but practitioners often use it to designate the five publicly available pretrained models. These models were built with the T5 family of language models and are available in different sizes depending on available memory and computation power. Table 5.1 summarizes each model's characteristics.

**Table 5.1 Characteristics of the available pretrained Chronos models**

| Model name | Parameters | Training time (hours) | Cost (USD) | Size (MB) |
|---|---|---|---|---|
| `chronos-t5-tiny` | 8 million | - | | 33.6 |
| `chronos-t5-mini` | 20 million | 7.68 | 252 | 81.8 |
| `chronos-t5-small` | 46 million | 7.73 | 253 | 185 |
| `chronos-t5-base` | 200 million | 17.96 | 588 | 806 |
| `chronos-t5-large` | 710 million | 63.05 | 2,066 | 2,840 |

In table 5.1, the reported cost is the cost of pretraining the model. Now that the models are pretrained and publicly available, no cost is associated with using them.

Overall, each model was pretrained on about 890,000 univariate time series, representing 84 billion tokens. The datasets cover many domains, including energy, transportation, nature, and the web. Chronos has been trained on time series with frequencies of 15 and 30 minutes, as well as hourly, daily, weekly, and monthly frequencies. Here, only the quarterly frequency has not been seen by the pretrained models.

The models were trained for 200,000 steps using eight graphics processing units (GPUs). The input sequence length was set to 512 time steps, and the forecasting horizon was set to 64 time steps. Keep in mind that forecasting on a horizon longer than 64 time steps can produce bad results.

### 5.4.3 Selecting the appropriate Chronos model

Before experimenting with Chronos in Python, let's reflect on how to choose a pretrained model. The `chronos-t5-large` model, for example, is the most performant. With more parameters, it captures more complex patterns in data, which translates to better zero-shot forecasting performance.

Thus, choosing a pretrained model boils down to available memory and computation power. If you have large memory space and GPUs for inference, opting for the largest model is the best solution. That model will likely produce the best performance, and inference time will be reasonable. If, however, you're running inference on a CPU only and don't have much memory space, `chronos-t5-small` or `chronos-t5-mini` is better. These models are relatively light, and inference time will be reasonable.

Usually, but not always, the bigger a model is, the better it is, but it also requires more memory and computation power to use it for inference and fine-tune it. If you select a model that takes too long to generate predictions or fine-tune, select a smaller model that is better adapted to your hardware.

## 5.5 Forecasting with Chronos

Unlike Lag-Llama, Chronos can be installed via `pip`, making it easy to use for time-series forecasting. Run the following command to complete the setup:

```
pip install git+https://github.com/amazon-science/chronos-forecasting.git
```

This command installs Chronos as a Python package, and it installs all the required libraries to run Chronos seamlessly. Now we're ready for zero-shot forecasting.

In this section, we'll use the dataset on weekly store sales in four Walmart stores (figure 5.8). This dataset is the same one we used in chapters 3 and 4.

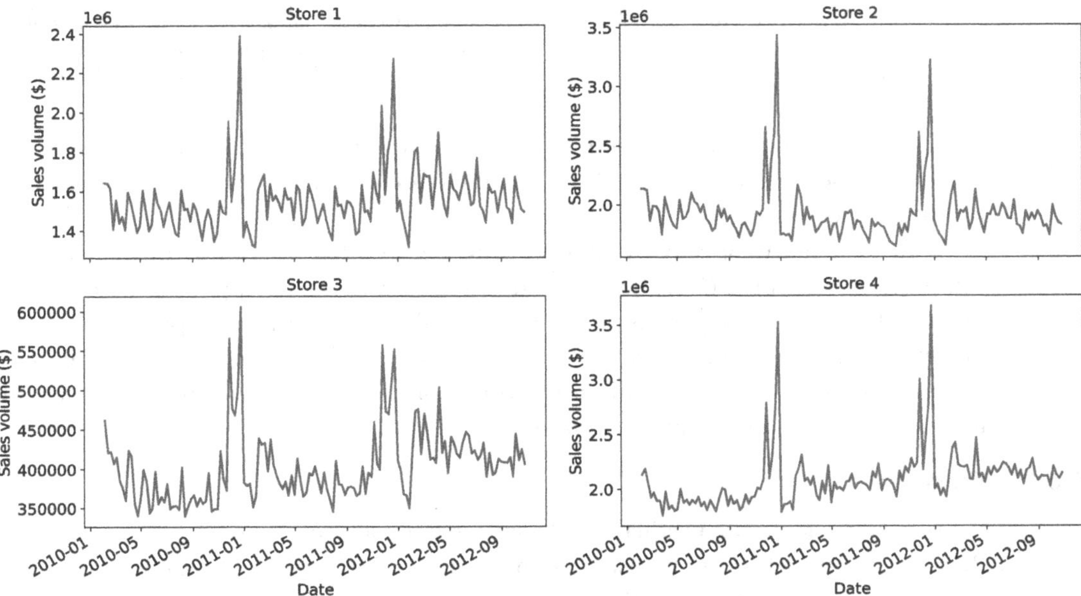


**Figure 5.8 Weekly sales of four Walmart stores**

### 5.5.1 Initial setup

Chronos expects a `torch.tensor` as input. Therefore, we take the `Weekly_Sales` column for all stores and store the information in a list of tensors, where each tensor is assigned to a store.

**Listing 5.1 Formatting the input for Chronos**

```
import torch

context = [torch.tensor(df.query("Store ==
➥ @i")['Weekly_Sales'].to_numpy()) for i in range(1, 5)]
```

We store the data from our target column in a tensor. Chronos doesn't work directly with DataFrames, so we need this little step to extract the data from the column to feed it to Chronos.

Next, we initialize the prediction pipeline. This step is where we specify the name of the pretrained model and what hardware to use for inference.

**Listing 5.2 Initializing the prediction pipeline**

```
from chronos import ChronosPipeline

pipeline = ChronosPipeline.from_pretrained(
    "amazon/chronos-t5-small",
    device_map="cpu",
    torch_dtype=torch.bfloat16,
)
```

Selects the pretrained model. You can choose any model from table 5.1.

Selects the device for inference. Use "cpu" for CPU inference, "mps" for Apple Silicon devices, or "cuda" for GPU inferences that support CUDA.

First, we choose the pretrained model to use. This example uses `chronos-t5-small`, but feel free to use any model from table 5.1 Keep in mind that using a different model will produce different results.

Next, we need to specify the hardware to be used for inference. In this chapter, inference is done on a CPU, but you can run inference on an Apple Silicon device or use a GPU. Finally, I suggest using the `bfloat16` data type because it speeds inference. `bfloat16` is a low-precision floating-point format that offers a good tradeoff between computational efficiency and numerical precision. The precision of forecasts may suffer a little, but running inference is faster.

### 5.5.2 Predictions

We're ready to generate predictions. Again, we'll use a forecast horizon of eight weeks. Because the model is probabilistic, we must specify the number of samples to draw to form the prediction intervals. We set this value to 20 samples. Note that increasing this value results in more robust intervals at the cost of slower inference.

**Listing 5.3 Making predictions with Chronos**

```
predictions = pipeline.predict(
    context=context,                  ◄— Passes the input sequences to predict
    prediction_length=8,              ◄— Specifies the forecast horizon
    num_samples=20,                   ◄— Number of samples to construct
)                                        the prediction intervals
```

Here, we use the `context` variable we created earlier to feed the input sequence to Chronos. Then we specify the forecast horizon and the number of samples to build the prediction intervals.

Figure 5.9 illustrates the `predictions` variable in an array that contains predictions for each store. Each element is an array itself, which has 20 samples for each step in the forecast horizon. Remember that the samples are used to build the prediction interval.

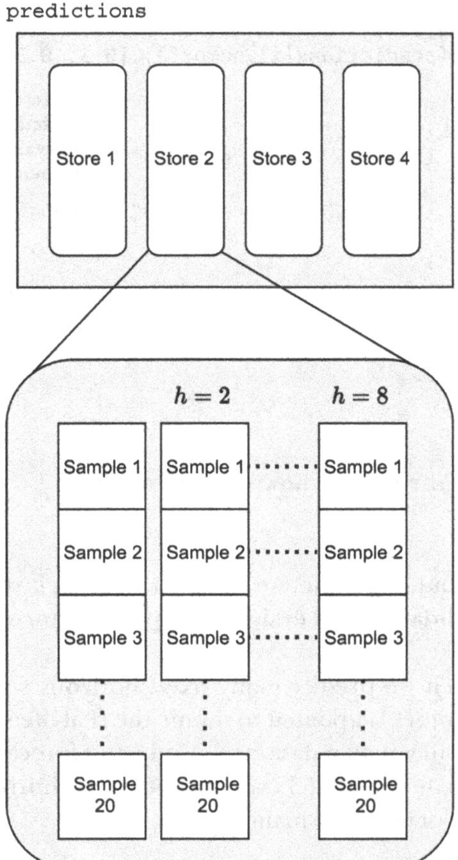


**Figure 5.9** The `predictions` variable contains the predictions for each store, each of which is itself an array with 20 samples for each step in the forecast horizon.

Thus, to extract the predictions and a 80% prediction interval, we can use the following code:

```
for i in range(4):
    low, median, high = np.quantile(predictions[i].numpy(), [0.1, 0.5,
    ➥ 0.9], axis=0)
```

Note that the median is considered the point forecast of Chronos. We can change the prediction interval by modifying the lower and upper bounds, however. For a 60% prediction interval, we would use `[0.2, 0.5, 0.8]`. At this point, we can plot the forecasts.

**Listing 5.4 Plotting the predictions from Chronos**

```
start_date = pd.to_datetime('2012-10-26')
forecast_dates =  [start_date + pd.DateOffset(weeks=i) for i in range(1, 9)]

fig, axes = plt.subplots(ncols=2, nrows=2, figsize=(14,8))

for i, ax in enumerate(axes.flatten()):
    store_id = i+1
    data = df.query("Store == @store_id")
    low, median, high = np.quantile(predictions[i].numpy(), [0.1, 0.5,
    ➥ 0.9], axis=0)                                    ◄── Extracts the predictions and intervals from Chronos

    ax.plot(data['Date'], data['Weekly_Sales'])
    ax.plot(forecast_dates, median, ls='--', color='green',
    ➥ label='Forecast')
    ax.fill_between(forecast_dates, low, high, color="green", alpha=0.3)

    ax.set_title(f"Store {store_id}")
    ax.set_xlabel('Date')
    ax.set_ylabel('Sales volume ($)')
    ax.legend(loc=1)

fig.autofmt_xdate()
plt.tight_layout()
```

Running the preceding code produces the results shown in figure 5.10.

## 5.6 Cross-validating with Chronos

Because we made predictions that are out of sample, we can't evaluate their quality. In this section, we see how to run cross-validation and evaluate the performance of Chronos in our scenario.

Cross-validation is a process in which we predict many fixed horizons within our dataset. After every prediction, the input set is updated to mimic the real-life situation: making forecasts, waiting to collect the new actual data, and producing forecasts based on the new data. This allows us to evaluate the model over many forecast horizons, giving us a more representative evaluation of its performance.

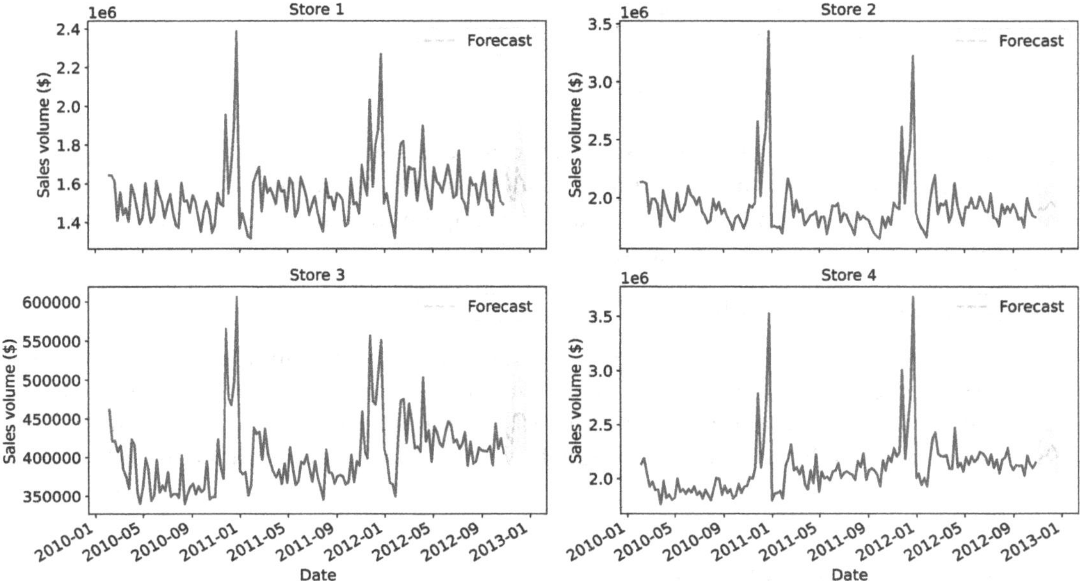


**Figure 5.10 Plotting the predictions from Chronos. The shaded areas represent a 80% prediction interval.**

Unlike TimeGPT, which comes with a built-in cross-validation function, Chronos requires us to define our own function. This function behaves exactly like the one in TimeGPT, creating nonoverlapping windows.

**Listing 5.5 Cross-validation function with Chronos**

```
def cross_validation_chronos(df, h, n_windows=4, target_col):

    lows = []
    medians = []
    highs = []

    for i in range(n_windows, 0, -1):          # Loops over all nonoverlapping windows
        context = torch.tensor(
                  df[target_col][:-(h * i)])   # Sets the input sequence as torch.tensor

        predictions = pipeline.predict(
            context=context,
            prediction_length=h,
            num_samples=20,
        )

        low, median, high = np.quantile(predictions[0].numpy(), [0.1, 0.5,
          0.9], axis=0)                        # Extracts the prediction and the 80% prediction interval

        lows.extend(low)
```

```
            medians.extend(median)
            highs.extend(high)

        return lows, medians, highs
```

In this listing, our `cross_validation_chronos` function takes a DataFrame, the horizon length, the number of cross-validation windows, and the name of the column with our target. The function loops over all nonoverlapping windows. We store the predictions as the input sequence is updated.

### 5.6.1 Running cross-validation

Let's apply cross-validation only to store 1, using four cross-validation folds and a horizon of eight weeks. Because we have four windows and a horizon of eight weeks, the model will return predictions for the last 32 time steps of our dataset. We'll store the actual and predicted values in a single DataFrame for easier plotting and evaluation.

**Listing 5.6 Running cross-validation**

```
df = df.query('Store == 1')

lows, medians, highs = cross_validation_chronos(df,       ◄ Runs cross-validation
                                                h=8,
                                                n_windows=4,
                                                target_col='Weekly_Sales')

test_df = df[['Store', 'Date', "Weekly_Sales"]]
➥ [-32:]                                    ◄ Gets the actual values that
                                               align with the predictions
test_df['low'] = lows                          from cross-validation
test_df['median'] = medians
test_df['high'] = highs
```

Now we can plot the predictions made during cross-validation (figure 5.11).

There, we can see some overlap between the forecasts and the actual values, which is a good sign.

### 5.6.2 Evaluating Chronos

Next, we'll evaluate the performance of Chronos using the `utilsforecast` library (chapter 3). Table 5.2 shows the results, along with the performance obtained by TimeGPT and Lag-Llama under the same conditions.

**Listing 5.7 Evaluating the performance of Chronos in cross-validation**

```
from utilsforecast.losses import mae, smape
from utilsforecast.evaluation import evaluate

evaluation = evaluate(
    test_df,
```

```
    metrics=[mae, smape],
    models=['median'],
    target_col='Weekly_Sales',
    id_col='Store'
)
```

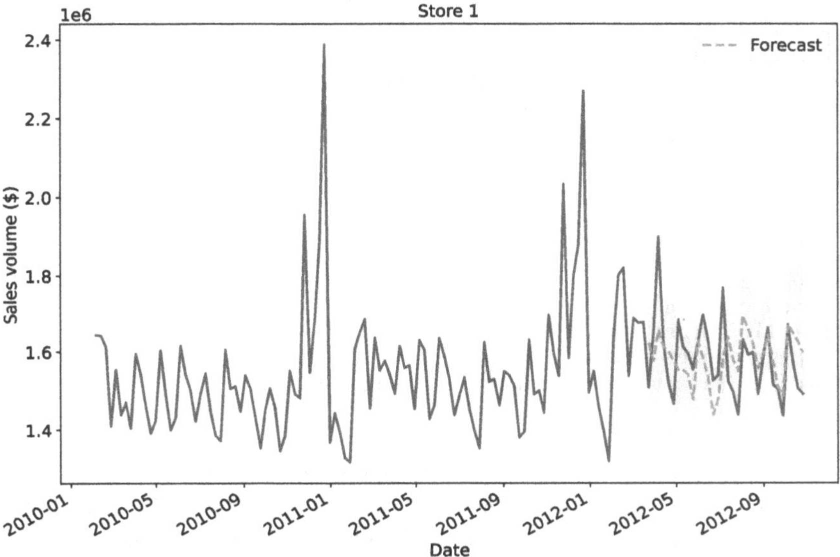


**Figure 5.11 Predictions obtained from running cross-validation with Chronos. The shaded area represents the 80% prediction interval.**

**Table 5.2 Performance metrics of large time models in cross-validation over four windows of eight weeks**

| Metric | TimeGPT (fine-tuned) | Lag-Llama (fine-tuned) | Chronos |
|---|---|---|---|
| MAE | 63544 | 72990 | 77657 |
| sMAPE (%) | 2.04 | 2.29 | 2.44 |

In listing 5.7, we use the MAE and the symmetric mean absolute percentage error (sMAPE) to evaluate the performance of Chronos as we evaluated the performance of TimeGPT in chapter 3. Here, Chronos achieves an MAE of 77657$ and a sMAPE of 2.44%. Under the same conditions, both TimeGPT and Lag-Llama achieved better results, although they were fine-tuned.

## 5.7 Fine-tuning Chronos

Up to now, we've used the pretrained models of Chronos without fine-tuning them. Usually, fine-tuning a model on our dataset leads to better results, as table 5.2 shows. Therefore, let's fine-tune our model to see the effect on performance.

**NOTE** To fine-tune Chronos, I highly recommend having access to a GPU; otherwise, training time can be prohibitively long. The code in this section was run inside Google Colab, which provides a free GPU environment.

### 5.7.1 Performing initial setup

First, we install the Chronos package and clone the repository to access the training scripts:

```
!pip install "chronos[training] @ git+https://github.com/amazon-
➥ science/chronos-forecasting.git"
!git clone https://github.com/amazon-science/chronos-forecasting.git
!cd chronos-forecasting/
```

We also import all the necessary packages for this step:

```
import pandas as pd
import numpy as np
from pathlib import Path
from typing import Union
from gluonts.dataset.arrow import ArrowWriter
import torch
```

If we want to fine-tune Chronos on a specific dataset, that dataset has to be in Apache Arrow format, a data format built for fast processing of large datasets. Let's create a function that transforms our CSV file to Arrow format. For simplicity, because we're working in Colab, we'll read the CSV file from the GitHub repository. In this listing , we read our dataset on weekly sales and select only store 1. The values are extracted and written to Arrow format.

**Listing 5.8 Converting CSV to Arrow**

```
def convert_csv_to_arrow(
    csv_url: str,
    arrow_path: Union[str, Path],
    store_id: int
):

    df = pd.read_csv(csv_url)          ◄── Reads the CSV file

    store_data = df[df['Store'] == store_id]     ◄── Selects a unique store id

    store_data['Date'] = pd.to_datetime(     ◄── Makes sure that the time
    ➥ store_data['Date'])                        column is datetime

    start_time = store_data['Date'].min()     ◄── Gets the starting date

    time_series = [store_data['Weekly_Sales']     ◄── Stores the value of the series
    ➥ .values]                                        as a list of numpy arrays

    dataset = [     ◄── Creates the dataset
```

```
        {"start": start_time, "target": ts} for ts in time_series
    ]

    ArrowWriter(compression="lz4")
        .write_to_file(dataset, path=arrow_path)     # Writes the dataset to Arrow format

csv_url =
    https://raw.githubusercontent.com/marcopeix/FoundationModelsForTimeSeri
    esForecasting/main/data/walmart_sales_small.csv

convert_csv_to_arrow(csv_url, "sales_data_store1.arrow", store_id=1)
```

### 5.7.2 Configuring the fine-tuning parameters

Next, we define the training configuration in a YAML (Yet Another Markup Language) file. We adapt the existing training configuration for fine-tuning mainly by specifying our desired horizon and reducing the number of training steps. The next listing defines the configuration file for fine-tuning Chronos, changing only a few parameters from the default configuration.

**Listing 5.9 Defining the configuration for fine-tuning Chronos**

```
import yaml

config = {                                    # Defines the training configuration
    'training_data_paths': [
        "/content/sales_data_store1.arrow"    # Places the path to the Arrow file containing our data
    ],
    'probability': [0.9],
    'context_length': 64,
    'prediction_length': 8,     # Specifies the horizon. Here, we use eight weeks in the future.
    'min_past': 60,
    'max_steps': 500,           # Maximum number of fine-tuning steps
    'save_steps': 250,
    'log_steps': 100,
    'per_device_train_batch_size': 32,
    'learning_rate': 0.001,
    'optim': 'adamw_torch_fused',
    'num_samples': 20,
    'shuffle_buffer_length': 100,
    'gradient_accumulation_steps': 1,
    'model_id': 'google/t5-efficient-small',    # Which model to use. We stick to T5-small.
    'model_type': 'seq2seq',
    'random_init': False,
    'tie_embeddings': True,
    'output_dir': './output/',     # The directory where the fine-tuned model will be stored
    'tf32': True,
    'torch_compile': True,
    'tokenizer_class': 'MeanScaleUniformBins',    # The tokenization strategy. Here, we use mean scaling and uniform binning.
    'tokenizer_kwargs': {
        'low_limit': -15.0,
        'high_limit': 15.0
```

```
    },
    'n_tokens': 4096,
    'lr_scheduler_type': 'linear',
    'warmup_ratio': 0.0,
    'dataloader_num_workers': 1,
    'max_missing_prop': 0.9,
    'use_eos_token': True
}                                                   Defines the path to save
                                                    the configuration file
yaml_file_path = 'fine-tune_config.yaml'  ◄

                                                    Saves the configuration file
with open(yaml_file_path, 'w') as yaml_file:  ◄
    yaml.dump(config, yaml_file, default_flow_style=False)
```

In the preceding code, we specify the path to the dataset that we transformed to Arrow format. We also set the horizon to eight, which is the forecast horizon we use throughout this chapter. Then we reduce the number of maximum training steps to 500. Remember that fine-tuning is meant to specialize the model on our scenario and still benefit from the pretrained data. Finally, we still use the `T5-small` model because we've worked with it throughout this chapter.

### 5.7.3 Launching the fine-tuning procedure

Now we can launch the fine-tuning process on the GPU instance of Colab:

```
!CUDA_VISIBLE_DEVICES=0 python chronos-
➥ forecasting/scripts/training/train.py --config /content/fine-
➥ tune_config.yaml
```

The preceding code block launches the process on a GPU with `CUDA_VISIBLE_DEVICES=0`. Then it runs the Python script for training and specifies the path to the configuration file defined previously.

At this point, we've fine-tuned a Chronos model on our sales dataset. To evaluate its performance, we use cross-validation with four windows and a horizon of eight weeks. That way, we can compare the results with those of the experiment in which the model was not fine-tuned. The following listing reads our CSV from the GitHub repository and redefines the cross-validation because we're working in Colab.

**Listing 5.10 Reading the data and defining the cross-validation function in Colab**

```
url =
➥ "https://raw.githubusercontent.com/marcopeix/
➥ FoundationModelsForTimeSeriesForecasting/
➥ main/data/walmart_sales_small.csv"

df = pd.read_csv(url, parse_dates=['Date'])
df = df.query('Store == 1')

def cross_validation_chronos(df, h, n_windows=4, target_col):
```

```
    lows = []
    medians = []
    highs = []

    for i in range(n_windows, 0, -1):
        context = torch.tensor(df[target_col][:-(h * i)])

        predictions = pipeline.predict(
            context=context,
            prediction_length=h,
            num_samples=20,
        )

        low, median, high = np.quantile(predictions[0].numpy(), [0.1, 0.5,
          0.9], axis=0)

        lows.extend(low)
        medians.extend(median)
        highs.extend(high)

    return lows, medians, highs
```

### 5.7.4 Forecasting with a fine-tuned model

To use our fine-tuned model, we use the `ChronosPipeline` object, but this time, we pass the path to the saved fine-tuned model. In listing 5.11, the path to the fine-tuned model is in `content/output/run-0` because we're working in Colab and specified (in the YAML file) saving the results in the `output` directory. Every time we launch the training process, a new `run-{id}` folder is created. Finally, the model files are stored in the `checkpoint-final` folder.

**Listing 5.11 Loading the fine-tuned model**

```
from chronos import ChronosPipeline

pipeline = ChronosPipeline.from_pretrained("/content/output/run-
  0/checkpoint-final/", device_map='cuda',
  torch_dtype=torch.bfloat16)
```

The fine-tuned model is always in the latest run in the checkpoint-final folder.

### 5.7.5 Evaluating the fine-tuned model

Now that the fine-tuned model is loaded, we can run cross-validation, get predictions, and evaluate performance. We compare the performance of fine-tuned mode with the base model (figure 5.12). We also update the performance table (table 5.3).

**Listing 5.12 Cross-validation and performance evaluation of the fine-tuned model**

```
from utilsforecast.losses import mae, smape
from utilsforecast.evaluation import evaluate
```

```
lows, medians, highs = cross_validation_chronos(df,
                                                h=8,
                                                n_windows=4,
                                                target_col='Weekly_Sales')

test_df = df[['Store', 'Date', 'Weekly_Sales']]
➥ [-32:]

test_df['low'] = lows
test_df['chronos-fine-tuned'] = medians
test_df['high'] = highs

evaluation = evaluate(
    test_df,
    metrics=[mae, smape],
    models=['chronos-fine-tuned'],
    target_col='Weekly_Sales',
    id_col='Store'
)
```

Runs cross-validation with the fine-tuned model

Gets the actual values that align with cross-validation

Stores the predicted values

Evaluates the model using MAE and sMAPE

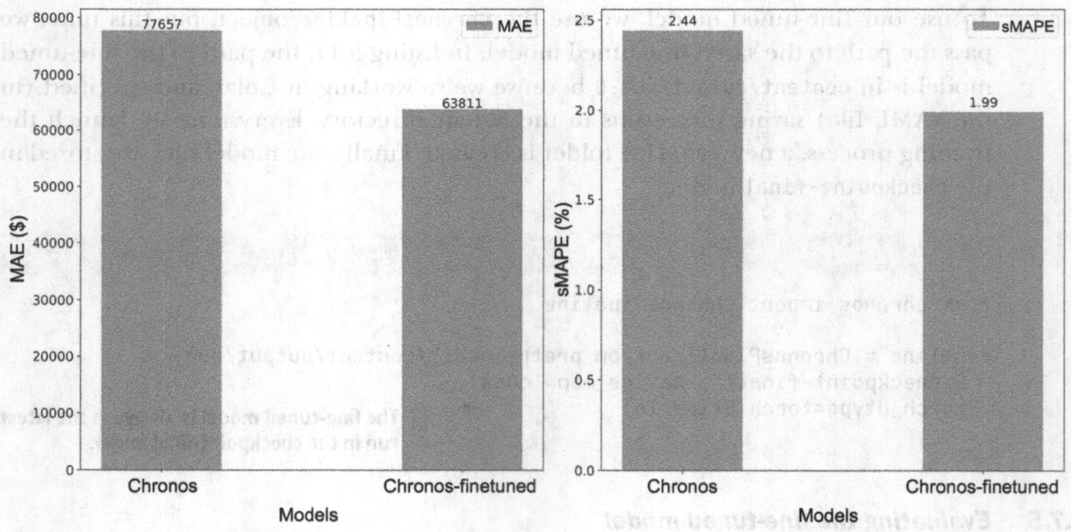


**Figure 5.12 Comparing the MAE and sMAPE before and after fine-tuning Chronos. Lower is better.**

We can see that fine-tuning Chronos improved forecasting performance. The MAE was reduced from 77657$ to 63811, and the sMAPE was reduced from 2.44% to 1.99% with the fine-tuned model. Thus, fine-tuning Chronos clearly resulted in more accurate forecasts.

**Table 5.3 Performance metrics of large time models in cross-validation over four windows of eight weeks**

| Metric | TimeGPT (fine-tuned) | Lag-Llama (fine-tuned) | Chronos (fine-tuned) |
|---|---|---|---|
| MAE | 63544 | 72990 | 63811 |
| sMAPE (%) | 2.04 | 2.29 | 1.99 |

Table 5.3 shows that Chronos performs best because it achieves lower metrics than TimeGPT and Lag-Llama. Once more, we cannot conclude that Chronos is better than the other models in an absolute sense. The main idea is to design robust experiments to compare models' performances and select the best model for a particular task. Up to this point, Chronos has been best at forecasting weekly sales for store 1.

## 5.8 Detecting anomalies with Chronos

Chronos doesn't natively support anomaly detection. But we can apply the logic from TimeGPT, making predictions using a 99% prediction interval. If the actual value falls outside the interval, it's considered an anomaly.

Let's use Chronos to detect anomalies in daily taxi rides in New York City. We used TimeGPT for the same task chapter 3. Figure 5.13 shows the dataset and the four anomalies we must detect, all previously labeled by humans.

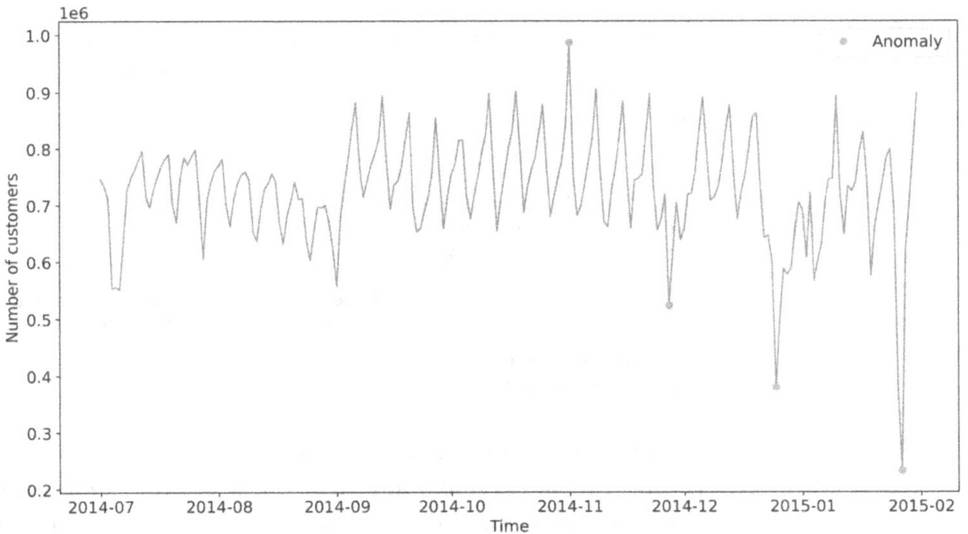


**Figure 5.13 The dots indicate labeled anomalies labeled in the daily number of customers of the New York City taxi service.**

First, let's build a function to detect anomalies with Chronos.

**Listing 5.13 Detecting anomalies with Chronos**

```
def anomaly_detection_chronos(df, h, n_windows, value_col, confidence=0.99):

    lows = []
    medians = []
    highs = []

    low_conf = (1 - confidence)/2    ◄── Gets the lower bound of the prediction interval

    for i in range(n_windows, 0, -1):    ◄── Makes predictions using cross-validation
        context = torch.tensor(df[value_col][:-(h * i)])

        predictions = pipeline.predict(
            context=context,
            prediction_length=h,
            num_samples=20,
            limit_prediction_length=False
        )

        low, median, high = np.quantile(predictions[0].numpy(), [low_conf,
        ➥ 0.5, 1-low_conf], axis=0)

        lows.extend(low)
        medians.extend(median)
        highs.extend(high)

    df_test = df[-(n_windows*h):]    ◄── Gets the actual values for the predicted sequence

    df_test['low'] = lows
    df_test['median'] = medians
    df_test['high'] = highs

    df_test['anomaly'] = ((df_test[value_col] < df_test['low']) |
    ➥ (df_test[value_col] > df_test['high']))
    ➥ .astype(int)    ◄── Labels as an anomaly if the actual value falls outside the prediction interval

    return df_test    ◄── Returns a DataFrame with actual and predicted values
```

We reuse the cross-validation logic, allowing us to detect anomalies over long periods without exceeding Chronos's maximum horizon of 64 time steps. The output of this function is a DataFrame with actual values, predicted values, and a label for anomalies.

Next, we can run anomaly detection on our dataset. Here, we use eight windows with a horizon of 23 time steps to detect anomalies over the last 184 time steps of the dataset. This recreates the conditions of TimeGPT, allowing us to compare the performance of both models in detecting anomalies. We also use a 99% prediction interval.

**Listing 5.14 Running anomaly detection**

```
df = pd.read_csv('../data/nyc_taxi_anomaly_daily.csv',
    parse_dates=['timestamp'])

anomaly_df = anomaly_detection_chronos(df,
                                        h=23,
                                        n_windows=8,
                                        value_col='value',
                                        confidence=0.99)
```

Figure 5.14 shows the result. The model found all labeled anomalies, but it also falsely labeled many normal points as anomalies. Because we used a 99% prediction interval, reducing the interval would lead to even more points being falsely labeled.

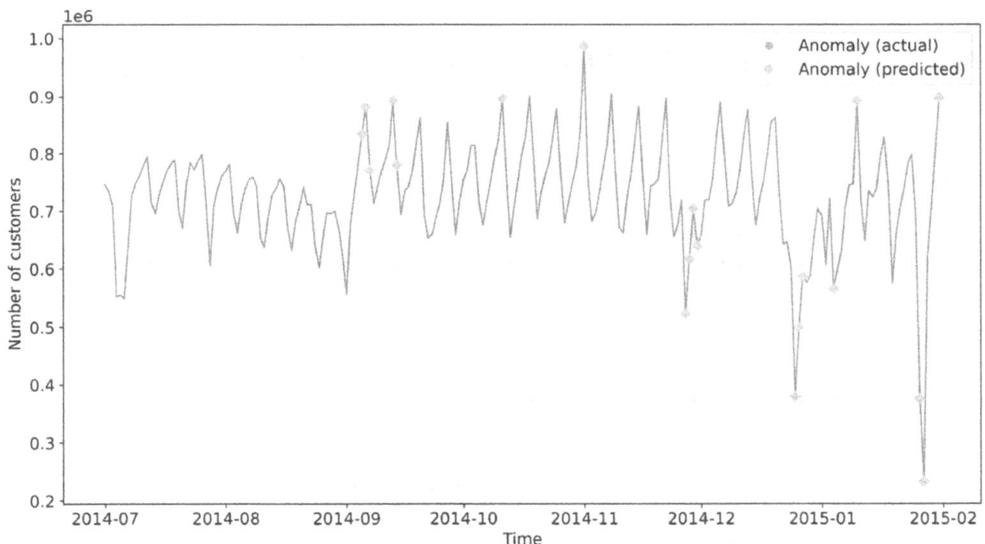


**Figure 5.14 Anomalies detected by Chronos**

Figure 5.15 shows the result of computing Chronos's precision, recall, and F1 Score. TimeGPT achieves higher precision and a higher F1 Score, so overall, it's a better model for detecting anomalies in this dataset. For Chronos, recall is 100%, but precision and F1 Score are lower than in TimeGPT. Chronos achieves a precision of 21%, meaning that among the points labeled as anomalies, only 21% are in fact anomalies. Once again, this example is not a comprehensive benchmark of either model's anomaly-detection capabilities.

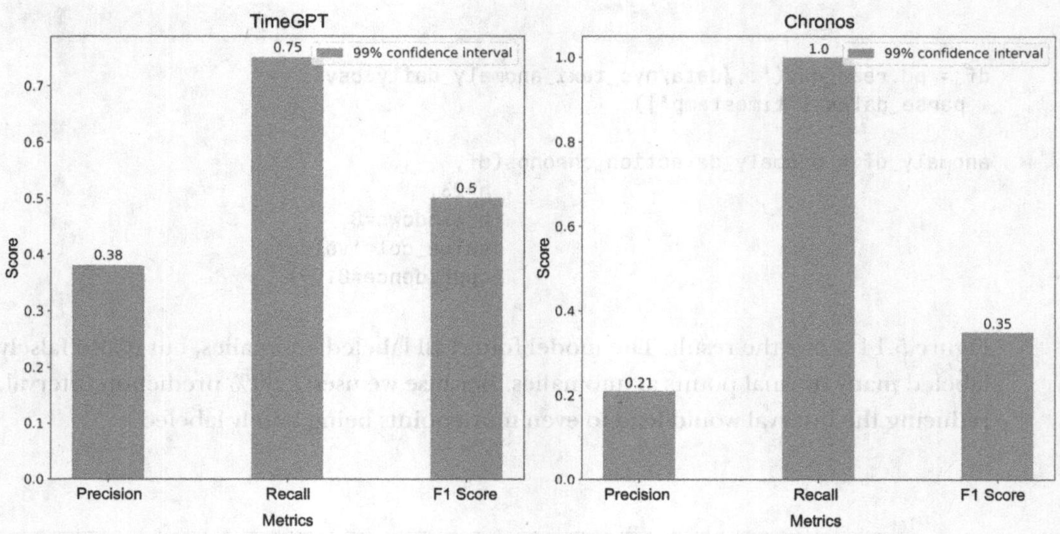


**Figure 5.15 Comparing the anomaly-detection performance of TimeGPT (left) and Chronos (right). Higher is better.**

## 5.9 Next steps

In this chapter, we discovered and applied Chronos. Although Chronos is technically a framework to pretrain existing language models for time series forecasting, it also designates a suite of pretrained forecasting models on the T5 family. Once more, let's update our summary of foundation models (table 5.4).

**Table 5.4 Pros and cons of each foundation forecasting model**

| Model | Pros | Cons | When to use |
|---|---|---|---|
| TimeGPT | Easy and fast to use<br>Comes with many native functions<br>Works on any device, regardless of hardware<br>Free plan | Paid product for a certain usage<br>Model may not be available if the server is down | Forecasting on long and short horizons with exogenous features<br>You need to fine-tune but do not have the local resources. |
| Lag-Llama | Open source model<br>Free to use | Awkward to use because we must clone the repository<br>Speed of inference depends on our hardware. | Quick proof of concept<br>Ideal for research-oriented projects |
| Chronos | Open source model<br>Free to use<br>Can be installed as a Python package | Speed and accuracy depend on our hardware.<br>Fine-tuning requires cloning the repository.<br>We must define some functions manually. | Forecasting on horizons shorter than 64 time steps<br>Forecasting series without strong trends |

Chronos is open-source and can be installed as a package, making it much easier to use than Lag-Llama. However, depending on the hardware available, we might be limited to using smaller models that do not perform as well as larger models.

It can be used for both forecasting and anomaly detection, but it requires some manual setup and defining some functions to make the experience more streamlined.

Keep in mind that Chronos was trained on a forecast horizon of 64 timesteps, so forecasting on longer periods may degrade the performance.

Furthermore, at the time of writing, it does not support the use of exogenous features when forecasting.

In chapter 6, we explore Moirai, a foundation model developed by Salesforce that aims to provide a unified solution to large-scale time-series forecasting.

## Summary

- Chronos is a framework that trains existing language models for time-series forecasting. It tokenizes time-series data using mean scaling and uniform binning to feed it to a language model.
- Existing pretrained models are based on the T5 architecture.
- Chronos can be installed as a package, making it easier to use in a production environment.
- It can be used for forecasting and anomaly detection, but it requires some manual setup and defining functions to streamline the process.
- Forecasting beyond 64 time steps may degrade the quality of forecasts.
- Chronos does not support exogenous features.
- The selection of a pretrained model depends on the available hardware. If a GPU is available for inference and you have the necessary memory space, opting for the largest model leads to the best results.

# 6 Moirai: A universal forecasting transformer

***This chapter covers***

- Discovering the Moirai model
- Zero-shot forecasting with Moirai
- Forecasting with exogenous features
- Detecting anomalies with Moirai

Until now, TimeGPT is the only foundation model covered in this book so far that supports exogenous features—external factors that affect our series, such as holidays. At this writing, Lag-Llama and Chronos can perform only univariate forecasting; they don't support exogenous features. Yet this support is a critical aspect of forecasting because future values of time series are often influenced by external factors. The sales of flowers and chocolates, for example, are likely influenced by holidays, so having a way to feed that information to our models will result in better performance.

Moirai is one of the first open source foundation models to support exogenous features out of the box. It's ideal to use when we have external variables, and it's also accessible via a Python package.

This chapter explores the architecture of Moirai to show how it processes the input series. We discover that the model was pretrained because the quality of a foundation model relies heavily on its pretraining protocol. Then we apply the model in our sales forecasting scenario and to anomaly detection.

## 6.1 Exploring Moirai

Moirai (the name is derived from *masked encoder-based universal time-series forecasting*) is a foundation forecasting model developed by Salesforce researchers [1]. It is a probabilistic forecasting model, meaning that it outputs a future distribution of values, like all the models we have explored so far. Later in this chapter, in section 6.3, we'll use the median as the point forecast and inherently calculate any prediction interval from the output distribution.

### 6.1.1 Viewing the architecture of Moirai

In addition to using only the encoder portion of the transformer architecture, Moirai uses patching to tokenize the input series. It also uses a mixture of distributions for the final predicted distribution, as shown in figure 6.1.

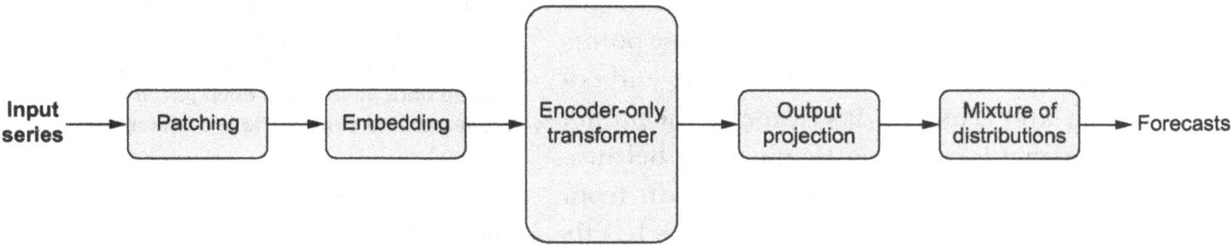


**Figure 6.1 Architecture of Moirai. Here, the series is patched before entering the encoder-only transformer. Then, a mixture of distributions generates a flexible output distribution of future values.**

With this architecture, Moirai attempts to be a universal forecaster, which is an especially challenging task because time-series data is highly heterogeneous. Depending on their domain, time series can depend on different variates, and of course, they have values on different scales. Also, the frequency of time series has a large effect on the observed patterns. Usually, high-frequency data, such as every second or minute, displays many variations, whereas low-frequency data, such as yearly or quarterly, tends to be smoother. Let's explore in detail how each component of Moirai architecture addresses the challenge of building a foundation forecasting model.

#### PATCHING

As shown in figure 6.1, the first step is patching the input time series. This concept was introduced for time-series forecasting in the PatchTST model [2].

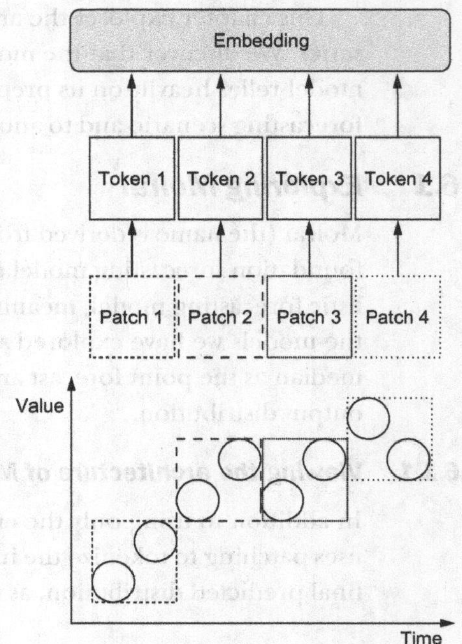


**Figure 6.2 The process of patching. Typically, each data point (circle) is a token that's sent to the embedding layer. With patching, we group data points, and each patch becomes a token that is sent to the embedding layer.**

> **NOTE** Grouping data points together to be tokenized allows the model to extract local relationships between past and future data points. It also reduces the number of tokens being set to the model, making it lighter and faster.

The idea is that instead of tokenizing each time step individually and sending it to the embedding layer, we create patches by grouping many time steps in a single token, as shown in figure 6.2.

Typically, every time-series point is tokenized and sent to the embedding layer of the transformer. The main drawback of this method is that it's difficult for the model to learn relationships between past and future data points.

Patching overcomes this challenge by grouping time-series points. Figure 6.2 shows an example of patching with a length of 2: we create groups of two data points that are tokenized and sent to the embedding layer. That way, it's easier for the model to extract local semantic meaning because now each token carries information from multiple data points. This approach has the added benefit of reducing the number of tokens being sent to the embedding layer. In figure 6.2, instead of sending eight individual tokens, we send four because each patch becomes a token. This makes the model lighter and faster and allows it to consider a longer input window, enabling the model to learn long-term variations in the series.

Whereas patches can overlap in PatchTST, they're strictly nonoverlapping in Moirai, as shown in figure 6.2. Furthermore, Moirai varies the length of the patch depending on the frequency of the data. Longer patches are used for high-frequency data, and shorter patches are used for low-frequency data. Table 6.1 summarizes possible patch lengths given a series' frequency.

**Table 6.1 Patch lengths used for frequencies in Moirai**

| Frequency | Patch length |
|---|---|
| Yearly, quarterly | 8 |
| Monthly | [8, 16, 32] |
| Weekly, daily | [16, 32] |

**Table 6.1 Patch lengths used for frequencies in Moirai (*continued*)**

| Frequency | Patch length |
|---|---|
| Hourly | [32, 64] |
| Every minute | [32, 64, 128] |
| Every second | [64, 128] |

If we pass yearly or quarterly data, a patch length of 8 is used, meaning that groups of eight data points are tokenized. If the data is monthly, the series is patched three times, with lengths of 8, 16 and 32. Each patched series is fed to its own embedding layer, so three different embedding layers for monthly data will be fed to the encoder-only transformer.

The lengths reported in table 6.1 were determined heuristically by the researchers. The idea behind setting a longer patch length for high-frequency data is to lower the computation cost because patching reduces the number of tokens. Also, with longer patches, the model can still consider long input windows, which are crucial for high-frequency datasets. Keep in mind that we don't choose the patch length when using Moirai. This setting is made automatically depending on the frequency of the data.

#### ANY-VARIATE ATTENTION IN THE ENCODER-ONLY TRANSFORMER

When the series is patched, it goes through the embedding layer (explored in chapter 1), and the data makes its way to the encoder-only transformer. The architecture of the encoder portion of the transformer remains unchanged in Moirai, but the researchers introduced a significant modification that allows the model to handle multivariate data.

Recall that the embedding layers map an input to a fixed-dimensional space, depending on the number of input series and the number of hidden layers. Therefore, using the traditional transformer architecture forces us to assume that variates are independent or set a maximum number of input series.

In the context of building a foundation model, this approach is too constraining. Moirai addresses that problem by flattening multivariate data into a single long sequence, as shown in figure 6.3.

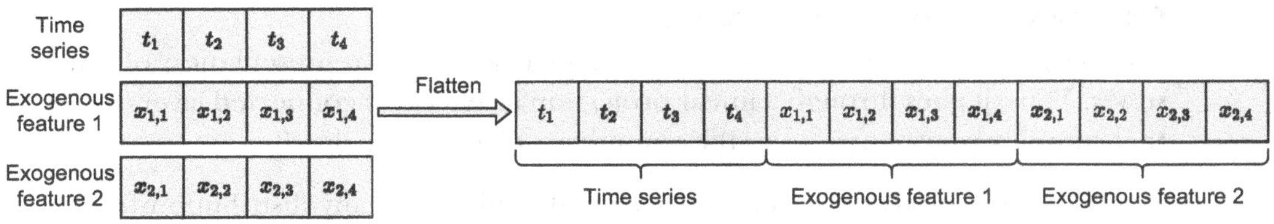


**Figure 6.3 To handle an arbitrary number of variates, Moirai flattens the data into a single series.**

In figure 6.3, an input with a target series and two exogenous features is flattened into one long sequence that is fed to the encoder, getting rid of the fixed-dimensionality problem because the transformer can already handle sequences of varying length. Therefore, adding or removing features merely changes the length of the input. But a new challenge arises because now the model must distinguish between input series. Thus, we introduce the binary attention bias, effectively creating an any-variate attention mechanism.

The *binary attention bias* is a simple mathematical trick that allows us to encode information about the relationship between features in the attention calculation. The formula for the binary attention bias is

$$u^{\{1\}} * \mathbb{1}_{\{m=n\}} + u^{(2)} * \mathbb{1}_{\{m \neq n\}} \tag{6.1}$$

where $\mathbb{1}$ is a conditional function defined as follows:

$$\mathbb{1}_{\{\text{cond}\}} = \begin{cases} 1, & \text{if cond} \\ 0, & \text{otherwise} \end{cases} \tag{6.2}$$

In equation 6.1, $u^{(1)}$ and $u^{(2)}$ are learnable parameters, and *m* and *n* are simple variate indices. If *m* equal *n*, the model is learning relationships with data coming from the same series. Therefore, the bias $u^{(1)}$ is added, and bias $u^{(2)}$ is canceled out because $\mathbb{1}$ equals 0 when *m* is not equal to *n*. Alternatively, if attention is being calculated with data coming from different variates, *m* is different from *n*, so bias $u^{(2)}$ is added.

With this simple mathematical trick, the model inherently knows whether it's learning information from a target series and its historical values or from data points that come from different series. Thus, the model can consider any number of series and exogenous features.

At this point, we know that the input data is flattened and patched with varying lengths depending on the frequency of the data. For each patch length, an embedding layer is learned, and that embedding is fed to an encoder-only transformer, where the attention mechanism is modified with the binary attention bias to help distinguish between each series in the flat sequence. The next step is generating output.

#### PROJECTION AND MIXTURE OF DISTRIBUTIONS

The output of the encoder-only transformer is a hidden representation of patched series. Thus, it goes through a linear projection layer, a fully connected layer that maps that complex representation to the parameters of a mixture distribution.

> **DEFINITION** A *mixture distribution* is a combination of many distribution functions called *components*. This is a way to create a hybrid version of many distributions, resulting in a more flexible distribution function.

This last element is critical in Moirai because it allows the creation of a more flexible distribution of future values. In Lag-Llama, only the Student's t-distribution is used, so Lag-Llama can model only symmetric distributions. Not all time-series data comes from symmetric distributions, which is where the mixture distribution comes into play. A mixture distribution is a weighted sum of different probability density functions:

$$f(x) = \sum_{i=1}^{n} w_i f_i(x) \tag{6.3}$$

In equation 6.3, $w_i$ is the mixing weight, and $f_i(x)$ is a distribution function that makes up the mixture distribution. In this case, the weight is the probability that a point is drawn from a given distribution function. Therefore, a mixture distribution is obtained by drawing points from different distribution functions, resulting in a new combination (figure 6.4).

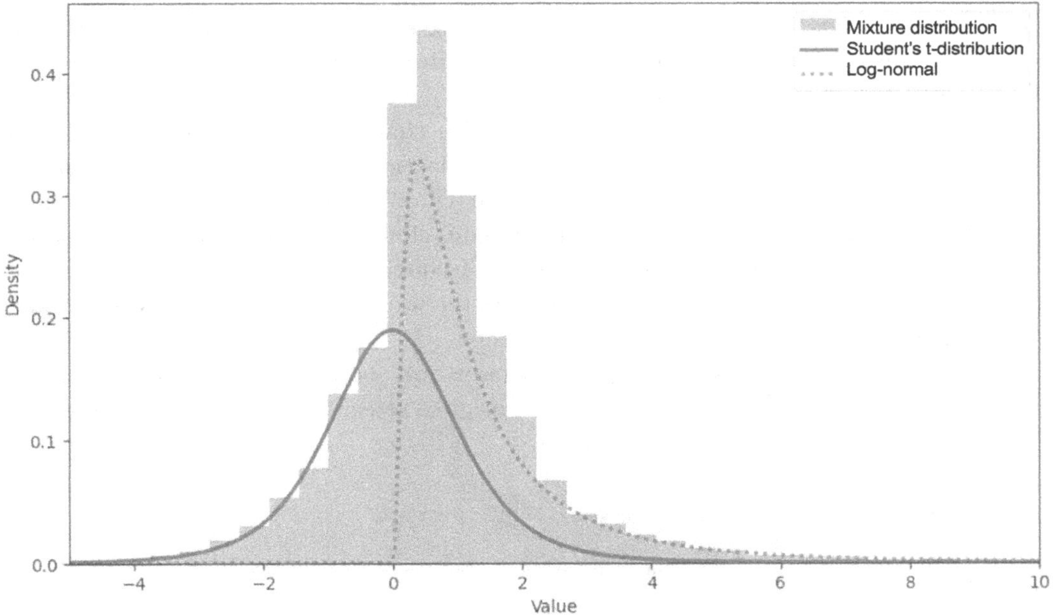


**Figure 6.4 A mixture distribution made of a Student's t-distribution and a log-normal distribution. For this plot, points have the same chance of being drawn from each distribution, and the result is a combination of both functions.**

The mixture distribution in figure 6.4 is illustrated by the bars. We see that the mixture has properties from both the Student's t-distribution and the log-normal. In the case of Moirai, the mixture is made up of four components:

- Student's t-distribution
- Log-normal distribution

- Negative binomial distribution
- Low-variance normal distribution

The Student's t-distribution was chosen because it represents a robust choice for the vast majority of time-series data. The log-normal is included to adapt for right-skewed data. The negative binomial distribution is useful for positive count data. Finally, the low-variance normal distribution helps make the prediction intervals tighter. For the latter, variance is set to 0.001. With a mixture distribution, Moirai can generate flexible asymmetric prediction intervals and potentially adapt to various time-series datasets without assuming any existing fixed distribution.

### 6.1.2 Pretraining Moirai

In chapter 2, I mentioned that one major challenge in building a foundation forecasting model is overcoming data scarcity. The reality is that there is less open source time-series data than for natural language data. Large language models (LLMs) are often trained on trillions of tokens, whereas time-series models are constrained to about 1 billion tokens or fewer.

The researchers behind Moirai tackled this challenge by compiling what at this writing is the largest open source time series dataset, with more than 27 billion data points. This dataset is the Large-Scale Open Time Series Archive (LOTSA). It spans nine domains: energy, transportation, climate, cloud operations, web, sales, nature, economics, and health care. It also covers all frequencies, from yearly to every second. The dataset is openly available, which paves the way for new large time-series models because data scarcity is not as great a challenge.

Table 6.2 summarizes the number of datasets and observations for each frequency in LOTSA. All information is taken from the original research paper [1], and numbers of observations were rounded for legibility.

**Table 6.2 Breakdown of LOTSA by frequency**

| Frequency | Number of datasets | Number of observations |
|---|---|---|
| Yearly | 4 | 0.87 million |
| Quarterly | 5 | 2.31 million |
| Monthly | 10 | 11.04 million |
| Weekly | 7 | 18.48 million |
| Daily | 21 | 709.02 million |
| Hourly | 31 | 19.88 billion |
| Every minute | 25 | 7.01 billion |
| Every second | 2 | 14.79 million |

Table 6.2 shows that some datasets represent a larger portion of LOTSA. Hourly datasets make up 72% of LOTSA, for example, whereas yearly datasets account only for

0.003% of the observations. Thus, to ensure that the model generalizes well at all frequencies, Moirai was pretrained by subsampling series from the entire dataset. If a dataset represents more than 0.1% of LOTSA, its probability of being sampled was set to 0.1%, ensuring that the model doesn't overspecialize in a certain frequency.

Next, varying input sequences were used, ranging from 2 to 512 time steps. The forecast horizon is sampled from the input windows, ranging from 15% to 50% of the input window. Moirai was trained to forecast at most 256 time steps into the future because this number represents 50% of the largest input length.

Like Chronos, Moirai has versions of pretrained models: small, base, and large. Table 6.3 summarizes the models' training steps and parameters. The small model has the fewest parameters and was trained for only 100,000 steps. The base and large models were trained for 1 million steps, so these models were given more opportunities to learn from the pretraining data and are therefore more performant.

**Table 6.3 Summary of pretrained Moirai models**

| Model | Pretraining steps | Number of parameters |
|---|---|---|
| Small | 100,000 | 14 million |
| Base | 1,000,000 | 91 million |
| Large | 1,000,000 | 311 million |

> **WARNING** Keep in mind the tradeoff among model size, speed of inference, and performance. Although larger models tend to be more accurate, they also require more memory and more computational power to run inference. Also, larger models can be slower to generate predictions if the hardware isn't suitable.

### 6.1.3 *Selecting the appropriate model*

As in Chronos, the largest model usually produces the best results, and the choice of that model implies that we need better hardware to run it. Therefore, if large computation resources are available, opting for the large model is the best option.

Alternatively, if only a CPU is available, using the base or small model is preferable. The choice is always a matter of balancing the time of inference and the available hardware. Small models may produce worse results, but inference time is faster. Larger models may producer better results, but inference time can be particularly long if the hardware isn't powerful enough.

## 6.2 *Discovering Moirai-MoE*

In October 2024, the researchers behind Moirai introduced an enhanced version of the model with a slightly different architecture that uses a decoder-only transformer and mixture of experts. This version is called Moirai-MoE, where *MoE* stands for *mixture of experts* [3]. Moirai-MoE makes small adjustments in the architecture but follows the same general pretraining and prediction-generating steps, as shown in figure 6.5.

> **DEFINITION** A *mixture of experts* is a group of feed-forward networks. Each network specializes in a particular pattern of a time series, so each network is called an *expert*. This layer is preceded by a gating function that determines which experts to activate. When not all experts are activated, we call this a *sparse mixture of experts*.

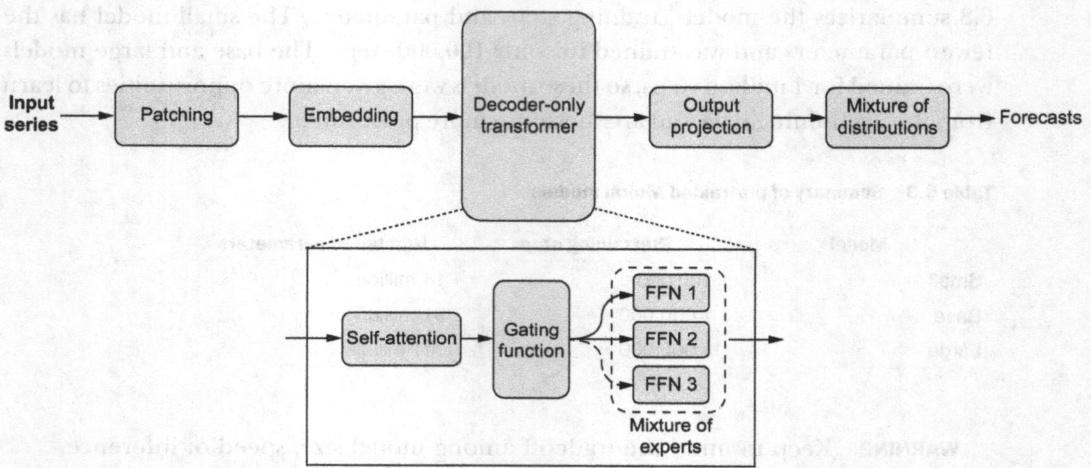


**Figure 6.5 Architecture of Moirai-MoE. Unlike the first version of Moirai, the new version uses a decoder-only transformer. Inside the decoder-only transformer, a gating function and a mixture-of-experts layer have been added. The gating function learns which expert to activate depending on the data, with a maximum of two experts being activated at the same time. The activation of an expert is indicated by a solid arrow.**

In figure 6.5, the first steps are the same, meaning that the series is still patched and embedded. The core model, however, is a decoder-only transformer instead of an encoder-only transformer. After the self-attention mechanism, a gating function and a mixture-of-experts layer are added. We explore these elements in more detail later in section 6.2.1. Finally, forecasts are obtained from an output projection layer and a mixture of distributions, as in the previous version of Moirai. These changes simplify the model and unlock greater performance. The following sections explore the components in detail to show the differences between the two versions of the model.

### 6.2.1 Patching and embedding

Like Moirai, Moirai-MoE uses patching before embedding the patched tokens and sending them to the transformer. Recall that Moirai uses heuristics to determine the patch length depending on the frequency of the data. Thus, different embedding layers are trained for each patch length, adding complexity and computational overhead during pretraining.

By contrast, Moirai-MoE uses a fixed patch length for all series, regardless of frequency, and generates nonoverlapping patches. Thus, a single input projection is trained, making the model more general because it isn't specializing in a particular frequency. In other words, all frequencies are patched and embedded the same way. This greatly simplifies the model's architecture and results in a more general architecture for a universal forecaster.

### 6.2.2 *Studying the decoder-only transformer*

Unlike Moirai, Moirai-MoE uses a decoder-only transformer. This change is significant because the encoder-only architecture predicted the entire forecast sequence in a single shot.

With a decoder-only transformer, the forecast sequence is generated one token at a time, and each predicted token informs the next predicted token. Keep in mind that a token is a patch of time steps, so it isn't forecasting one time step at a time; it's forecasting one group of time steps at a time.

#### MIXTURE OF EXPERTS

As shown in figure 6.5, a gating function and a mixture-of-experts layer were added after the self-attention mechanism, replacing the usual feed-forward network in the classical architecture of a decoder-only transformer.

In Moirai-MoE, the sparse mixture-of-experts layer consists of 32 experts, each of which is a feed-forward network that specializes in a particular time-series pattern. There could be an expert for each frequency of data, an expert for increasing trend, another one for decreasing trends, and so on. The idea is that Moirai-MoE tokenizes and embeds all series the same way, regardless of frequency; the mixture-of-experts layer specializes in particular aspects of time-series sequences.

**NOTE** Moirai-MoE uses a sparse mixture of experts, meaning that not all experts are activated, effectively speeding the inference process.

#### GATING FUNCTION

The next main challenge is designing a function to activate the right expert, which is the responsibility of the gating function. Traditionally, the gating function uses a learned weighted function. The gating function must be learned from scratch. Some experts are activated often, and others are rarely used. To counter that situation, the researchers proposed a gating function based on token clusters. They used the token representations previously learned by Moirai and applied k-means clustering to obtain centroids. Here, the number of centroids corresponds to the number of experts, which is 32.

Then, for each new input token, the Euclidean distance is calculated between the input token and each centroid. The distances are converted to probabilities using the softmax function, which routes the token to the right expert. Therefore, tokens with the smallest distance to a particular centroid are routed to their respective expert. That way, the model isn't learning the routing from scratch and uses the natural clustering of token representations during pretraining, which better reflects the actual distribution of patterns in the data.

### 6.2.3 Pretraining Moirai-MoE

The pretraining protocol of Moirai-MoE is identical to that of Moirai. The researchers pretrained and released two sizes of Moirai-MoE: small and base. The small model contains 117 million parameters, and the base model has 935 million parameters. These figures are significantly larger than in the previous Moirai architecture, which had 14 million parameters for the small configuration and 91 million parameters for the base configurations.

This doesn't mean that the inference time is slower for Moirai-MoE. The increase in parameters comes from the mixture of experts. Because not all experts are activated, however, at the time of inference, Moirai-MoE is faster than its predecessor.

## 6.3 Forecasting with Moirai

The workflow of forecasting with Moirai is a mix of the Lag-Llama and Chronos workflows. First, Moirai comes as a Python package, so we can run the command line to install the required dependencies and use a pretrained Moirai model:

```
pip install uni2ts
```

Then, like Lag-Llama, Moirai borrows the formats and functionalities of GluonTS to handle data preprocessing, create a predictor, and make predictions. We'll reuse some logic implemented in chapter 4 and adapt it to the Moirai model.

> **NOTE** I use the small model in this book to ensure that most readers can run the code. If you have access to a graphics processing unit (GPU) or more powerful computation resources, feel free to use the base or large model. Also, I use the original Moirai architecture in the code. Both versions take the same input parameters; you have to change only the model name, as specified in the code blocks.

### 6.3.1 Zero-shot forecasting with Moirai

In this section, we'll stick to our scenario of predicting weekly sales in four Walmart stores so we can focus on using Moirai without loading and learning a new dataset.

#### READING THE DATA

We start by reading our dataset. We're using the same dataset from chapter 3, so we're not plotting the time series again. Because Moirai expects a `PandasDataset`, a format from GluonTS, we also set the `date` column as the index, exactly as in Lag-Llama.

**Listing 6.1 Reading the dataset**

```
df = pd.read_csv('../data/walmart_sales_small.csv', parse_dates=['Date'])
df = df[['Store', 'Date', 'Weekly_Sales']]
df = df.set_index('Date')

ds = PandasDataset.from_long_dataframe(df, target='Weekly_Sales',
    item_id='Store')
```

Excludes the exogenous features (annotation on `df = df[['Store', 'Date', 'Weekly_Sales']]`)

#### INITIALIZING THE MODEL

Now that the dataset is in the format Moirai expects, we can initialize the model. Here, we specify the prediction length, which is eight weeks into the future. The context length is the entire historical data, and we generate 100 samples from the future distribution. In this case, we're not working with the available exogenous features, but we'll use them in section 6.3.3.

**Listing 6.2 Initializing the Moirai model**

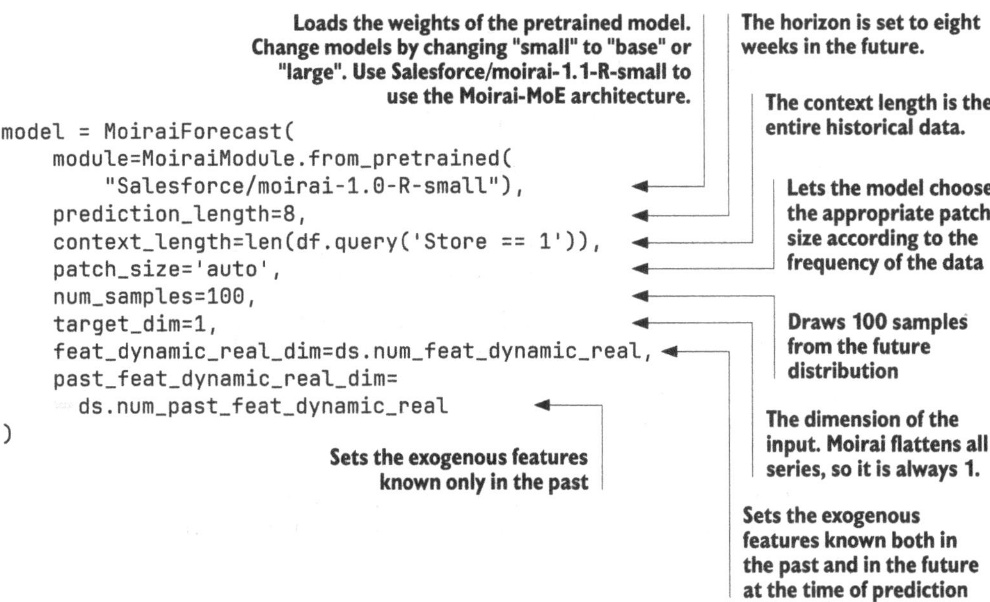

```
model = MoiraiForecast(
    module=MoiraiModule.from_pretrained(
        "Salesforce/moirai-1.0-R-small"),
    prediction_length=8,
    context_length=len(df.query('Store == 1')),
    patch_size='auto',
    num_samples=100,
    target_dim=1,
    feat_dynamic_real_dim=ds.num_feat_dynamic_real,
    past_feat_dynamic_real_dim=
        ds.num_past_feat_dynamic_real
)
```



In listing 6.2, the last two parameters set the exogenous features. These are attributes of the `ds` object, so we don't have to set them manually. We're not using exogenous features here, but we will in section 6.3.3.

#### MAKING PREDICTIONS

When the model is initialized, we can create a `predictor` object and generate forecasts.

**Listing 6.3 Generating predictions with Moirai**

```
predictor = model.create_predictor(batch_size=32)
forecasts = predictor.predict(ds)
forecasts = list(forecasts)
```

At this point, the `forecasts` variable contains an array of arrays. Each array represents the predictions for each store. Then, inside each array, we have 100 samples for each time step in the future, as in Lag-Llama and Chronos. Therefore, we reintroduce the `get_median_and_ci` function to extract the median as the point forecast and get the boundaries of a user-defined prediction interval. This function is the same as in chapters 4 and 5, so I won't explain its logic again.

**Listing 6.4 Extracting the median and bounds for a given confidence**

```
def get_median_and_ci(data,
                      start_date,
                      horizon,
                      freq,
                      id,
                      confidence=0.95):
    n_samples, n_timesteps = data.shape

    medians = np.median(data, axis=0)

    lower_percentile = (1 - confidence) / 2 * 100
    upper_percentile = (1 + confidence) / 2 * 100

    lower_bounds = np.percentile(data, lower_percentile, axis=0)
    upper_bounds = np.percentile(data, upper_percentile, axis=0)

    pred_dates = pd.date_range(start=start_date, periods=horizon, freq=freq)
    formatted_dates = pred_dates.strftime('%m-%d-%Y').tolist()

    df = pd.DataFrame({
    'Date': formatted_dates,
    'Store': id,
    'Moirai': medians,
        f'Moirai-lo-{int(confidence*100)}': lower_bounds,
        f'Moirai-hi-{int(confidence*100)}': upper_bounds
    })

    return df
```

Next, we use this function to format the predictions into a DataFrame for each store. In this case, we keep the default 95% prediction interval.

**Listing 6.5 Formatting predictions for each store**

```
preds = [
    get_median_and_ci(
```

```
            data=forecasts[i].samples,
            start_date='11-02-2012',
            horizon=8,
            freq='W-FRI',
            id=i+1
        )
        for i in range(4)
]

preds_df = pd.concat(preds, axis=0, ignore_index=True)
preds_df['Date'] = pd.to_datetime(preds_df['Date'])
```

We can plot the historical data and the zero-shot predictions made by Moirai as shown in figure 6.6.

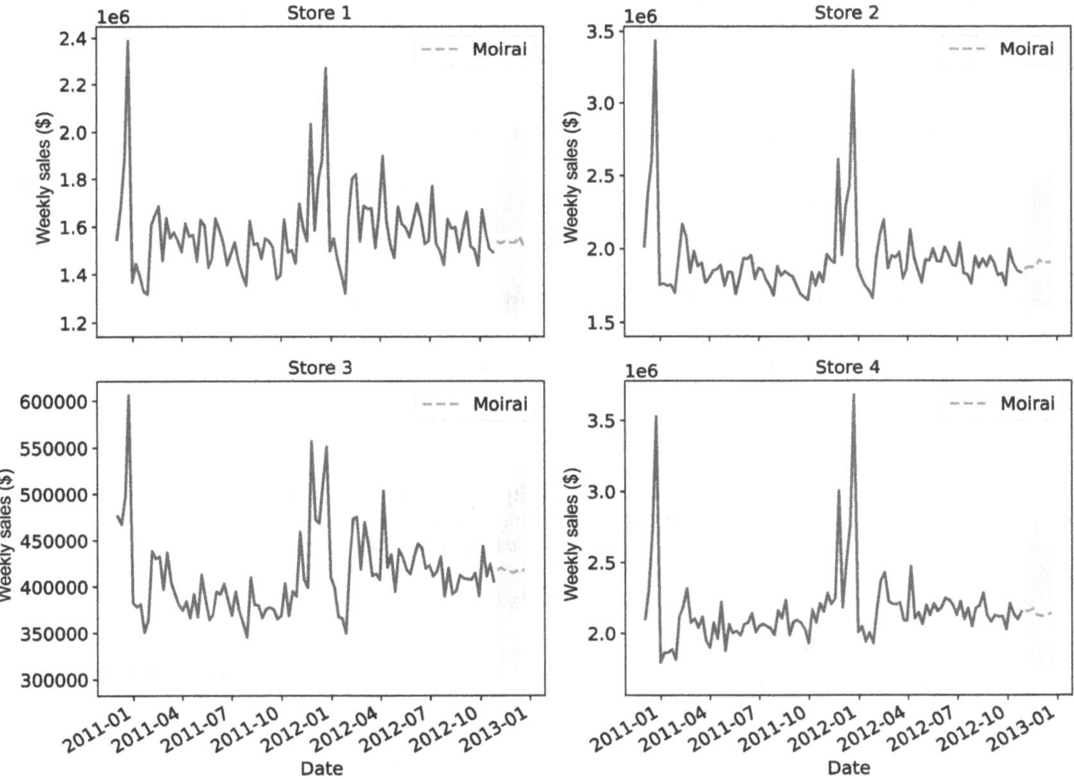


**Figure 6.6 Zero-shot forecasts of the weekly sales of four stores eight weeks into the future. The shaded area represents the 95% prediction interval.**

In figure 6.6, the predictions are the dashed lines, and the prediction interval is displayed as a shaded area. We can't assess the performance of the model because we generated predictions for dates we have no known values for. Therefore, we must perform cross-validation to evaluate the performance of Moirai.

### 6.3.2 Cross-validation with Moirai

With cross-validation, we can evaluate the performance of large time models by forecasting multiple windows and comparing the predicted and actual values.

#### READING THE DATA FOR STORE 1

We read the dataset again to start with a clean slate. We don't use the exogenous features here, but we'll use them in the next section to see how including them affects the model's performance.

**Listing 6.6 Reading and formatting the dataset**

```
df = pd.read_csv('../data/walmart_sales_small.csv', parse_dates=['Date'])
df = df.query("Store == 1")
df = df[['Store', 'Date', 'Weekly_Sales']]
df = df.set_index('Date')

ds = PandasDataset.from_long_dataframe(df,
                                       target="Weekly_Sales",
                                       item_id="Store")
```

#### RUNNING CROSS-VALIDATION

Next, we use a GluonTS function to create the cross-validation windows automatically. To stay consistent with preceding chapters, we use four windows with a horizon of 8 time steps, reserving the last 32 time steps for testing.

**Listing 6.7 Creating cross-validation windows**

```
train, test_template = split(ds, offset=-32)

test_data = test_template.generate_instances(
    prediction_length=8,
    windows=4,
    distance=8
)
```

- `split(ds, offset=-32)`: Splits the dataset, specifying how many time steps are reserved for testing. The negative means we take the last data points of the dataset.
- `prediction_length=8`: Sets the horizon of the forecast
- `windows=4`: Sets the number of windows
- `distance=8`: Sets the distance equal to the horizon to have nonoverlapping windows

In listing 6.7, the `distance` parameter determines how many time steps separate the start of each cross-validation window. We set it to the same value as the horizon to avoid overlapping windows.

Next, we initialize the pretrained Moirai model. Again, we use the small version, but feel free to use any version you want. We shorten the input length here because part of the data is reserved for testing. When the model is initialized, we can generate predictions.

**Listing 6.8 Initializing Moirai and making predictions**

```
model = MoiraiForecast(
    module=MoiraiModule.from_pretrained(f"Salesforce/moirai-1.0-R-small"),
    prediction_length=8,
    context_length=100,
    patch_size="auto",
    num_samples=100,
    target_dim=1,
    feat_dynamic_real_dim=ds.num_feat_dynamic_real,
    past_feat_dynamic_real_dim=ds.num_past_feat_dynamic_real,
)

predictor = model.create_predictor(batch_size=32)
forecasts = predictor.predict(test_data.input)
forecasts = list(forecasts)
```

At this point, we must extract the predictions for each cross-validation window. Again, we use the `get_median_and_ci` function to format them in a DataFrame. We also add the actual values of the test set to that DataFrame to make evaluation and plotting easier.

**Listing 6.9 Extracting and formatting predictions**

```
start_dates = ["2012-03-23", "2012-05-18",
➥ "2012-07-13", "2012-09-07"]          ◄── The starting dates of the
                                            cross-validation windows
cv_preds = [
    get_median_and_ci(
        data=forecasts[i].samples,
        start_date=start_dates[i],
        horizon=8,
        freq='W-FRI',
        id=1
    )
    for i in range(4)
]

cv_preds_df = pd.concat(cv_preds, axis=0, ignore_index=True)
cv_preds_df['Date'] = pd.to_datetime(cv_preds_df['Date'])
cv_preds_df['Weekly_Sales'] = df.iloc[-32:]['Weekly_Sales'].values
```

Then we can plot the predictions against the actual values, as shown in figure 6.7.

#### EVALUATING THE MODEL

A visual evaluation isn't enough to assess the performance of a model, so we must calculate the mean absolute error (MAE) and symmetric mean absolute percentage error (sMAPE), as shown in listing 6.10.

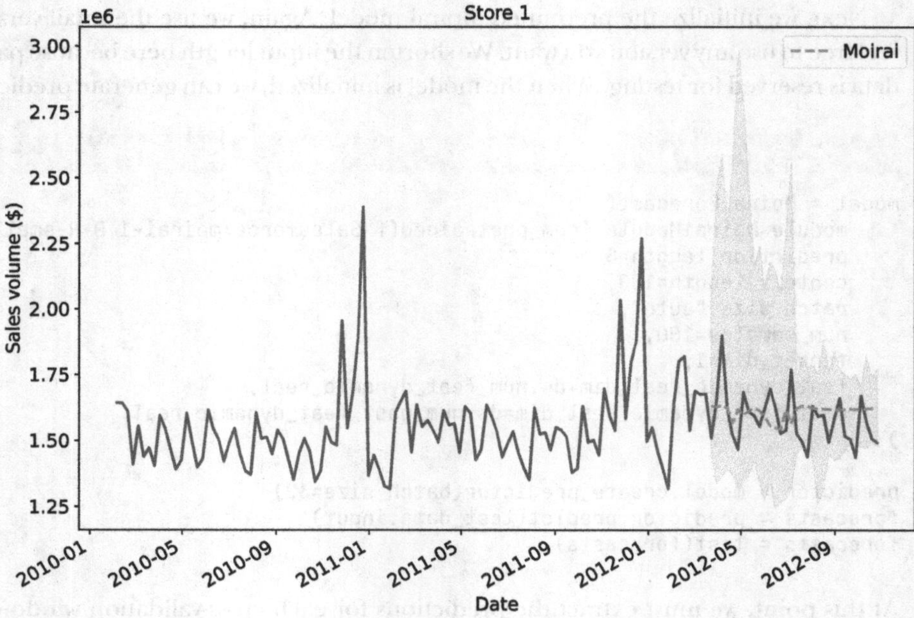


**Figure 6.7 Predictions from running cross-validation with Moirai. The shaded area represents the 95% prediction interval. Some overlap occurs, but Moirai doesn't seems to forecast the seasonal variations correctly.**

**Listing 6.10 Evaluating Moirai**

```
from utilsforecast.losses import mae, smape
from utilsforecast.evaluation import evaluate

evaluation = evaluate(
    cv_preds_df,
    metrics=[mae, smape],
    models=['Moirai'],
    target_col='Weekly_Sales',
    id_col='Store'
)
```

Table 6.4 compares Moirai's performance with that of the other foundation models we've used.

**Table 6.4 Performance metrics of large time models in cross-validation over four windows of eight weeks**

| Metric | TimeGPT (fine-tuned) | Lag-Llama (fine-tuned) | Chronos (fine-tuned) | Moirai (univariate) |
|---|---|---|---|---|
| MAE | 63544 | 72990 | 63811 | 84140 |
| sMAPE (%) | 2.04 | 2.29 | 1.99 | 2.64 |

This table reports an MAE of 84140$ and a sMAPE of 2.64% for Moirai. Keep in mind, however, that we haven't used the available exogenous features in the dataset to inform the predictions. Section 6.3.3 includes those features in the model so we can measure their effect on the forecasts' accuracy.

### 6.3.3 *Forecasting with exogenous features*

Up to now, we've used only historical sales data to predict our target. But Moirai supports the use of exogenous features, which can lead to better results.

#### READING THE DATA WITH EXOGENOUS FEATURES

We start by reading the dataset again, this time keeping all other rows for the exogenous features.

**Listing 6.11 Reading the data with all exogenous features**

```
df = pd.read_csv('../data/walmart_sales_small.csv', parse_dates=['Date'])
df = df.query("Store == 1")
df = df.set_index('Date')
```

Then, when we create the `PandasDataset`, we must specify the types of exogenous features. Here, there are two types of features:

- `past_feat_dynamic_real`—The first type designates features that are known only in the past. In our current scenario, these features include temperature, fuel price, Consumer Price Index (CPI), and unemployment rate. We have historical data for all these features but can't know their exact values at the time we make predictions.
- `feat_dynamic_real`—The second type designates features that are known both in the past and in the future. In our current scenario, those features are holiday dates. We know that holidays have been celebrated on the same date in the past and will keep being celebrated on the same date in the future.

We could argue that we could predict features such as temperature and unemployment rate over the forecast horizon and use those predictions to inform the forecast of our target. That approach is valid, but keep in mind that all forecasts contain some errors, and using predictions to generate more predictions can magnify those errors. By contrast, we know the future values of calendar features such as holidays with absolute certainty.

Thus, we create our `PandasDataset` specifying the column names for each feature type. In this case, we use only the historical values of temperature, fuel price, CPI, and unemployment rate, and we use both past and future values of the holiday flag.

**Listing 6.12 Creating the dataset and assigning exogenous features**

```
ds = PandasDataset.from_long_dataframe(
    df,
    target='Weekly_Sales',
```

```
    item_id='Store',
    past_feat_dynamic_real=["Temperature", "Fuel_Price", "CPI",
    ➥ "Unemployment"],
    feat_dynamic_real=["Holiday_Flag"]
)
```

These features are known only in the past.

These features are known in the past and in the future at the time of prediction.

#### MAKING PREDICTIONS WITH EXOGENOUS FEATURES

We follow the same steps as before to split our dataset, create cross-validation windows, and make predictions. This time, however, the model is using exogenous features.

**Listing 6.13 Cross-validating with Moirai**

```
train, test_template = split(
    ds, offset=-32
)

test_data = test_template.generate_instances(
    prediction_length=8,
    windows=4,
    distance=8
)

model = MoiraiForecast(
    module=MoiraiModule.from_pretrained(f"Salesforce/moirai-1.0-R-small"),
    prediction_length=8,
    context_length=100,
    patch_size="auto",
    num_samples=100,
    target_dim=1,
    feat_dynamic_real_dim=ds.num_feat_dynamic_real,
    past_feat_dynamic_real_dim=ds.num_past_feat_dynamic_real,
)

predictor = model.create_predictor(batch_size=32)
forecasts = predictor.predict(test_data.input)
forecasts = list(forecasts)
```

Again, we extract the predictions into a DataFrame and join the actual values for easier plotting and evaluation.

**Listing 6.14 Extracting and formatting predictions**

```
start_dates = ["2012-03-23", "2012-05-18", "2012-07-13", "2012-09-07"]

cv_feat_preds = [
    get_median_and_ci(
        data=forecasts[i].samples,
        start_date=start_dates[i],
        horizon=8,
```

```
        freq='W-FRI',
        id=1
    )
    for i in range(4)
]

cv_feat_preds_df = pd.concat(cv_feat_preds, axis=0, ignore_index=True)
cv_feat_preds_df['Date'] = pd.to_datetime(cv_feat_preds_df['Date'])

cv_feat_preds_df['Weekly_Sales'] = df.iloc[-32:]['Weekly_Sales'].values
```

The predictions informed by the exogenous features are plotted in figure 6.8.

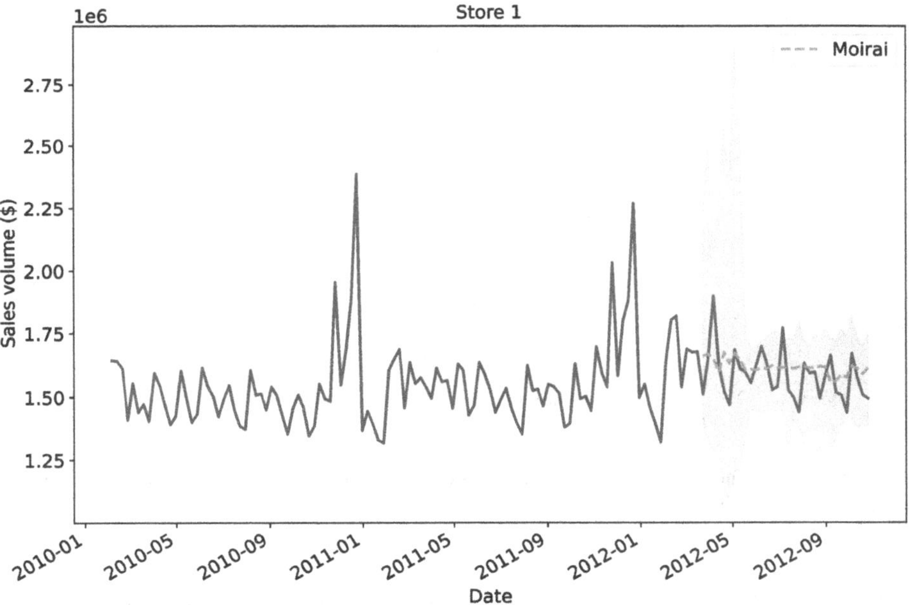


**Figure 6.8 Predictions obtained from running cross-validation with Moirai and using exogenous features. The shaded area represents the 95% prediction interval.**

Despite including exogenous features, the model still can't predict cyclical changes. We're using the smallest version of the Moirai model, however; using a larger version might result in better performance.

#### EVALUATING PREDICTIONS

Next, we evaluate the performance of Moirai when it uses exogenous features and compare it to the performance of Moirai when it uses only historical values, as shown in figure 6.9.

Listing 6.15 Evaluating Moirai with exogenous features

```
evaluation = evaluate(
    cv_feat_preds_df,
    metrics=[mae, smape],
    models=['Moirai'],
    target_col='Weekly_Sales',
    id_col='Store'
)
```

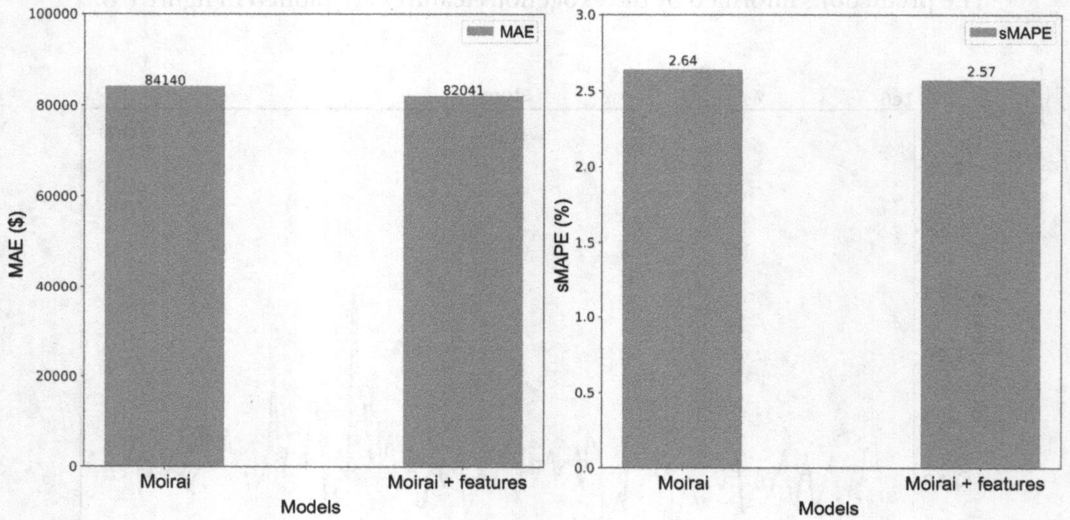


**Figure 6.9 Both performance metrics are improved when exogenous features are included, indicating a boost in performance. Lower is better in this plot.**

We also update the model performance comparison with this new experiment (table 6.5).

**Table 6.5 Performance metrics of large time models in cross-validation over four windows of eight weeks**

| Metric | TimeGPT (fine-tuned) | Lag-Llama (fine-tuned) | Chronos (fine-tuned) | Moirai | Moirai + exog |
|---|---|---|---|---|---|
| MAE | 63544 | 72990 | 63811 | 84140 | 82041 |
| sMAPE (%) | 2.04 | 2.29 | 1.99 | 2.64 | 2.57 |

Including exogenous features lowered Moirai's MAE from 84140$ to 82041$ and its sMAPE from 2.64% to 2.57%, representing an average improvement of roughly 2.5% across both metrics. Clearly, in this situation, using exogenous features has a positive effect on Moirai's performance. This example also exemplifies the importance of supporting exogenous features for large time models: including information from good features usually results in better performance.

## 6.4 Detecting anomalies with Moirai

For this experiment, we use the dataset from previous chapters to detect abnormal volumes of taxi rides in New York City. The natural first step is reading the dataset.

**Listing 6.16 Reading the dataset for anomaly detection**

```
df = pd.read_csv('../data/nyc_taxi_anomaly_daily.csv',
➥ parse_dates=['timestamp'])
```

To perform anomaly detection, we apply the same logic as we did in Chronos and TimeGPT. We perform rolling forecasts over many windows of the dataset, and if actual values fall outside a set prediction interval, we label it an anomaly.

To perform anomaly detection, we define a function that returns a DataFrame with the actual values, actual label, predicted label, predicted values, and predicted bounds.

**Listing 6.17 Function for anomaly detection with Moirai**

```
def anomaly_detection_moirai(df,
                             target_col,
                             id_col,
                             date_col,
                             h,
                             n_windows,
                             freq,
                             confidence=0.99):

    ds = PandasDataset.from_long_dataframe(      ← Creates the PandasDataset that Moirai expects
        df,
        target=target_col,
        item_id=id_col,
    )

    train, test_template = split(      ← Creates cross-validation windows
    ds, offset=-(n_windows*h)      ← The offset corresponds to the period for which we want to detect anomalies.
    )

    test_data = test_template.generate_instances(      ← Generates the test instances
        prediction_length=h,
        windows=n_windows,
        distance=h
    )

    model = MoiraiForecast(      ← Initializes the Moirai model
        module=MoiraiModule.from_pretrained(
        ➥ f"Salesforce/moirai-1.0-R-small"),
        prediction_length=h,
```

```
        context_length=100,
        patch_size="auto",
        num_samples=100,
        target_dim=1,
        feat_dynamic_real_dim=ds.num_feat_dynamic_real,
        past_feat_dynamic_real_dim=ds.num_past_feat_dynamic_real,
    )

    predictor = model.create_predictor(batch_size=32)
    forecasts = predictor.predict(test_data.input)
    forecasts = list(forecasts)

    df_test = df[-(n_windows*h):]          ◄── Corresponds to the actual values
                                               for the period for which we're
    list_dates = df_test[date_col]             performing anomaly detection
    start_dates = list(list_dates[::h])

    cv_preds = [                           ◄── Extracts predictions
        get_median_and_ci(                     as a DataFrame
            data=forecasts[i].samples,
            start_date=start_dates[i],w
            horizon=h,
            freq=freq,
            id=0,
            confidence=confidence
        )
        for i in range(n_windows)
    ]

    cv_preds_df = pd.concat(cv_preds, axis=0, ignore_index=True)
    cv_preds_df['Date'] = pd.to_datetime(cv_preds_df['Date'])

    df_test.rename(columns={date_col: 'Date'}, inplace=True)
    df_test = pd.merge(df_test, cv_preds_df, on='Date')
    df_test['anomaly'] = ((df_test[target_col] < df_test['Moirai-lo-99']) |
    ➥ (df_test[target_col] > df_test['Moirai-hi-99']))
    ➥ .astype(int)                        ◄── Labels an anomaly if the
                                               actual values are outside
    df_test = df_test.drop('Store', axis=1)    the prediction interval

    return df_test
```

In listing 6.17, we recognize many of the steps we used for forecasting. First, we create the `PandasDataset`; then we generate the cross-validation windows. This time, however, the windows must span the period for which we want to perform anomaly detection. Next, we initialize the model, make predictions, and write some logic so that when the actual values are outside the prediction intervals, they are labeled anomalies.

Now we can run this function and perform anomaly detection. Here, we use 23 windows and a horizon of eight, resulting in anomaly detection over the last 184 time steps. This replicates the conditions of the experiments made with TimeGPT and Chronos, making the results comparable.

**Listing 6.18 Running anomaly detection with Moirai**

```
df['unique_id'] = 0

anomaly_df = anomaly_detection_moirai(df,
                                      target_col="value",
                                      id_col="unique_id",
                                      date_col="timestamp",
                                      h=23,
                                      n_windows=8,
                                      freq='D',
                                      confidence=0.99)
```

The function expects a unique identifier. We set a constant value because we have only one series.

Then we can plot the points that the model considered anomalies, as shown in figure 6.10.

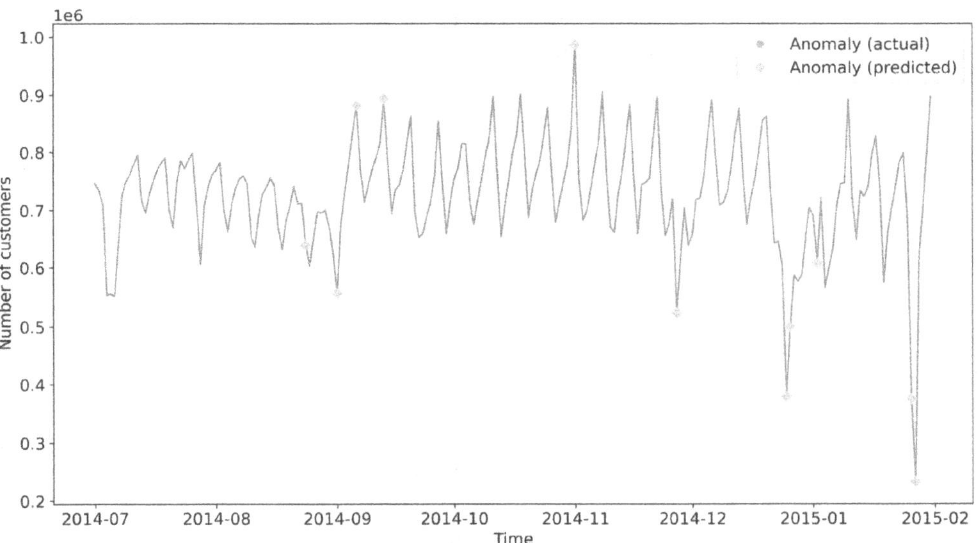


**Figure 6.10 Anomalies detected by Moirai**

The figure shows that Moirai flagged all actual anomalies but incorrectly labeled many other points as anomalies. This result indicates high recall but low precision for this experiment We can reuse the `evaluate_anomaly_detection` function from chapters 3 and 5 to calculate the precision, recall, and F1 Score of Moirai.

**Listing 6.19 Evaluating the performance of anomaly detection**

```
def evaluate_anomaly_detection(df, preds_col, actual_col):
    tp = ((df[preds_col] == 1) & (df[actual_col] == 1)).sum()
```

```
    tn = ((df[preds_col] == 0) & (df[actual_col] == 0)).sum()

    fp = ((df[preds_col] == 1) & (df[actual_col] == 0)).sum()

    fn = ((df[preds_col] == 0) & (df[actual_col] == 1)).sum()

    precision = tp / (tp + fp) if (tp + fp) != 0 else 0

    recall = tp / (tp + fn) if (tp + fn) != 0 else 0

    f1_score = 2 * (precision * recall) / (precision + recall) if
    ➥(precision + recall) != 0 else 0

    return precision, recall, f1_score

precision, recall, f1_score = evaluate_anomaly_detection(
➥anomaly_df[-182:], 'anomaly', 'is_anomaly')
```

For simplicity, we compare only the F1 Scores of models previously used for anomaly detection, as it is a geometric average of precision and recall in figure 6.11.

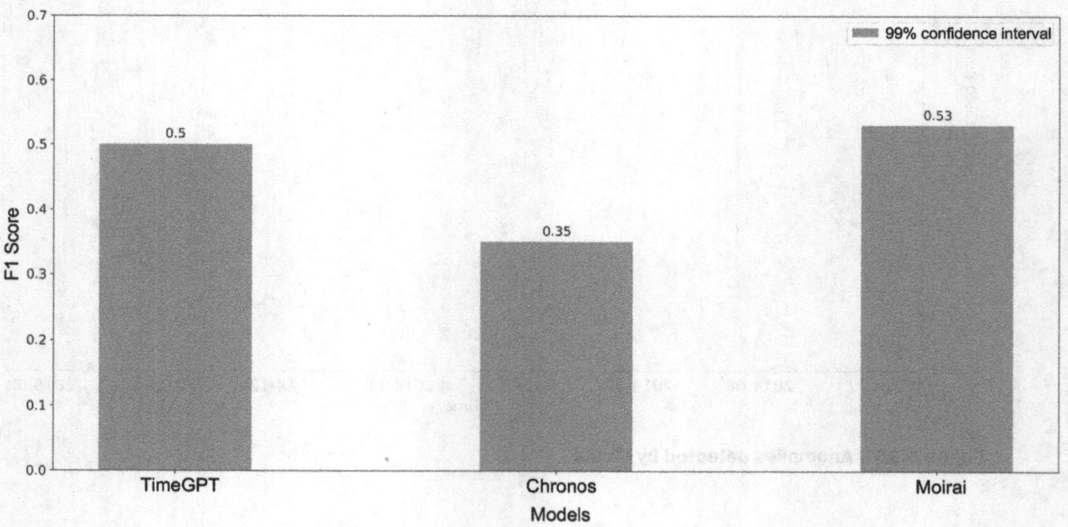


**Figure 6.11 F1 Scores of foundation models used for anomaly detection. Here, Moirai achieves the best overall result. Higher is better.**

In this scenario, Moirai achieves the best performance with an F1 Score of 0.53, and Chronos achieves the lowest performance on this task. This result doesn't represent benchmarks of those models' anomaly-detection capabilities because we're experimenting on only one dataset.

## 6.5 *Next steps*

In this chapter, we discovered Moirai, which is an encoder-only transformer model that supports exogenous features and is open source. We can update our summary table of the large time models explored so far (table 6.6).

**Table 6.6 Pros and cons of each foundation forecasting model**

| Model | Pros | Cons | When to use |
|---|---|---|---|
| TimeGPT | Easy and fast to use<br>Comes with many native functions<br>Works on any device, regardless of hardware<br>Free plan | Paid product for a certain usage<br>Model may not be available if the server is down | Forecasting on long and short horizons with exogenous features<br>You need to fine-tune but do not have the local resources. |
| Lag-Llama | Open source model<br>Free to use | Awkward to use because we must clone the repository<br>Speed of inference depends on our hardware. | Quick proof of concept<br>Ideal for research-oriented projects |
| Chronos | Open source model<br>Free to use<br>Can be installed as a Python package | Speed and accuracy depend on our hardware.<br>Fine-tuning requires cloning the repository.<br>We must define some functions manually. | Forecasting on horizons shorter than 64 time steps<br>Forecasting series without strong trends |
| Moirai | Open source model<br>Free to use<br>Supports exogenous features<br>Can be installed as a Python package | Speed and accuracy depend on the hardware.<br>We must define helper functions when we're not working entirely with GluonTS. | You have exogenous features.<br>Forecasting on horizons shorter than 256 time steps |

Moirai can be installed as a Python package, which is highly convenient, although it does rely on functionalities of GluonTS, which can represent a learning curve for practitioners who are not used to this library. Moirai comes with LOTSA, which has more than 27 billion data points. It represents a major contribution to the scientific community because it solves the problem of data scarcity when building a large time model.

In chapter 7, we explore TimesFM, a foundation forecasting model developed by Google researchers.

## Summary

- Moirai is a large time model developed by Salesforce researchers. It uses patching and an encoder-only transformer for probabilistic forecasting. The model is open source and can be installed as a Python library.
- It natively supports exogenous features.
- Using the largest model may lead to the best results, although it requires better hardware for reasonable inference times.
- LOTSA is the largest collection of open source time-series data and an important contribution to the development of future large time models.

# 7 Deterministic forecasting with TimesFM

***This chapter covers***

- Exploring the architecture of TimesFM
- Zero-shot forecasting with TimesFM
- Predicting with exogenous features

All foundation models we've explored so far are probabilistic forecasting models, which output a future probability distribution for each step in the forecast horizon. This allows us to derive arbitrary quantiles and quantify the uncertainty of the outcome as prediction intervals.

Although this approach provides a more complete view of the future, a model's output requires more processing steps. Also, we may be interested in only the point forecast, not the intervals. This approach is especially useful when a definitive forecast, rather than a range of possible values, is necessary for planning purposes.

**DEFINITION** *Deterministic forecasting* (or *point forecasting*) gives a single forecast value for a future time step. By contrast, *probabilistic forecasting* gives a range of possible values for a future time step. In deterministic forecasting, uncertainty is not accounted for.

TimesFM comes into play in this scenario. This model is a deterministic foundation forecasting model developed by Google Research [1]. Because it returns point forecasts, it can't be used for anomaly detection, which relies on uncertainty quantification to label anomalies. Still, TimesFM is ideal for forecasting values only, not ranges of values.

In this chapter, we explore the architecture of TimesFM, which borrows many components from Moirai but in a decoder-only transformer. We also examine the pretraining protocol and apply the model for zero-shot forecasting.

## 7.1 Examining TimesFM

TimesFM (which stands for Time-Series Foundation Model) is a deterministic model, meaning that it returns a point forecast. It's contrary to all the foundation models we've explored thus far, all of which are probabilistic forecasting models that output a distribution.

TimesFM is trained to take an input sequence and output a future sequence as follows, where $L$ is the length of the input sequence and $H$ is the length of the forecast horizon:

$$f : (y_{1:L}) \rightarrow \hat{y}_{L+1:L+H} \tag{7.1}$$

Because the model is deterministic, it's trained with a loss function that quantifies the distance from the predicted values and the actual values, such as the mean absolute error (MAE) or mean squared error (MSE). In the case of TimesFM, the MSE was used as a loss function, which penalizes large errors more heavily and should result in a better model overall.

### 7.1.1 Architecture of TimesFM

The discussion of TimesFM's architecture and inner workings is shorter than the comparable discussions in chapters 3 through 6 because many concepts from previous models are reused here. TimesFM is similar to Moirai (chapter 6), which also uses patching on the input series. Unlike Moirai, however, it uses a decoder-only transformer architecture, and it uses residual blocks to embed the input patches and map the output of the transformer to a sequence of predicted values, as shown in figure 7.1.

Figure 7.1 shows some familiar concepts, such as the transformer and patching, although their inner workings are slightly different from what we've explored in other models. The following sections explore the steps in detail.

#### PATCHING

The first step in TimesFM is patching the series. Each patch is contiguous and non-overlapping. As we saw in chapter 6, this step speeds inference because grouping data points reduces the number of tokens fed to the transformer.

Traditionally in transformers, the output is generated in an autoregressive fashion, where each piece of the output is fed back to the decoder to generate the next piece of

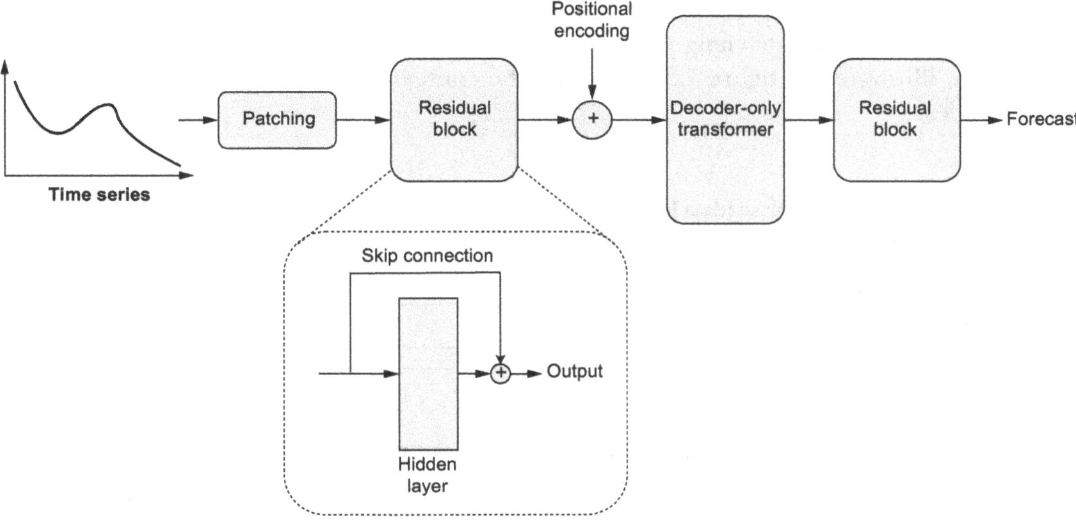


**Figure 7.1 Architecture of TimesFM. The input series is patched and set to a residual block that maps the input patches to a vector. The residual block is a multilayer perceptron with one hidden layer and a skip connection. The output vector is added to positional encoding and sent to the decoder-only transformer. The output of the transformer is sent to another residual block that returns a sequence of predicted values.**

output, as discussed in chapter 1. But this approach is less accurate in time-series forecasting, especially on long horizons. Ideally, the model outputs the entire sequence directly without feeding back its output. That is possible, of course, only if the horizon is set to a fixed value—not a possibility when we're building a foundation model because technically, the user can specify any arbitrary horizon.

To overcome this issue, TimesFM is trained to forecast longer output patches, as shown in figure 7.2. That way, it takes fewer steps to predict longer horizons, which makes predictions better.

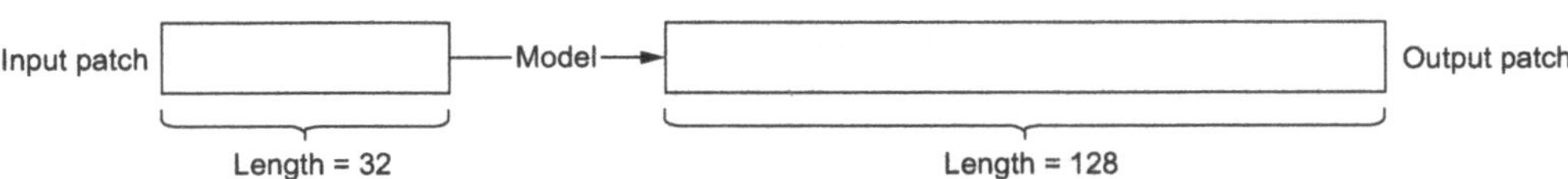


**Figure 7.2 In TimesFM, the output patch is longer than the input patch. Because the model performs fewer autoregressive steps when forecasting longer horizons, performance is better.**

In figure 7.2, the input patch length is 32 time steps, and the output patch length is 128 time steps. Thus, if the model is tasked with forecasting 256 time steps into the future, this technique requires only two autoregressive steps. If the output patch length were the same as the input patch length, the technique would require eight autoregressive steps.

To avoid building a mode that functions well only when the context length is a multiple of the input patch length, the researchers employed a random patch-masking strategy, illustrated in figure 7.3. Note that the context length is the length of the input series.

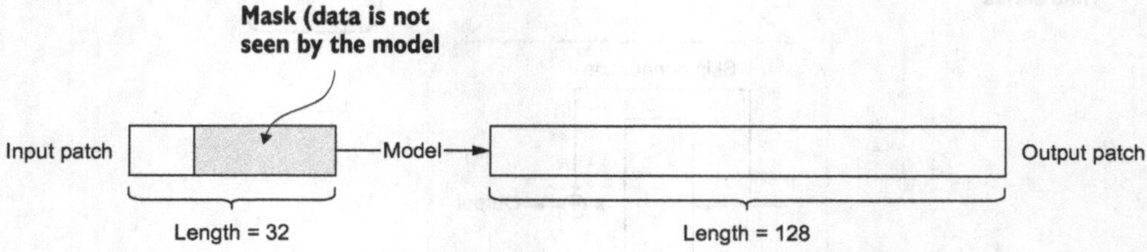


**Figure 7.3 Input patch-masking strategy during the training phase of TimesFM**

In the figure, we see that part of the input patch can be masked so that the model doesn't see these data points during training. With this random masking strategy, the model is trained to predict output patches with varying context lengths, even as small as a single data point. That way, TimesFM can handle many context lengths. Input masking is done only during the pretraining phase, of course. At the time of inference, the model sees the entire input sequence.

#### EMBEDDING WITH THE RESIDUAL BLOCK

The patched series is sent to a residual block, which maps the input to a vector with dimensions that match the hidden dimensions of the decoder-only transformer. A residual block uses a skip connection that adds the input to the output of the multilayer perceptron that passed through its hidden layers (refer to figure 7.1). This architecture choice is common in deep learning models with many hidden layers because it prevents the model from forgetting earlier information. It also mitigates the problem of vanishing or exploding gradients, which result respectively in the model's not learning or failing to optimize correctly.

The output of the residual block is summed with positional encoding, as in the traditional transformer that we explored in chapter 1.

#### GOING INSIDE THE DECODER-ONLY TRANSFORMER

The input patches and positional encoding are sent to a decoder-only transformer, which contains many stacked decoder layers all using multihead attention, as shown in figure 7.4.

We recognize the decoder portion of the transformer that we explored in chapter 1; TimesFM uses the same architecture.

Recall that during training, parts of the input patches may be masked, so the model will not attend, or see, the masked entries. This allows the model to handle varying input lengths.

#### GENERATING PREDICTIONS

The output of the transformer is in the form of patches, which go through another network of residual blocks that map those tokens to the final predictions over a given horizon. When the horizon exceeds the output patch length, the predictions are done recursively by feeding the last predictions back into the model to predict the next set of values. If the horizon is shorter than the output patch length, the values are truncated.

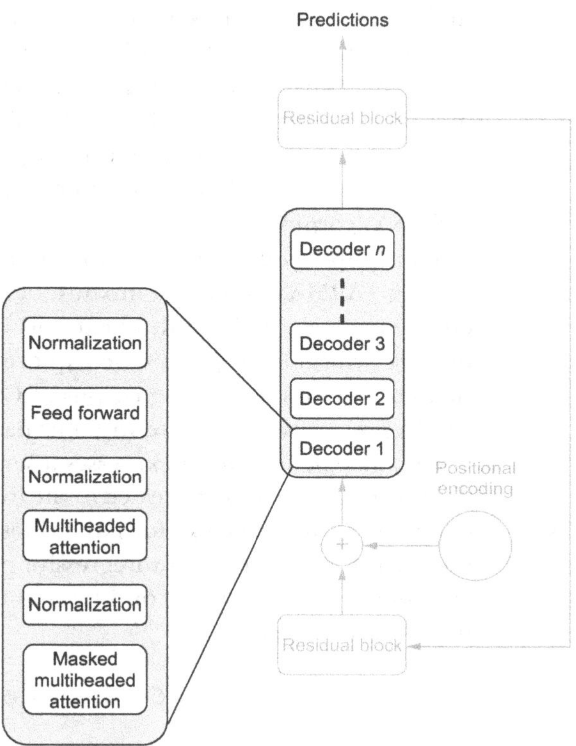


**Figure 7.4 Focusing on the decoder-only portion of TimesFM. The decoder is made of many decoder layers, each using multiheaded attention.**

### 7.1.2 *Pretraining TimesFM*

TimesFM is a deterministic model, meaning that it outputs point forecasts. Therefore, the model was pretrained to minimize the mean squared error (MSE) of its predictions. Because it uses the MSE, the model is penalized more heavily when it makes large errors, which should result in a better forecasting model.

To pretrain TimesFM, the researchers assembled a massive dataset of more than 207 million unique time series for a total exceeding 380 billion data points. Table 7.1 breaks down the series used in the training dataset.

**Table 7.1 Datasets used for pretraining TimesFM**

| Dataset | Frequencies | Number of data points |
|---|---|---|
| Synthetic | - | 6.1 billion |
| M4 | Yearly, quarterly, monthly, daily, and hourly | 26.7 million |
| Wiki Pageviews | Monthly, weekly, daily, and hourly | 374.5 billion |
| Google Trends | Monthly, weekly, daily, hourly | 536.4 million |
| Others | Daily, hourly, 15 minutes, and 10 minutes | 199.2 million |

The M4 dataset is the same one we used to pretrain our own small foundation model in chapter 2. Most of the training data comes from the web-traffic domain. Google

Trends, for example, quantifies search interest over time from millions of queries. In this case, the researchers used data from 22,000 search queries and aggregated them at different frequencies. Similarly, Wiki Pageviews tracks the hourly views of all Wikimedia pages. The data was aggregated at daily, weekly, and monthly frequencies, resulting in a total corpus of more than 374 billion data points, representing roughly 98% of the entire dataset. Therefore, this corpus doesn't have the same diversity in domain as foundation models such as Moirai and its Large-Scale Open Time Series Archive (LOTSA) corpus.

Finally, the synthetic dataset consists of generated series using autoregressive moving average (ARMA) processes, mixture of sines and cosines for seasonal series at different frequencies, series with linear and exponential trends, and step functions. Most of these synthetic properties are explored in chapter 5; the KernelSynth method uses them to enrich the training corpus of Chronos. TimesFM, however, is the first to use ARMA processes to generate synthetic data.

An *autoregressive process* expresses a series in which future values are linearly dependent on past values, as expressed in the following equation, where $C$ denotes a constant, $\Phi$ represents a coefficient for past values, and $\epsilon$ represents an error term. Also, $p$ represents the order of the autoregressive process, determining how many past values to consider. If $p$ is set to 1, we consider only the previous value. If $p$ is set to 10, we consider the 10 previous values:

$$y_t = C + \phi_1 y_{t-1} + \phi_2 y_{t-2} + \ldots + \phi_p y_{t-p} + \epsilon_t \quad (7.2)$$

Then a moving average process states that the future values depend on the mean of the series and past error terms. In other words, we can think of a moving average process as deviations from an average value at different time steps, as follows, where $\mu$ represents the mean, $\theta$ represents coefficients for past error terms, and $\epsilon$ still represents error terms. Here, the order of a moving average process is denoted as $q$ and also determines how many past error terms are considered:

$$y_t = \mu + \epsilon_t + \theta_1 \epsilon_{t-1} + \theta_2 \epsilon_{t-2} + \ldots + \theta_q \epsilon_{t-q} \quad (7.3)$$

Combining both processes results in the following ARMA process, where both $p$ and $q$ affect the final model:

$$y_t = C + \phi_1 y_{t-1} + \phi_2 y_{t-2} + \ldots + \phi_p y_{t-p} + \mu + \epsilon_t + \theta_1 \epsilon_{t-1} + \theta_2 \epsilon_{t-2} + \ldots + \theta_q \epsilon_{t-q} \quad (7.4)$$

Thus, by varying the order of $p$ and $q$ and varying the coefficients in the autoregressive and moving portions, we can generate a virtually infinite number of unique time series.

TimesFM was pretrained using an input patch length of 32 and an output patch length of 128 time steps. The data was sampled so that 80% came from real-world data and 20% came from the synthetic dataset. The maximum context length was set to 512 for long series. Series with a weekly frequency weren't long enough to accommodate that context length, so it was reduced to 256 for them. It was further reduced to 64 for monthly, quarterly, and yearly series.

In TimesFM, the longest input sequence contains 512 time steps. The model truncates any longer sequence. Also, because the output patch length was set to 128, any horizon exceeding 128 time steps triggers the autoregressive generation of future values.

TimesFM was pretrained in three sizes with 17 million, 70 million, and 200 million parameters. Only the largest model is publicly available. On one hand, we know that the larger a model is, the better it tends to perform, so we can access the best version of the model. On the other hand, the computational requirements to use TimesFM are higher because we can use only the largest model. In fact, we need at least 16 GB of RAM just to load TimesFM and its dependencies.

## 7.2 Forecasting with TimesFM

Before using TimesFM for zero-shot forecasting, I must mention some points to keep in mind when working with this model:

- *The model is univariate.* When we pass multiple series, each series is predicted individually, but the series' interdependence is not considered. As we'll see in section 7.2.3, the model can handle exogenous variables, which means we can predict only one series.
- *When this book was written, known issues occurred when the model's requirements were installed on Windows and macOS machines.* Some packages work only on Linux systems. Therefore, the following code was run in Google Colab, which is the easiest way for all readers to get, set up, and use the model.
- *Although the model was developed by Google Research, it's not an official product maintained by Google.* The community on GitHub can address any issues you may encounter.
- *The model was updated when this section was written.* Both versions can be accessed through different checkpoints. The previous version, `google/timesfm-1.0-200m-pytorch`, has 200 million parameters and a maximum context length of 512 time steps. The latest version is `google/timesfm-2.0-500m-pytorch`, which follows the same pretraining procedure and architecture that we've already explored but supports a maximum input length of 2,048 time steps. Also, as the name suggests, this version is larger, with 500 million parameters. This section uses the latest version, but you can change the name of the checkpoint to use the previous version.
- *The available model outputs experimental quantiles* (as we'll see in section 7.2.1). Therefore, the model generates prediction intervals, but the researchers state that this feature is experimental and the quantiles are not calibrated. At this time, we should focus solely on the point forecasts of TimesFM.

To install TimesFM, run this command:

```
pip install timesfm
```

Some errors may be returned, but it's safe to ignore them. Then restart the Colab kernel. We're ready to make zero-shot predictions.

### 7.2.1 *Zero-shot forecasting with TimesFM*

We'll use the same dataset we've used since chapter 3 so we can focus on applying different foundation models and compare their performance.

**Listing 7.1 Reading the data**

```
df =
➥pd.read_csv("https://raw.githubusercontent.com/marcopeix/FoundationMode
➥lsForTimeSeriesForecasting/main/data/walmart_sales_small.csv")
```

When the data is in memory, we can load TimesFM. We have to modify only two parameters depending on the scenario: `context_len` and `horizon_len`. These parameters correspond to the length of the input series and the horizon forecast, respectively. Then we must fix the rest of the parameters to load the model correctly.

**Listing 7.2 Loading TimesFM**

```
tfm = timesfm.TimesFm(
      hparams=timesfm.TimesFmHparams(
          backend="cpu",                          ← Use gpu if a GPU is available.
          per_core_batch_size=32,                 ← Do not change. This is specific to the model.
          horizon_len=8,                          ← Specifies the forecast horizon
          num_layers=50,                          ← Do not change. This is specific to the model.
          use_positional_embedding=False,         ← Sets to False for faster inference
          context_len=2048,                       ← Must be a multiple of 32. For the current endpoint,
                                                    the maximum value is 2048. For the previous endpoint,
                                                    the maximum value is 512.
      ),
      checkpoint=timesfm.TimesFmCheckpoint(
          huggingface_repo_id=
          ➥"google/timesfm-2.0-500m-pytorch"),   ← Loads the latest endpoint of TimesFM.
                                                    The previous endpoint is loaded with
                                                    "google/timesfm-1.0-200m-pytorch".
)
```

In this code, `context_len` must be a multiple of 32, and the value should not exceed `2048`. If a longer sequence is sent to the model, the model truncates it.

We can't change some parameters. `num_layers` and `per_core_batch_size`, for example, are fixed values for the model; if we change them, the model won't load properly.

Also, as specified in the model's documentation, we set `use_positional_embedding` to `False` to speed inference.

TimesFM comes with the `forecast_on_df` method, which can take an input DataFrame and outputs another DataFrame with the predictions. This method borrows some logic from Nixtla and its packages, and it requires the date column to be named `ds` and the identifier column to be named `unique_id`. Although Nixtla packages allow us to designate those columns as parameters, TimesFM requires this specific nomenclature. Thus, we must rename some columns before forecasting.

**Listing 7.3 Renaming columns for TimesFM**

```
df = df.rename(columns={"Store": "unique_id", "Date": "ds"})
df['ds'] = pd.to_datetime(df['ds'])
```

When the columns are renamed, we can use the `forecast_on_df` method to generate predictions. The method uses an input of 128 time steps to forecast the next eight data points because that's how we loaded the model (refer to listing 7.2).

To forecast, we pass the DataFrame and specify the frequency and name of the target column. In this case, the frequency is weekly, and our target is `Weekly_Sales`.

**Listing 7.4 Zero-shot forecasting on a DataFrame**

```
preds_df = tfm.forecast_on_df(
    inputs=df,                      # Passes the input DataFrame
    freq="W",                       # Specifies the frequency
    value_name="Weekly_Sales",      # Specifies the name of the target column
    num_jobs=-1                     # Set to -1 to use all available resources for inference.
)
```

When we specify the frequency in `forecast_on_df`, TimesFM internally maps it to a categorical value (table 7.2). Thus, the model maps the frequency parameter to high (`0`), medium (`1`), and low (`2`) categories. At this point, we have our predictions for the stores and can plot them as shown in figure 7.5.

**Table 7.2 Frequency parameters and their categories in TimesFM**

| Frequency parameter | Meaning | Category in TimesFM |
|---|---|---|
| S | Every second | `0` |
| MIN | Every minute | `0` |
| H | Hourly | `0` |
| D | Daily | `0` |
| B | Business day | `0` |

**Table 7.2 Frequency parameters and their categories in TimesFM (*continued*)**

| Frequency parameter | Meaning | Category in TimesFM |
|---|---|---|
| W | Weekly | 1 |
| M | Monthly | 1 |
| Q | Quarterly | 2 |
| Y | Yearly | 2 |

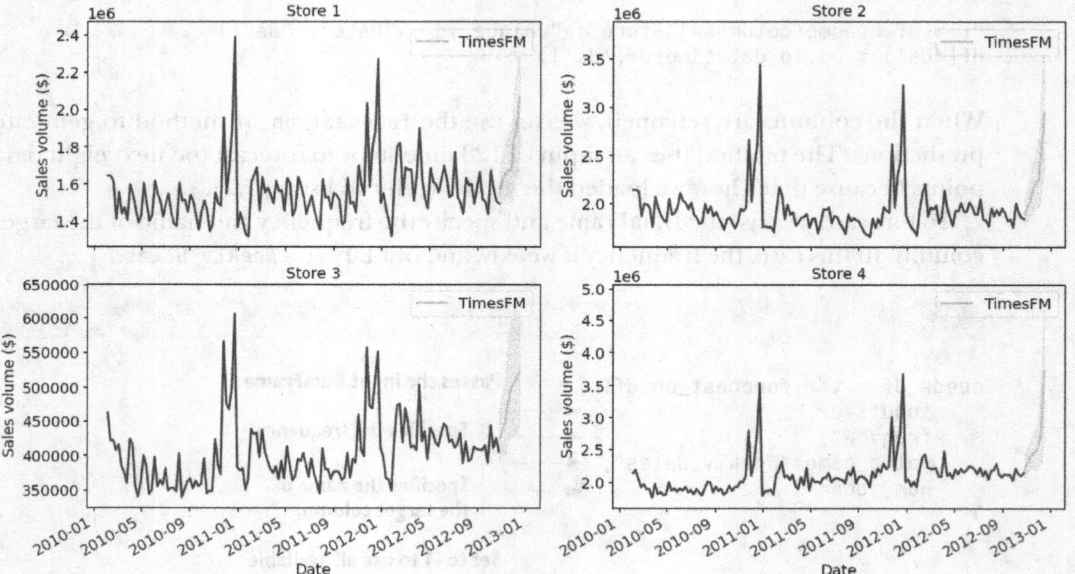


**Figure 7.5 Zero-shot predictions of the weekly sales for each store**

The shaded area designates a 90% prediction interval, but remember that it comes from experimental quantiles that were not calibrated. Therefore, these intervals may not be valid.

TimesFM requires much less coding than Chronos, Lag-Llama, and Moirai, in which we had to define functions to format the predictions. Here, a DataFrame is returned, making the forecasting process much faster and more streamlined. These predictions are out of sample, of course, and we can't evaluate the model's performance, so we must do cross-validation to evaluate the accuracy of its predictions.

### 7.2.2 *Cross-validation with TimesFM*

Unfortunately, no functions perform cross-validation in TimesFM. We must define our own function that reuses the `forecast_on_df` method.

**Listing 7.5 Function for cross-validation with TimesFM**

```
def cross_validation_timesfm(df, h, n_windows, target_col, freq):
  all_preds = []

  for i in range(n_windows, 0, -1):
    input_df = df.iloc[:-(h*i)]

    preds_df = tfm.forecast_on_df(
    inputs=input_df,
    freq=freq,
    value_name=target_col,
    num_jobs=-1
    )

    all_preds.append(preds_df)

  preds = pd.concat(all_preds, axis=0,
    ignore_index=True)

  return preds
```

The input DataFrame gradually has more context as we advance in the for loop.

Uses the forecast_on_df method to predict

Appends the DataFrame to the list that will contain all DataFrames

Concatenates all DataFrames into a single DataFrame with all predictions

In this listing, our function takes a DataFrame as well as the forecasting horizon, number of cross-validation windows, name of the target column, and frequency. Then we initialize a list that will contain the prediction DataFrame for each window.

Next, we start a `for` loop where we feed an initial input sequence to TimesFM and make predictions with the `forecast_on_df` method. At the next iteration of the `for` loop, the input sequence is updated with the next set of values to generate the next sequence of predictions until we run out of windows. Finally, we add the predictions DataFrame to our list and concatenate all DataFrames inside the list to return a single DataFrame with all predictions.

Now let's run cross-validation for store 1 only, as we did in previous chapters. For consistency, we use the same settings: a horizon of eight time steps and four cross-validation windows.

**Listing 7.6 Cross-validation with TimesFM**

```
cv_df = df.query("unique_id == 1")
cv_preds = cross_validation_timesfm(
    df=cv_df,
    h=8,
    n_windows=4,
    target_col="Weekly_Sales",
    freq="W")
```

We can plot the predictions obtained from cross-validation as shown in figure 7.6.

The figure shows that TimesFM failed to predict the more sudden changes in the series, but some overlap occurs between predicted and actual values. To quantify the

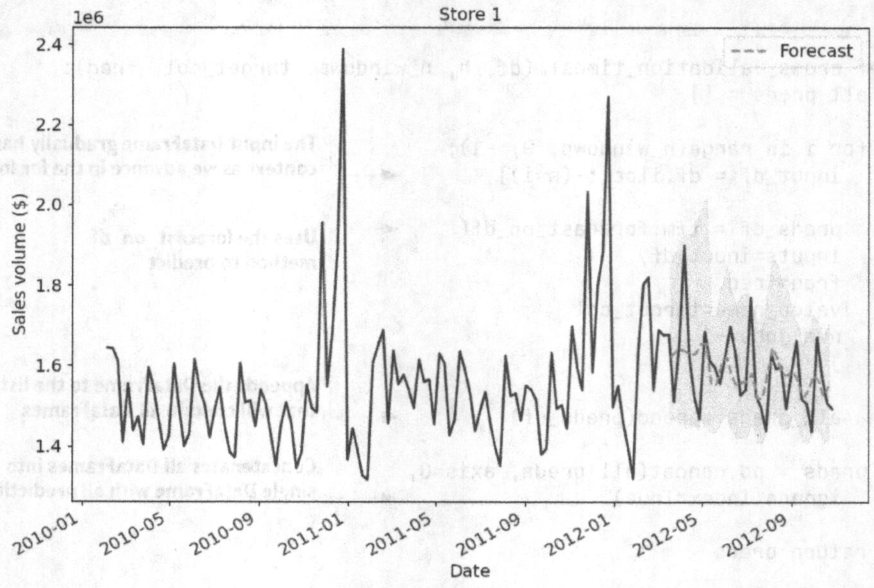


**Figure 7.6 Predictions obtained from cross-validation with TimesFM. The shaded area represents a 90% prediction interval obtained from experimental quantiles that were not calibrated, so it may not be valid.**

performance of the model, we measure the MAE and sMAPE. We also add its performance to our comparison table (table 7.3).

**Listing 7.7 Evaluating TimesFM**

```
eval_df = cv_preds[['unique_id', 'ds', 'timesfm']]        ◄ Removes unnecessary columns to focus on the predicted values
eval_df['Weekly_Sales'] =
➥ cv_df['Weekly_Sales'][-32:].values                      ◄ Takes the actual values that align with cross-validation

evaluation = evaluate(
    eval_df,
    metrics=[mae, smape],
    models=[<timesfm'],
    target_col='Weekly_Sales',
    id_col='unique_id'
)
```

**Table 7.3 Performance metrics of large time models in cross-validation over four windows of eight weeks**

| Metric | TimeGPT (fine-tuned) | Lag-Llama (fine-tuned) | Chronos (fine-tuned) | Moirai + exog | TimesFM |
|---|---|---|---|---|---|
| MAE | 63544 | 72990 | 63811 | 82041 | 64578 |
| sMAPE (%) | 2.04 | 2.29 | 1.99 | 2.57 | 2.02 |

TimesFM achieves an MAE of 64,578$ and a sMAPE of 2.02% with zero-shot forecasting. This performance is better than Moirai's and closely approaches that of fine-tuned TimeGPT and Chronos. This comparison is not representative of a model's performance on an absolute scale, however, because we are evaluating only on a single dataset with a limited test size.

### 7.2.3 Forecasting with exogenous features

TimesFM supports the use of exogenous features, but they have to be available for future time steps as well. By contrast, Moirai supports both historical and future exogenous values. Let's see how we can forecast using information from external variables with TimesFM.

The way that TimesFM handles exogenous features is outside the TimesFM model itself. It uses a simple ridge regression with exogenous features to calculate their contribution to the final forecast, as shown in figure 7.7.

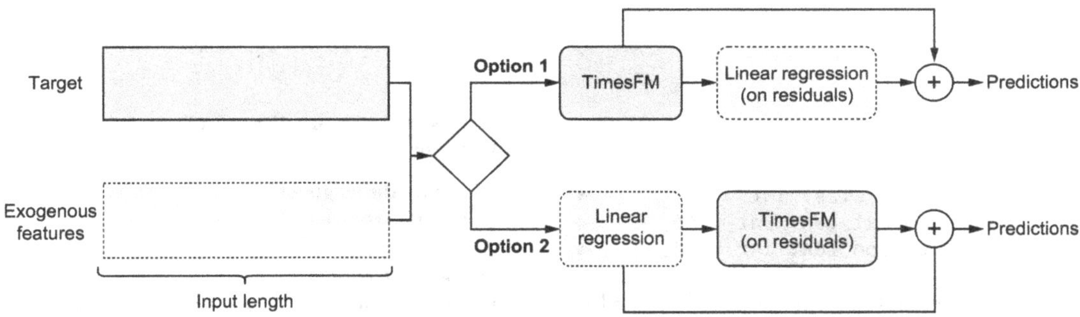


**Figure 7.7 Two options for handling exogenous features in TimesFM**

We have two options for considering exogenous features:

- *We can predict the target itself using TimesFM.* Then we remove the fitted values of TimesFM on the input sequence, which gives us residuals. Next, we use linear regression to model the relationship between the residuals and the exogenous features. Finally, we add the predictions from both TimesFM and the linear regression.
- *We use the same process but reverse the order.* First, we fit a linear regressor with the exogenous features. The fitted values are removed from the input, giving us residuals. Then TimesFM forecasts using the input sequence of residuals, and both predictions are added to give the final forecast. Ultimately, this method works because a model's fitted values always carry some kind of errors, denoted as residuals, because no fit can be perfect.

TimesFM's way of handling exogenous features is very different from Moirai's. Moirai's architecture is built to handle external variables natively; TimesFM uses another regression model.

For this experiment, we forecast a horizon of 32 time steps in a single shot. Let's split our data into a training and test set for evaluation.

**Listing 7.8 Splitting data into a training set and a test set**

```
train = cv_df[:-32]
test = cv_df[-32:]
```

To forecast with covariates, we must use the `forecast_with_covariates` method. This method doesn't take a DataFrame as input; instead, it takes batches of data from a generator function.

Thus, we adapt the function presented in the official documentation of TimesFM to our scenario. Because we need to know the future values of our exogenous variables, we use the feature `Holiday_Flag`, which is the only one we can know with certainty in the future.

**Listing 7.9 Generator function to pipeline data for TimesFM**

```
def get_batched_data_fn(
    batch_size: int = 2,
    context_len: int = 64,
    horizon_len: int = 32,
):
    examples = defaultdict(list)

    num_examples = 0
    for start in range(0, len(cv_df) - (context_len + horizon_len),
    ➥horizon_len):
        num_examples += 1
        examples["inputs"].append(train["Weekly_Sales"][start:(context_end
        ➥:= start + context_len)].tolist())
        examples["Holiday_Flag"].append(train["Holiday_Flag"][start:context
        ➥_end + horizon_len].tolist())
        examples["outputs"].append(train["Weekly_Sales"][context_end:(conte
        ➥xt_end + horizon_len)].tolist())

    def data_fn():
        for i in range(1 + (num_examples - 1) // batch_size):
            yield {k: v[(i * batch_size) : ((i + 1) * batch_size)] for k, v
            ➥in examples.items()}

    return data_fn
```

Specifies the batch size. Use a small value if the dataset is small, as here.

Specifies the length of the input sequence

Specifies the length of the output sequence

Makes the input sequence of the target

Yields batches of data

Makes the output sequence of the target

Makes the sequence of the exogenous variable. It must cover the input and output lengths.

This listing has a lot to unwrap. First, we must ensure that the `batch_size` is appropriate for our dataset. Here, the dataset is fairly small, so we must use a small value as well. Then we specify the lengths of the input and output sequences. Next, the function builds a dictionary with the input sequence and its corresponding output sequence. This step is also where we add sequences of our exogenous variables. Then the function returns another function, `data_fn()`, that yields batches of data, the expected input of the `forecast_with_covariates` method in TimesFM.

Next, we initialize another instance of the TimesFM model to match the context and horizon lengths of our function.

**Listing 7.10 Initializing a TimesFM model**

```
tfm_h32 = timesfm.TimesFm(
      hparams=timesfm.TimesFmHparams(
          backend="cpu",  # "gpu" if CUDA is available
          per_core_batch_size=32,
          horizon_len=32,
          num_layers=50,
          use_positional_embedding=False,
          context_len=2048,
      ),
      checkpoint=timesfm.TimesFmCheckpoint(
          huggingface_repo_id="google/timesfm-2.0-500m-pytorch"),
  )
```

We run the data pipelining function and loop through all examples to get the predictions over the entire horizon.

**Listing 7.11 Making predictions with covariates**

```
input_data = get_batched_data_fn()                    # Creates batches of input data

for i, example in enumerate(input_data()):
    cov_forecast, _ =
      tfm_h32.forecast_with_covariates(               # Makes predictions with forecast_with_covariates
        inputs=example["inputs"],
        dynamic_numerical_covariates={},
        dynamic_categorical_covariates={              # Our feature is a dynamic categorical variable.
            "Holiday_Flag": example["Holiday_Flag"],
        },
        static_numerical_covariates={},
        static_categorical_covariates={},
        freq=[1] * len(example["inputs"]),            # The frequency is encoded as 1, as in table 7.2.
        xreg_mode="xreg + timesfm",                   # We fit a linear regression first, and TimesFM predicts residuals.
        ridge=0.0,                                    # Controls the L2 regularization parameter
        force_on_cpu=False,
        normalize_xreg_target_per_input=True,
    )
```

In this listing, we see that forecasting with covariates is much less intuitive than zero-shot forecasting with DataFrames. Still, let's unpack what is happening.

First, we create the batches of data as described in listing 7.9. Then we use the `forecast_with_covariates` method of TimesFM. Next, we feed the input sequence to the model and specify the type of exogenous features we have. In this case, `Holiday_Flag` is a dynamic categorical feature because it changes over time (dynamic) and indicates whether there is a holiday (categorical).

TimesFM also supports other types of features, such as a *dynamic numerical covariate*, another real-valued time series that varies over time. A *static numerical covariate* is a real-valued sequence that stays constant over time. Similarly, a *static categorical covariate* expresses a category that remains constant, such as a product category.

We also have to specify a `freq` sequence for the model. Here, we encode it as `1` because we must do it manually in this function. Our weekly frequency corresponds to `1`, as shown in table 7.2.

The `xreg_mode` parameter determines which option to use when dealing with covariates. It decides whether or not we fit TimesFM first. In this case, we fit TimesFM last.

Finally, the `ridge` parameter controls the L2 regularization parameter in the regression model. When this parameter is set to `0`, there is no penalty, and it defaults to a linear regression. Increasing this parameter pushes some of the weights toward `0`, decreasing the complexity of the regressor.

To evaluate the effect of using covariates, let's make baseline predictions using TimesFM only. Figure 7.8 compares both methods.

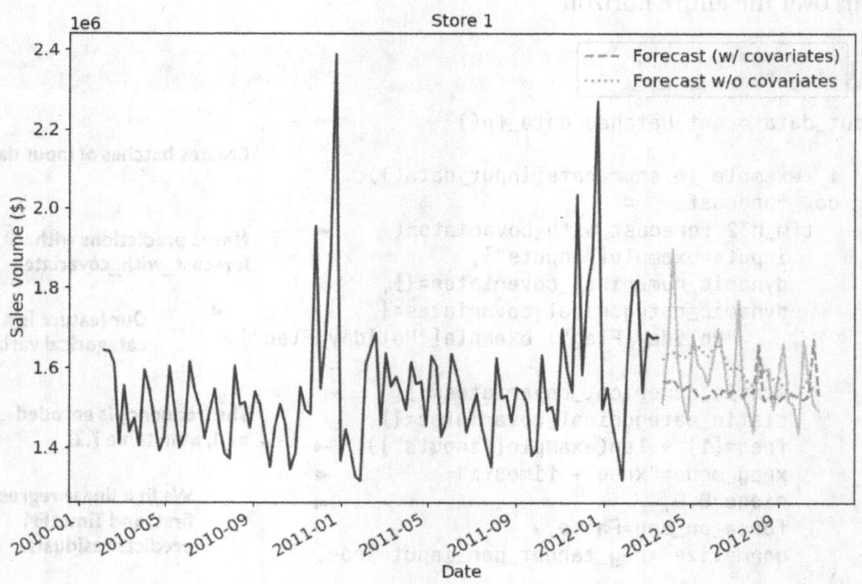


**Figure 7.8 Comparing the forecasts obtained with and without covariates**

**Listing 7.12 Baseline predictions without covariates**

```
no_cov_preds = tfm_h32.forecast_on_df(
    inputs=train,
    freq="W",
    value_name="Weekly_Sales",
    num_jobs=-1
)
```

In figure 7.8, we see that with covariates, the model can predict some future peaks in sales. Nevertheless, we compute the MAE and sMAPE of both methods to see which results in better performance. Figure 7.9 shows the MAE and sMAPE for both methods.

**Listing 7.13 Evaluating TimesFM with and without covariates**

```
eval_df = test[['unique_id', 'ds', 'Weekly_Sales']]
eval_df['timesfm_cov'] = cov_forecast[0]
eval_df['timesfm'] = no_cov_preds['timesfm'].values

evaluation = evaluate(
    eval_df,
    metrics=[mae, smape],
    models=['timesfm', 'timesfm_cov'],
    target_col='Weekly_Sales',
    id_col='unique_id'
)
```

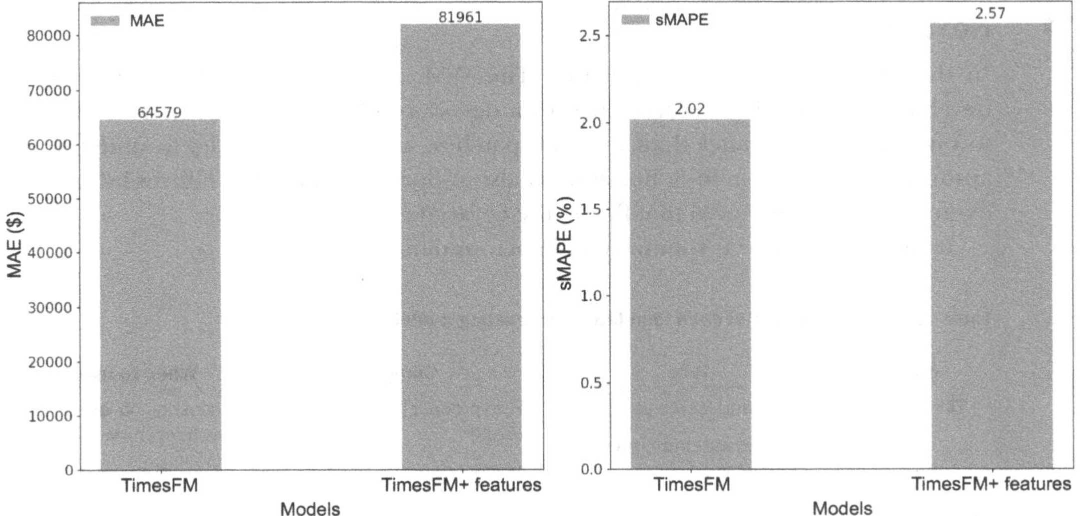


**Figure 7.9 MAE and sMAPE for forecasting with covariates and without covariates. Lower is better. Here, using covariates results in a less accurate forecast from TimesFM.**

We see that using covariates worsens the performance of TimesFM because both the sMAPE and MAE increased when we used exogenous features. Although using features allowed the model to predict some peaks in future sales, it seems that the predictions are worse overall than when we used only historical data for this situation.

## 7.3 Fine-tuning TimesFM and anomaly detection

One key characteristic of foundation models is their ability to be fine-tuned to specific datasets. We saw in previous chapters how to fine-tune foundation models, which generally improves the accuracy of their predictions.

At this writing, the documentation for fine-tuning TimesFM is sparse and requires knowledge of JAX, a library developed by Google for array-oriented numerical computation with just-in-time compilation enabling faster calculations for machine learning models. Thus, fine-tuning TimesFM requires the user to write their own training loop and batch processing functions in JAX, which is beyond the scope of this book. It also means that practitioners who are unfamiliar with JAX will have a hard time fine-tuning the model. For those reasons, I don't cover fine-tuning TimesFM in this book.

As for anomaly detection, TimesFM can't perform this task because the model is deterministic. We could argue that experimental quantiles are available, but we can generate a maximum prediction interval of only 90%. Therefore, it's unreasonable to label a point as an anomaly if it exceeds only the 90% prediction interval. Also, these quantiles are experimental and were not calibrated, so they may not be valid intervals. Therefore, TimesFM is not suitable for anomaly detection.

## 7.4 Next steps

In this chapter, we studied and used TimesFM, a deterministic foundation model developed by Google Research. It uses a decoder-only architecture that was trained to output longer patches than its input patches, allowing the model to undergo less autoregressive steps on long horizons. It also supports exogenous features by using an external regression model that fits on the covariates.

Table 7.4 updates our summary table of foundation models.

**Table 7.4 Pros and cons of each foundation forecasting model**

| Model | Pros | Cons | When to use |
|---|---|---|---|
| TimeGPT | Easy and fast to use<br>Comes with many native functions<br>Works on any device, regardless of hardware<br>Free plan | Paid product for a certain usage<br>Model may not be available if the server is down | Forecasting on long and short horizons with exogenous features<br>You need to fine-tune but do not have the local resources. |

**Table 7.4 Pros and cons of each foundation forecasting model (*continued*)**

| Model | Pros | Cons | When to use |
|---|---|---|---|
| Lag-Llama | Open source model<br>Free to use | Awkward to use because we must clone the repository<br>Speed of inference depends on our hardware. | Quick proof of concept<br>Ideal for research-oriented projects |
| Chronos | Open source model<br>Free to use<br>Can be installed as a Python package | Speed and accuracy depend on our hardware.<br>Fine-tuning requires cloning the repository.<br>We must define some functions manually. | Forecasting on horizons shorter than 64 time steps<br>Forecasting series without strong trends |
| Moirai | Open source model<br>Free to use<br>Supports exogenous features<br>Can be installed as a Python package | Speed and accuracy depend on the hardware.<br>We must define helper functions when not working entirely with GluonTS. | You have exogenous features.<br>Forecasting on horizons shorter than 256 time steps |
| TimesFM | Open source model<br>Free to use<br>Can be installed as a Python package<br>Supports exogenous features | Only the largest model is available.<br>Restrictive requirements for use (16 GB of RAM, Linux-based system to install dependencies)<br>Knowledge of JAX is required for fine-tuning.<br>Can't perform anomaly detection because it is a deterministic model | Ideal for deterministic forecasting in which prediction intervals are not required<br>You want to feed a long input series. |

Although TimesFM is open source and free to use, only the largest model is available, so we need decent computational power to run the model (16 GB of RAM just to load the model and its dependencies). Also, fine-tuning requires knowledge of JAX, which makes it less accessible than the models we explored in earlier chapters. Furthermore, because the model is deterministic, we can't use it for anomaly detection. Although the model outputs prediction quantiles, the user can't set them; also, they are still in the experimental stage and were not calibrated, so they may not be valid.

This concludes the part of the book on large time models. Throughout these chapters, we made many comparisons between predicting the next value in a time series and the next word in a sentence. This is especially true in the case of Chronos, which adapts LLMs for time-series forecasting. In part 3, we turn our attention to LLMs to see whether we can prompt them to forecast time-series data.

## Summary

- TimesFM is a deterministic foundation model developed by Google Research. It uses a decoder-only transformer for point forecasting.
- The model is open source and free to use, but only the largest version is available.
- It supports exogenous features by using an external linear regression algorithm.
- Because the model is deterministic, it can't perform anomaly detection.
- Fine-tuning the model requires knowledge of JAX, making it inaccessible to practitioners who are unfamiliar with the technology.

# Part 3

# Using LLMs for time-series forecasting

Having explored models specifically built for time-series forecasting, we wonder whether we can use LLMs directly. After all, LLMs are large models that are trained for the analogous task of generating a sequence of words based on an input sentence.

To that end, in chapter 8, we use Flan-T5 and Llama for time-series forecasting, using prompting techniques such as few-shot and chain-of-thought prompting. We also use these models for anomaly detection and realize that although they work, they may not be the best solution for all use cases. In chapter 9, we explore Time-LLM, which greatly improves the performance of LLMs in time-series forecasting by reprogramming some of their components.

# 8 Forecasting as a language task

**_This chapter covers_**

- Framing a forecasting problem as a language task
- Forecasting with large language models
- Cross-validating with LLMs
- Detecting anomalies with LLMs

In previous chapters, we discovered and experimented with many large time models that are specifically built for time-series forecasting. Still, as highlighted by the researchers of Chronos, predicting the next value of a time series is analogous to predicting the next word in a sentence. Although Chronos is a framework for retraining existing LLMs for forecasting, in this chapter, we experiment with prompting LLMs to solve forecasting tasks.

This approach has already been studied and named PromptCast [1]. The idea is simple: turn a numerical prediction task into a natural language task that LLMs can understand.

Framing a forecasting problem as a language task involves processing the input and the output. First, the values of the input series must be formatted as a prompt.

Then we feed this prompt to the language model, which also outputs a string. This string must be processed to extract the predictions. Thus, we should use these models only if we already have access to an LLM, need a natural language interface, and know how to construct robust prompts to guide the model.

In this chapter, we experiment with this approach by using the Flan-T5 and `Llama-3.2-3b-instruct` models. We develop functions to create prompts programmatically and format the output of the LLMs, as well as perform various experiments in forecasting with LLMs.

## 8.1 Overview of LLMs and prompting techniques

Although this book focuses on using foundation models for forecasting, it's important to highlight some key elements of LLMs and prompt engineering. Feel free to skip this section if you've interacted with LLMs before. This section contains the prerequisites for understanding the rest of this chapter, which covers the main characteristics of Flan-T5 and `Llama-3.2-3b-instruct` and explores some prompt engineering techniques.

### 8.1.1 Exploring Flan-T5 and Llama-3.2

As we've seen throughout this book, foundation models have specific characteristics that result in better performance in certain situations or have a specific way of interacting with them. TimeGPT, for example, can work directly with DataFrames, whereas Chronos works with tensors, and Moirai works with GluonTS data formats. The same logic applies to LLMs.

#### FLAN-T5

Flan-T5 [2] is an enhanced version of T5 that has been fine-tuned on different tasks. We explored the T5 family of models in chapter 5 because Chronos applied its framework to the T5 language models. Flan-T5 was fine-tuned on more than 1,800 tasks, including question answering, arithmetic reasoning, and text categorization. As a result, the performance of the model on different tasks increased significantly.

Flan-T5 is especially good at answering questions. Thus, we typically interact with Flan-T5 through a question-and-answer message. We don't ask Flan-T5 to forecast, which represents an instruction; instead, we ask the model what the future values will be. That way, we're framing the task as a question, which should result in better performances.

The models in the Flan-T5 family are open source and available in different sizes, from `flan-t5-small` (77 million parameters) to `flan-t5-xxl` (11.3 billion parameters).

#### LLAMA-3.2-3B-INSTRUCT

Llama 3 is a series of language models developed by researchers at Meta [3]. At this writing, it's the latest version of the Llama family of models, first released in 2023.

The Llama models use the Transformer architecture, explored in detail in chapter 1, with its input embeddings, positional encoding, and self-attention mechanism. The models were fine-tuned and adapted on a range of tasks. We can see them as more advanced than Flan-T5 because they're capable of handling dialogue and code generation.

In this chapter, we'll use `Llama-3.2-3B-instruct`. From the name, we see that the model has 3 billion parameters and is adapted to follow instructions. Therefore, we typically interact with this model by specifying a clear set of instructions.

**NOTE** At this writing, Llama 3 models are publicly available but for research purposes only. Their license specifically prohibits their use for commercial purposes.

### 8.1.2 Understanding the basics of prompting

*Prompting* refers to the technique of structuring instructions that LLMs can understand. With prompting, we can turn a numerical prediction task into a natural language task that LLMs understand, as illustrated in figure 8.1.

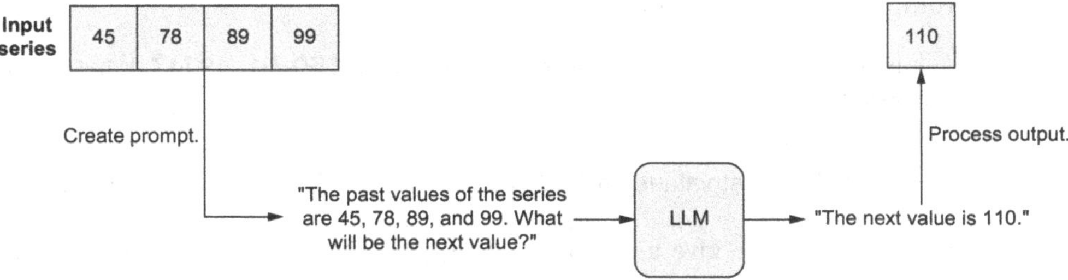


**Figure 8.1 General steps of forecasting with LLMs**

Unlike the foundation models we've explored so far, which are specifically designed for forecasting, LLMs are fine-tuned on thousands of different tasks. Therefore, we must specify in the prompt what is expected from them.

Here, the prompt takes the form of a natural language question or instruction. We can't feed a sequence of values to an LLM without specifying what we expect, such as forecasting the next values or detecting an anomaly, because all LLMs are trained and fine-tuned on natural language data.

The three main methods of prompting a language model are zero-shot prompting, few-shot prompting, and chain-of-thought prompting. In the following sections, we explore each method in detail.

#### Zero-shot prompting

Zero-shot prompting is the most basic and natural way of interacting with an LLM. It involves writing the question or instruction and feeding it to the model. Here is an example of zero-shot prompting an LLM in the context of forecasting:

 The past values are: 10, 15, 21, 26, 32, 28. What will be the next value?

In the prompt, we're framing our forecasting problem as a question-answering task. We specify the input values and ask the model what the next value will be. We don't specify anything else in the prompt. The model is free to generate an answer in any format, so the following is a possible answer:

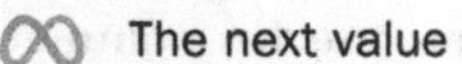

The next value will be 35.

This output might be fine in a conversational context, but for time-series forecasting, we need to extract numerical values from sentences, so we need to write lengthier code and processing logic. We can use few-shot prompting to nudge the model to answer in the format we prefer.

#### FEW-SHOT PROMPTING

With few-shot prompting, we specify how we want the model to answer our question directly in the input prompt. In the context of forecasting with an LLM, a few-shot prompt could look like this:

 Input: The past values of the series are: 30, 45, 50, 51, 49, 47. What will be the next value?

Output: 44

Input: The past values are: 10, 15, 21, 26, 32, 28. What will be the next value?

In this prompt, we give an example of a question-and-answer pair to tell the model how we expect the output. In this case, we want the model to output a single numerical value instead of a complete sentence. In the last part of the prompt, we write the actual question we want the model to answer.

Using few-shot prompting is a great way to control the output of an LLM and also increase its performance because we give the model an example of how to carry out our instructions. We'll use this technique often to interact with the Flan-T5 model.

#### CHAIN-OF-THOUGHT PROMPTING

The final technique we can use for prompting LLMs is the chain-of-thought technique. Whereas few-shot prompting gives an example of the expected output, chain-of-thought prompting goes a step further by specifying the steps to perform to get the right answer. We could specify the steps to perform anomaly detection this way:

 Input: The past values of the series are: 10, 11, 12, 10, 11, 23, 12. Which values are anomalous?

1 The majority of values are close to 10.
2 23 is a value that is abnormally large compared to the rest of the values.
3 23 must be an anomaly.

Output: 23.

Input: The past values of the series are: 10, 15, 18, 20, 45, 23, 25. Which values are anomalous?

In this prompt, we specify the thinking process to identify anomalous values. First, we determine that most values are close to 10; then we realize that 23 is large compared with all other values. Therefore, 23 must be an anomaly, and we specify in the prompt to output only the anomalous value.

With chain-of-thought prompting, we can improve the performance of LLMs on more complex tasks. Ultimately, choosing the right prompting technique is part of the experimentation process. In the models covered earlier in this book, we could experiment with different input lengths or exogenous features, but with LLMs, we can try different prompt structures and techniques to see how they affect the output of the model.

The next two sections focus on forecasting with Flan-T5 and Llama 3. Flan-T5 will be used as a local model, and Llama 3 will be accessed via API calls.

## 8.2 Forecasting with Flan-T5

In this section, we use Flan-T5 locally to perform zero-shot forecasting and anomaly detection. We'll use the model `flan-t5-base`, which has 278 million parameters. If your hardware allows it, feel free to use a larger version of Flan-T5. As always, we'll reuse the weekly sales forecasting scenario, so I won't reproduce the plot here.

The natural first step is downloading the model locally, which is convenient to do with the `transformers` library. We load the model itself as well as its tokenizer. The tokenizer preprocesses the input so the LLM can understand it and processes the output as a sentence in natural language.

**Listing 8.1 Loading Flan-T5 locally**

```
model_name = "google/flan-t5-base"
flant5_model = AutoModelForSeq2SeqLM.from_pretrained(model_name)
flant5_tokenizer = AutoTokenizer.from_pretrained(model_name, use_fast=True)
```

**Use any model size you want. Larger models take longer to generate output.**

### 8.2.1 Function to forecast with Flan-T5

Next, we build a function to perform forecasting with Flan-T5. This function completes a series of steps to translate the forecasting task to a language task; then it extracts and processes the output (figure 8.2).

The first step is scaling the data so we don't work with large numbers. The LLM outputs pieces of words and sentences autoregressively, so the next piece of information depends on the previous prediction. Thus, if we force the model to output large

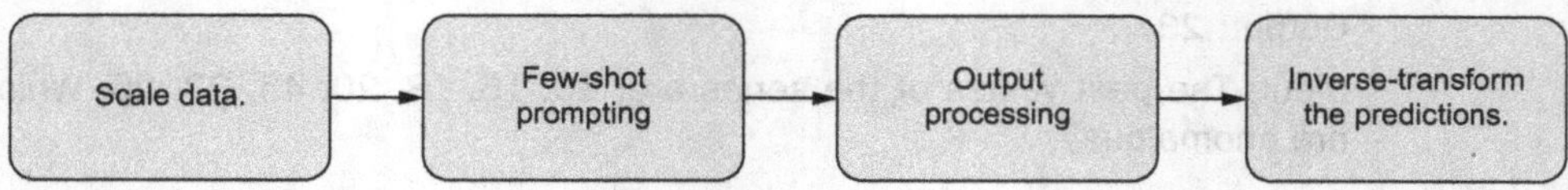


**Figure 8.2 Steps to forecast with an LLM like Flan-T5**

numbers, the model has more chances to make mistakes. Scaling the data minimizes this possibility.

Next, we use few-shot prompting. This approach allows us to nudge the model to generate only numbers so we avoid having complete sentences that require more processing steps.

When the model has generated a series of predictions, we must process that output to cast it as numbers because LLMs work only with strings. We may also need to add a few steps to extend or truncate the predictions because Flan-T5 is better at answering questions than following instructions.

Finally, we inverse transform the numbers to bring them back to the original scale of the dataset, making it easy to evaluate forecast performance. The following listing shows the entire forecasting function.

**Listing 8.2 Forecasting function with a local LLM**

```
def llm_forecast(
    df,
    model,
    tokenizer,
    horizon,
    context_len,
    target_col,
    max_new_tokens=100,
    temperature=1.0
):
    scaler = MinMaxScaler(feature_range=(0, 1))

    all_values = df[target_col].values.reshape(-1, 1)     # Fits the scaler on the data
    scaler.fit(all_values)

    context_values = df[target_col].tail(context_len).values.reshape(-1, 1)
    scaled_context_values = scaler.transform(context_values)
    ➥ .flatten()
                                                          # Scales the input sequence
    few_shot_examples = """
    Input: The last 8 scaled values of Weekly_Sales were 0.5283317,
    ➥ 0.58826193, 0.71939157, 0.95514386, 0.43612893, 0.45639017,
    ➥ 0.45729709,0.46355804. What will be the next values?
    Output: 0.53329332, 0.55390031, 0.59245479, 0.52100866, 0.52860909,
    ➥ 0.50953767, 0.53251093
    """                                                   # Creates an example for few-shot prompting

    values_str = ", ".join(map(lambda x: f"{x:.4f}", scaled_context_values))
```

```
    prompt = f"""
    {few_shot_examples}
    Input: The last {context_len} scaled values of {target_col} were
    ➥ {values_str}.
    What will be the next {horizon} scaled values? Remember to provide
    ➥ exactly {horizon} comma-separated numbers between 0 and 1.
    """                                                    Builds the prompt using
                                                           the input sequence
    prompt += "\nOutput:"

    inputs = tokenizer(prompt, return_tensors='pt')        Generates the next
    with torch.no_grad():                                  values using the LLM
        output = tokenizer.decode(
            model.generate(
                inputs["input_ids"],
                max_new_tokens=max_new_tokens,
                temperature=temperature
            )[0],                                          Repeats values if the
            skip_special_tokens=True                       output sequence is
        )                                                  shorter than the horizon
    print("Raw model output:", output)
    output = output.rstrip('.')                            Extracts numerical
                                                           values from the output
    try:
        scaled_preds = [float(x.strip()) for x in output.split(',') if
        ➥ x.strip()]
    except ValueError:
        print(f"Warning: Could not convert all outputs to float. Using only
        ➥ valid floats.")
        scaled_preds = [float(x.strip()) for x in output.split(',') if
        ➥ x.strip() and x.replace('.', '').isdigit()]

    if len(scaled_preds) < horizon:
        print(f"Warning: Did not generate enough predictions. Only
        ➥ generated {len(scaled_preds)} out of {horizon}")
        last_valid = scaled_preds[-1] if scaled_preds else 0.5  # Use 0.5
        ➥ if no valid predictions
        scaled_preds.extend([last_valid] * (horizon - len(scaled_preds)))
    elif len(scaled_preds) > horizon:
        scaled_preds = scaled_preds[:horizon]
                                                  Ensures that all predictions are
    scaled_preds = np.clip(scaled_preds, 0, 1)    between 0 and 1 (due to scaling)

    preds = scaler.inverse_transform(np.array(scaled_preds)
    ➥ .reshape(-1, 1)).flatten()
                                                  Inverse-transforms the predictions
    return preds.tolist()
```

Many steps are carried out in this listing, so let's explore them in detail. First, we'll consider the input parameters of the function, which are standard inputs that we've already seen except `max_new_tokens` and `temperature`. The `max_new_tokens` parameter controls the length of the output. Here, because we want to keep the output fairly short and straight to the point, we use a fairly small value. The `temperature` parameter controls the randomness of variability of the LLM's output. A low value (closer to `0`) makes the output more deterministic if we feed the same prompt many times. A high value increases variability, and the model will output different answers to the same prompt. Because we want to focus on learned patterns and have constant outputs, we'll set `temperature` to a fairly low value of `1`.

The next six lines focus on scaling the input sequence using the `MinMaxScaler`, which forces all the values to be between `0` and `1`. The idea is that the model won't have to predict long sequences of numbers and therefore should be more performant.

Next, we build an example of the completed task for our few-shot prompt. We show the model that we want it to output only a sequence of numbers separated by commas—nothing else. Then we build the entire prompt by showing the example first and asking the question again, using the input sequence extracted programmatically.

When the prompt is complete, we feed it to the model. First, the input is sent to the tokenizer, and the output is also sent through the tokenizer. That way, we can interact with the LLM in natural language, and the output is a sentence.

Next, we process the output. Because the model generates a sentence made of numbers separated by commas, we need to process that string to extract those numbers and cast them as such. The LLM may not output all the necessary values for a given horizon; if that happens, we repeat the last prediction until we get the required number of predictions.

The last step is ensuring that all predictions are between `0` and `1` because no values should exceed those boundaries due to scaling. Then we inverse the transformation and return a list of values that are in the original scale of the data.

### 8.2.2 Forecast with Flan-T5

Now that we understand each step of our function, let's run it to predict the sales of each store on a horizon of eight weeks, as in previous chapters.

**Listing 8.3 Predicting sales for each store**

```
store1_t5_preds = llm_forecast(data.query("Store == 1"),
                               model=flant5_model,
                               tokenizer=flant5_tokenizer,
                               horizon=8,
                               context_len=8,
                               target_col='Weekly_Sales')

store2_t5_preds = llm_forecast(data.query("Store == 2"),
                               model=flant5_model,
                               tokenizer=flant5_tokenizer,
                               horizon=8,
                               context_len=8,
                               target_col='Weekly_Sales')

store3_t5_preds = llm_forecast(data.query("Store == 3"),
                               model=flant5_model,
```

```
                                  tokenizer=flant5_tokenizer,
                                  horizon=8,
                                  context_len=8,
                                  target_col='Weekly_Sales')

store4_t5_preds = llm_forecast(data.query("Store == 4"),
                                  model=flant5_model,
                                  tokenizer=flant5_tokenizer,
                                  horizon=8,
                                  context_len=8,
                                  target_col='Weekly_Sales')
```

We set up the function so we can inspect the raw output of the model and print out warnings if it does not generate all values to cover the horizon. In this case, for the first store, we get

Raw model output: 0.2872, 0.2872, 0.2872, 0.2872, 0.2872, 0.2872
Warning: Did not generate enough predictions. Only generated 6 out of 8

The model generated only constant values when predicting the sales of store 1. Also, although we asked for the next eight values, only six values were generated. Therefore, we repeated the last prediction to complete the sequence.

All our predictions are in separate lists, so let's combine them for easier plotting and evaluation.

**Listing 8.4 Combining all predictions in a DataFrame**

```
def combine_predictions(
    predictions,
    start_date,
    horizon,
    freq,
    model_name
):
    date_range = pd.date_range(start=start_date, periods=horizon,
      freq=freq)                                        <-- Defines the dates
                                                            for the predictions
    data = []

    for store_id, store_predictions in enumerate(predictions, start=1):
        for date, prediction in zip
          (date_range, store_predictions):       <-- Combines all predictions
            data.append({                            in a DataFrame
                'Store': store_id,
                'Date': date,
                f"{model_name}": prediction
            })

    df = pd.DataFrame(data)
    df = df.sort_values(['Store', 'Date'])

    return df
```

```
all_preds = [store1_t5_preds, store2_t5_preds, store3_t5_preds,
➥ store4_t5_preds]

preds_df = combine_predictions(all_preds,                    ◄── Runs the function
                               start_date='11-02-2012',
                               horizon=8,
                               freq='W-FRI',
                               model_name="FlanT5")
```

When all the predictions are in a single DataFrame, we can plot them as shown in figure 8.3.

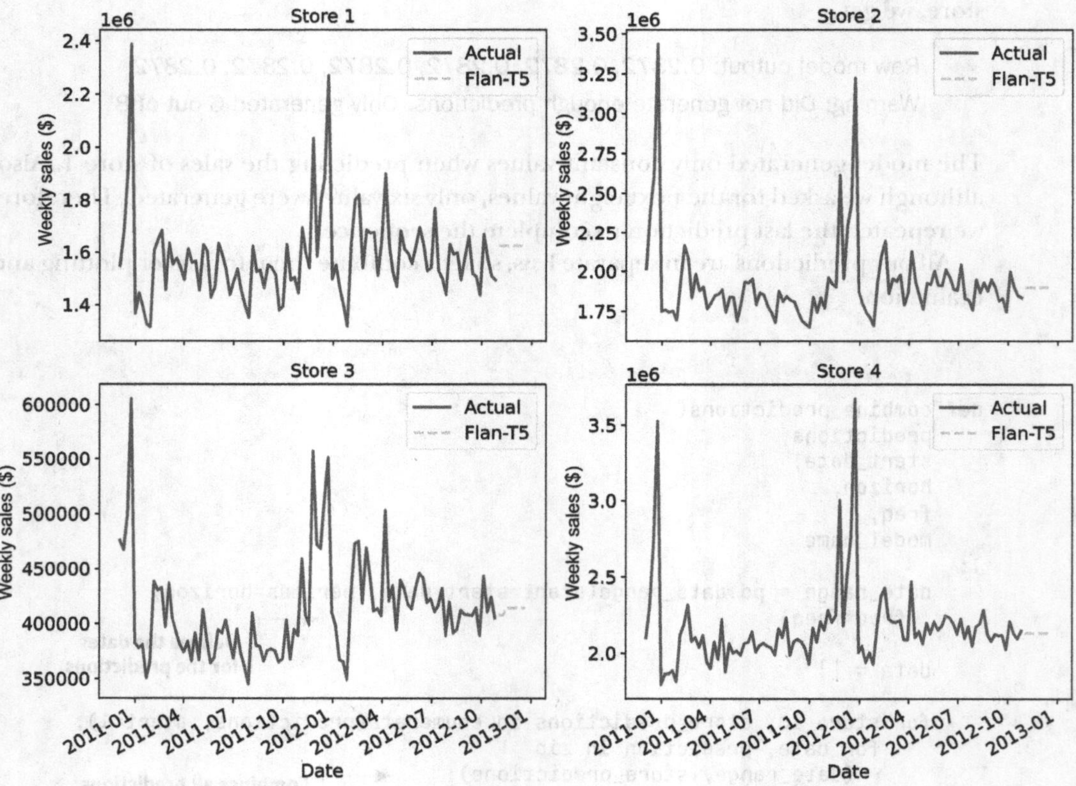


**Figure 8.3 Zero-shot predictions using Flan-T5**

In the figure, most of the predictions for all stores are constant because the model outputs the same value repeatedly and can't generate a sequence that covers the entire horizon, forcing us to repeat the last prediction to complete the sequence. Ultimately, these predictions are underwhelming; they almost correspond to using a naïve model such as predicting the mean of the series or predicting the last known value. Nevertheless, we achieved forecasting using an LLM.

## 8.3 Cross-validation with Flan-T5

It's hard to evaluate the performance of the model because we're forecasting over dates for which we don't know the actual values, so let's perform cross-validation with Flan-T5. As in previous chapters, applying cross-validation is essential for conducting a robust evaluation of a model's performance. Thus, we adapt the cross-validation function developed in chapter 5 for Chronos to use with Flan-T5. The main difference is that here, we use the `llm_forecast` function to generate the predictions.

**Listing 8.5 Cross-validation with Flan-T5**

```
def cross_validation_llm(df, h, n_windows, target_col, model, tokenizer):

    preds = []

    for i in range(n_windows, 0, -1):
        input_df = df.iloc[:-(h * i)]

        forecast = llm_forecast(
            input_df,
            model=model,
            tokenizer=tokenizer,
            horizon=h,
            context_len=h,
            target_col=target_col
        )                                  ◄── Use the llm_forecast function
                                               to make predictions.
        preds.extend(forecast)

    return preds
```

### 8.3.1 Running cross-validation

We run cross-validation by running the following function. Here, we run it for only the first store.

**Listing 8.6 Running cross-validation**

```
store1_cv = cross_validation_llm(data.query("Store == 1"),
                                h=8,
                                n_windows=4,
                                target_col='Weekly_Sales',
                                model=flant5_model,
                                tokenizer=flant5_tokenizer)
```

We can see the raw output of the model and study its behavior. In this case, we get the following:

```
Raw model output: 0.2982, 0.4534, 0.4696, 0.2077, 0.3347
Warning: Did not generate enough predictions. Only generated 5 out of 8
Raw model output: 0.1911, 0.1911, 0.3432, 0.2747
Warning: Did not generate enough predictions. Only generated 4 out of 8
Raw model output: 0.2872, 0.2872, 0.2929, 0.1970, 0.2087
Warning: Did not generate enough predictions. Only generated 5 out of 8
Raw model output: 0.1989, 0.1989, 0.1989, 0.1989, 0.1989, 0.1989
Warning: Did not generate enough predictions. Only generated 6 out of 8
```

Again, the model isn't predicting the entire horizon, meaning that the final predictions repeated the last predicted value. We get four warnings because we specified four cross-validation windows. The predictions are plotted as shown in figure 8.4.

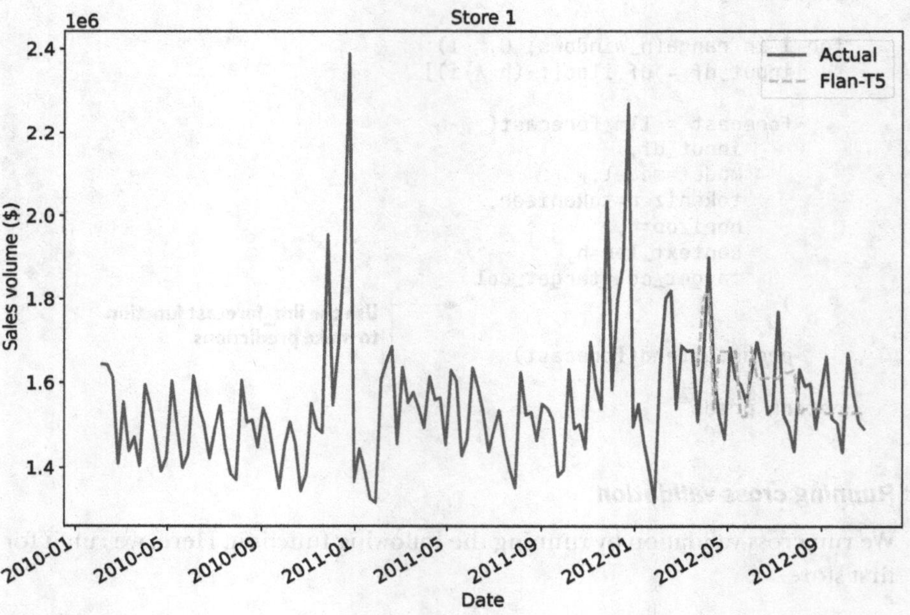


**Figure 8.4 Predictions obtained from cross-validation with Flan-T5**

### 8.3.2 Evaluating Flan-T5

The predictions seem to be reasonable because they overlap some of the actual values. Still, inspecting forecasts visually isn't robust, so we measure the mean absolute error (MAE) and the symmetric mean absolute percentage error (sMAPE). Then we compare its performance with that of all previous models in table 8.1.

**Listing 8.7 Running an evaluation of Flan-T5**

```
test_df = data.query("Store == 1").iloc[-32:]
test_df['FlanT5'] = store1_cv

evaluation = evaluate(
    test_df,
    metrics=[mae, smape],
    models=['FlanT5'],
    target_col='Weekly_Sales',
    id_col='Store'
)
```

**Table 8.1 Performance metrics of foundation models in cross-validation over four windows of eight weeks**

| Model | MAE | sMAPE (%) |
|---|---|---|
| TimeGPT (fine-tuned) | 63544 | 2.04 |
| Lag-Llama (fine-tuned) | 72990 | 2.29 |
| Chronos (fine-tuned) | 63811 | 1.99 |
| Moirai + exog | 82041 | 2.57 |
| TimesFM | 64578 | 2.02 |
| Flan-T5 | 83721 | 2.62 |

From this evaluation, we get an MAE of 83721$ and a sMAPE of 2.62%. This performance is comparable to that of Moirai, which achieved an MAE of 82041$ and a sMAPE of 2.57% in chapter 7, although that model was not fine-tuned and used exogenous features. Still, it's interesting to see this kind of performance, especially coming from an LLM that isn't trained to forecast time series. Nevertheless, this result is not representative of true performance because we're working on only a single dataset.

## 8.4 Forecasting with exogenous features with Flan-T5

Up to now, we've used the past values of the series without using any of the available exogenous features. Let's include them to see how they affect the performance of the model. To forecast using exogenous features, we apply the same logic as with Moirai and TimeGPT, providing the exogenous features in the output but also specifying their future values at the time of prediction. Thus, we work mainly with the holiday indicator because it's a covariate whose future values are certain.

### 8.4.1 Including exogenous features with Flan-T5

To work with exogenous features, we extend the `llm_forecast` function to take in the future values of exogenous features. We also change the example in our few-shot prompt to indicate to the model that it must use this new information when forecasting.

**Listing 8.8 Function to forecast with exogenous features**

```
def llm_forecast(
    df,
    model,
    tokenizer,
    horizon,
    context_len,
    target_col,
    future_exog,                    ◄ Parameter to accommodate future values of the exogenous features
    max_new_tokens=100,
    temperature=1.0
):
    scaler = MinMaxScaler(feature_range=(0, 1))

    all_values = df[target_col].values.reshape(-1, 1)
    scaler.fit(all_values)

    context_values = df[target_col].tail(context_len).values.reshape(-1, 1)
    scaled_context_values = scaler.transform(context_values).flatten()

    few_shot_examples = """            ◄ Adds the information of exogenous features in the example of the few-shot prompt
    Input: The last 8 scaled values of Weekly_Sales were 0.5283317 ,
    ➥ 0.58826193, 0.71939157, 0.95514386, 0.43612893, 0.45639017,
    ➥ 0.45729709, 0.46355804.
    The last values for Holiday_Flag were 0, 1, 0, 0, 0, 0, 0, 0. What will
    ➥ be the next values of Weekly_Sales knowing the next values of
    ➥ Holiday_Flag are 0, 0, 0, 0, 0, 0, 0, 0
    Output: 0.53329332, 0.55390031, 0.59245479, 0.52100866, 0.52860909,
    ➥ 0.50953767, 0.53251093
    """

    values_str = ", ".join(map(lambda x: f"{x:.4f}", scaled_context_values))

    prompt = f"""                    ◄ Adds the past and future values of the features for prediction
    {few_shot_examples}
    Input: The last {context_len} scaled values of {target_col} were
    ➥ {values_str}.
    What will be the next {horizon} scaled values knowing the next values
    ➥ of Holiday_Flag are {future_exog}? Remember to provide exactly
    ➥ {horizon} comma-separated numbers between 0 and 1.
    """

    prompt += "\nOutput:"

    inputs = tokenizer(prompt, return_tensors='pt')
    with torch.no_grad():
        output = tokenizer.decode(
            model.generate(
                inputs["input_ids"],
                max_new_tokens=max_new_tokens,
                temperature=temperature
            )[0],
            skip_special_tokens=True
        )
```

```
    print("Raw model output:", output)
    output = output.rstrip('.')

    try:
        scaled_preds = [float(x.strip()) for x in output.split(',') if
          x.strip()]
    except ValueError:
        print(f"Warning: Could not convert all outputs to float. Using only
          valid floats.")
        scaled_preds = [float(x.strip()) for x in output.split(',') if
          x.strip() and x.replace('.', '').isdigit()]

    if len(scaled_preds) < horizon:
        print(f"Warning: Did not generate enough predictions. Only
          generated {len(scaled_preds)} out of {horizon}")
        last_valid = scaled_preds[-1] if scaled_preds else 0.5  # Use 0.5
          if no valid predictions
        scaled_preds.extend([last_valid] * (horizon - len(scaled_preds)))
    elif len(scaled_preds) > horizon:
        scaled_preds = scaled_preds[:horizon]

    scaled_preds = np.clip(scaled_preds, 0, 1)

    preds = scaler.inverse_transform(np.array(scaled_preds).
        reshape(-1, 1)).flatten()

    return preds.tolist()
```

### 8.4.2 Extracting future values of exogenous variables

Next, we extract the future values of `Holiday_Flag` to feed to the model. The following code returns a dictionary of four sequences of eight values, which correspond to the four cross-validation windows with a horizon of eight that we used earlier.

**Listing 8.9 Getting the future values of exogenous features**

```
def values_to_str(df, column_name):
    last_values = df[column_name].tail(32).values     # Gets the last 32 values

    chunk1 = last_values[0:8]      # Separates the values into four sequences of eight values
    chunk2 = last_values[8:16]
    chunk3 = last_values[16:24]
    chunk4 = last_values[24:32]

    string1 = ", ".join(map(str, chunk1))     # Turns the sequences into strings
    string2 = ", ".join(map(str, chunk2))
    string3 = ", ".join(map(str, chunk3))
    string4 = ", ".join(map(str, chunk4))

    return string1, string2, string3, string4

hf1, hf2, hf3, hf4 = values_to_str(
```

```
➥data, 'Holiday_Flag')          ◀ Runs the values_to_str function

future_exog_dict = {0: hf1, 1:hf2, 2:hf3, 3:hf4}    ◀ Stores the sequences
                                                      in a dictionary
```

### 8.4.3 Cross-validating with external features

Next, we extend the cross-validation function to accept exogenous features.

**Listing 8.10 Cross-validation with exogenous features**

```
def cross_validation_llm_exog(df, h, n_windows,
➥target_col, model, tokenizer):

    preds = []

    for i in range(n_windows, 0, -1):
        input_df = df.iloc[:-(h * i)]
        window_idx = n_windows - i

        forecast = llm_forecast(
            input_df,
            model=model,
            tokenizer=tokenizer,
            horizon=h,
            context_len=h,
            target_col=target_col,
            future_exog=future_exog_dict[window_idx]
        )                                  ◀ Passes the future
                                             values of the features
        preds.extend(forecast)

    return preds
```

Then we can run cross-validation and plot the predictions in figure 8.5.

**Listing 8.11 Running cross-validation with features**

```
store1_cv_exog = cross_validation_llm_exog(data.query("Store == 1"),
                                           h=8,
                                           n_windows=4,
                                           target_col='Weekly_Sales',
                                           model=flant5_model,
                                           tokenizer=flant5_tokenizer)
```

Again, when running cross-validation, the model doesn't manage to forecast the entire horizon, as the following output shows:

Raw model output: 0.0023, 0.2982, 0.4534, 0.4696, 0.2077, 0.3469, 0.3347
Warning: Did not generate enough predictions. Only generated 7 out of 8
Raw model output: 0.53329332, 0.2840, 0.1911, 0.1419, 0.3432, 0.2747

```
Warning: Did not generate enough predictions. Only generated 6 out of 8
Raw model output: 0.53329332, 0.59245479, 0.52100866, 0.52860909
Warning: Did not generate enough predictions. Only generated 4 out of 8
Raw model output: 0.53329332, 0.55390031, 0.59245479, 0.52100866,
0.52860909
Warning: Did not generate enough predictions. Only generated 5 out of 8
```

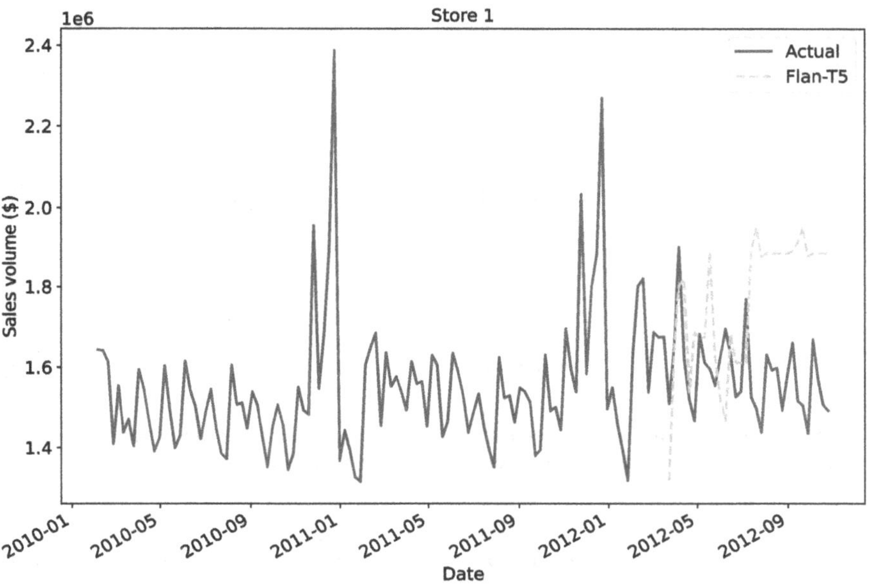


**Figure 8.5 Cross-validation with exogenous features. Here, the quality of the predictions has clearly degraded compared with not using features.**

### 8.4.4 *Evaluating Flan-T5 forecasts with exogenous features*

From figure 8.5, it's clear that using an exogenous feature significantly degraded the performance of the model because the values no longer overlap well. This conclusion is further supported by the following evaluation and the comparison in figure 8.6.

**Listing 8.12 Comparing performance with and without exogenous features**

```
test_df['FlanT5-exog'] = store1_cv_exog

evaluation = evaluate(
    test_df,
    metrics=[mae, smape],
    models=['FlanT5', 'FlanT5-exog'],
```

```
    target_col='Weekly_Sales',
    id_col='Store'
)
```

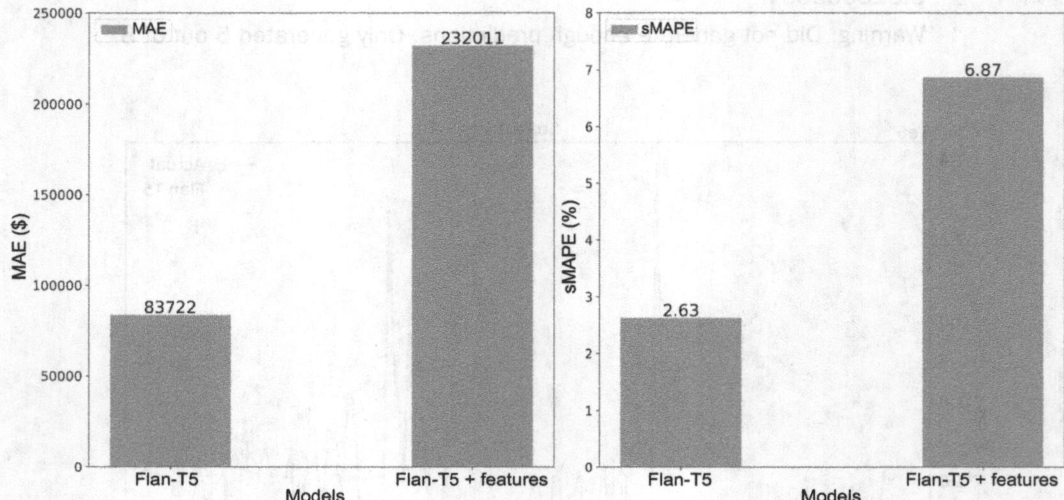


**Figure 8.6 Comparing the performance between using and not using features. Lower is better. Here, the model that uses features is significantly worse than the model that doesn't use features.**

In figure 8.6, we see that adding information from `Holiday_Flag` increased all evaluation metrics, which have more than doubled. Thus, the feature may not be predictive, or the model may have had a lot of trouble handling this particular covariate. Nevertheless, we've developed a method of forecasting with covariates using an LLM.

## 8.5 Detecting anomalies with Flan-T5

In previous chapters, we used probabilistic models to perform anomaly detection. If a value fell outside the prediction interval, it was considered an anomaly. In this case, even though the LLM is not making probabilistic forecasts, we can still ask it to perform anomaly detection using chain-of-thought prompting.

In addition to feeding a sequence of values, we compute some basic statistics, including the mean and the values of the 5th (lower bound) and 995th millile (upper bound). Then we specify that the model should look at all values and spot those that are smaller than the lower bound or larger than the upper bound. The prompt could be like this:

For each value, output 1 if it's an anomaly or 0 if it's normal.
Return ONLY a sequence of 0s and 1s separated by commas, with no other text.

Example 1:

Statistics:

Mean: 1000

Q1: 800

Q3: 1200

Values: 900, 1800, 1000, 500, 1100

Anomalies are values that are lower than Q1 or higher than Q3.

Output: 0,1,0,1,0

### 8.5.1 Defining a function for anomaly detection with Flan-T5

To achieve this task, we build a function that's similar to `llm_forecast`, but we modify the prompt to specify the task of anomaly detection, and we process the output differently.

**Listing 8.13 Anomaly detection with LLMs**

```
def detect_anomalies_llm(
    df,
    model,
    tokenizer,
    value_col,
    chunk_size = 10,
    max_new_tokens = 100
):
    mean_value = df[value_col].mean()          ◄── Calculates basic statistics
    std_value = df[value_col].std()                 of the input data
    q1 = df[value_col].quantile(0.995)
    q3 = df[value_col].quantile(0.005)

    anomalies = []

    stats_info = f"""Dataset Statistics:
Mean: {mean_value:.2f}
Standard Deviation: {std_value:.2f}
Q1: {q1:.2f}
Q3: {q3:.2f}
"""

    few_shot_examples = f"""For each value, output 1 if it's an anomaly or
➥ 0 if it's normal.
Return ONLY a sequence of 0s and 1s separated by commas,
➥ with no other text.

Example 1:
Statistics:
Mean: 1000
Q1: 800
Q3: 1200
Values: 900, 1800, 1000, 500, 1100
```

```
Anomalies are values that are lower than Q1 or higher than  Q3.
Output: 0,1,0,1,0

Example 2:
Statistics:
Mean: 500
Q1: 400
Q3: 600
Values: 450, 900, 500, 480, 470
Anomalies are values that are lower than Q1 or higher than  Q3.
Output: 0,1,0,0,0

Now analyze these values:"""

    for i in range(0, len(df), chunk_size):
        chunk = df.iloc[i:i + chunk_size]
        values_str = ", ".join([f"{x:.2f}" for x in chunk[value_col]])

        prompt = f"""{few_shot_examples}

{stats_info}
Values: {values_str}
Anomalies are values that are lower than Q1 or higher than  Q3.

Output exactly {len(chunk)} numbers (0 or 1) separated by commas:"""

        inputs = tokenizer(prompt, return_tensors='pt')
        with torch.no_grad():
            output = tokenizer.decode(
                model.generate(
                    inputs["input_ids"],
                    max_new_tokens=max_new_tokens,
                    temperature=0.3,
                    do_sample=False,
                )[0],
                skip_special_tokens=True
            )

        print(f"\nProcessing chunk {i//chunk_size + 1}:")
        print(f"Values: {values_str}")
        print(f"Model output: {output}")

        try:
            binary_value = next(int(c) for c in output if c in ['0', '1'])
            binary_values = [binary_value] * len(chunk)
            print(f"Extending {binary_value}
                ➥ to {len(chunk)} values")

        except (StopIteration, ValueError) as e:
            print(f"Error parsing output: {e}. Using 0 as default.")
            binary_values = [0] * len(chunk)

        anomalies.extend(binary_values)

    return anomalies
```

Generates a chain-of-thought prompt to show the model how to process each value

Feeds chunks of the sequence to the model to avoid feeding large sequences

Extracts binary labels. If the length of the output is not long enough, we repeat the predictions.

If the model fails, it defaults to labeling values as normal.

In this listing, the logic is essentially the same as in forecasting. Here, the input data is processed in chunks to avoid sending too many values to the LLM, which can result in poor performance.

We adapt the prompt for anomaly detection and use a chain-of-thought prompt to show the model how it should evaluate each value in the sequence. Then, when processing the output, we look for binary values, where `0` means the value is normal and `1` means the value is an anomaly. In case the model doesn't output a label for each value, we repeat the last prediction. Finally, if the model doesn't output a binary label, we default to a normal value.

Although this function seems long, that's due mostly to the large few-shot prompt that we feed to the model to ensure that it behaves as expected.

### 8.5.2 Running anomaly detection

Now we can run the function and detect anomalies.

**Listing 8.14 Running anomaly detection**

```
anomalies_flant5 = detect_anomalies_llm(
    df=df_anomaly,
    model=flant5_model,
    tokenizer=flant5_tokenizer,
    value_col='value'
)
```

Once again, we can inspect the raw output of the model. For the first chunk of data, we get the following response:

Processing chunk 1:

Values: 745967.00, 733640.00, 710142.00, 552565.00, 555470.00, 550285.00, 636570.00, 726535.00, 748567.00, 761596.00

Model output: 0

Extending 0 to 10 values

We obtain a similar response for all chunks. The model fails only to predict a single label with a value of `0`. In other words, it says the first value of the sequence is normal, forcing us to extend that prediction to the rest of the values. As a result, all values are labeled as normal, so the model fails at detecting anomalies. If we were to compute the precision, recall, and F1 Score, we'd obtain a value of `0` for all metrics because the model isn't detecting any anomalies.

This result is underwhelming. The model seemed to be able to generate reasonable forecasts earlier, but it fails at anomaly detection. This behavior may be normal, however, because Flan-T5 is not specifically trained to handle time-series data, and we're trying to adapt it using only prompting techniques.

## 8.6 Forecasting with Llama-3.2

Now that we've experimented with Flan-T5, let's perform the same tests with Llama-3.2, which is a bigger, more advanced model; it has more parameters and can handle dialogue and code generation. In this section, we work with `llama-3.2-3b-instruct`. The `instruct` portion of the name means that this model should be good at following instructions.

We'll interact with the model through API calls. That way, we don't have to download and set up the model locally, which can create various challenges depending on the available hardware. Thus, to reproduce the code and results, we'll create a free account on OpenRouter (https://openrouter.ai). This platform allows us to interact with both free and paid LLMs through an API, eliminating the hassle of setting everything locally and giving us the opportunity to interact with powerful models no matter what our local hardware is.

After our account is created, we must generate an API key, a secret token that authenticates us when we use the platform and allows us to send data to models and retrieve a response. This secret information is stored in the `OPENROUTER_API_KEY` variable throughout this section.

> **NOTE** The models in the Llama family are for research purposes only and can't be used in a commercial setting. The following code can be adapted to any LLM through OpenRouter, so make sure to use those models according to their licenses.

### 8.6.1 Performing initial setup

Let's start by defining a system prompt. This prompt is an instruction that specifies the context, tone, and boundaries of an LLM. In this prompt, we can ask the model to be humoristic in its response, to be a helpful assistant, or to answer only in rhyme. In other words, the prompt shapes the behavior of the LLM. We want the model to be expert at handling time-series data and predict the next sequence of values, so we set the system prompt as shown in the following listing.

**Listing 8.15 Setting the system prompt**

```
system_prompt = """
    You are a helpful assistant that performs time series predictions.
    The user will provide a sequence and you will predict the next
    sequence.
    The sequence is represented by decimal numbers as strings separated by
    commas.
    """
```

### 8.6.2 Creating a function to forecast via API call

Now we can write a function to forecast with Llama-3.2 via API. We'll make a request to the server with our prompt. The response is parsed as a JSON object from which we extract the output of the model.

**Listing 8.16 Function to forecast via API call**

```
def prompt_forecast(
    df,
    horizon,
    context_len,
    target_col
):
    input_values = df[f'{target_col}'].iloc[-context_len:]
      .values.tolist()

    response = requests.post(
      url="https://openrouter.ai/api/v1
        /chat/completions",
      headers={
        "Authorization":
          f"Bearer {OPENROUTER_API_KEY}",
      },
      data=json.dumps({
        "model":
          "meta-llama/llama-3.2-3b-instruct:free",
        "messages": [
            {
               "role": "system",
                "content": system_prompt
            },
          {
            "role": "user",
            "content": f"The past values of the series are {input_values}.
              What will be the next {horizon} values? Just output the
              next values and nothing else."
          }
        ]

      })
    )

    response_json = response.json()
    content = response_json['choices'][0]
      ['message']['content']
    if content.startswith('[') and content.endswith(']'):
        preds = json.loads(content)
    else:
        wrapped = f'[{content}]'
        preds = json.loads(wrapped)

    return preds
```

Annotations:
- Makes a list with the input sequence
- Makes a POST request to the server to send our data to the model
- We use this URL because we want the model to answer our prompt.
- Make sure to use your own API key.
- The data must be in JSON format when it's sent to the server.
- We use the free version of the model. Change this value to any model from OpenRouter if you want.
- Sends the system prompt
- Prompts to make the model forecast the input series
- Parses the response as a JSON object
- Extracts the answer from the LLM
- Parses the answer as a list

Let's break down in detail what's happening in this listing. First, we create a list from the input dataset, as we did when working with Flan-T5. Then, to interact with the server, we make a `POST` request because we're sending data to the server to get a response from the language model, That's why we use `requests.post()`. Inside the request, we specify the URL and pass the API key to authenticate us and allow us to make the request.

Next, in the data parameter, we format the information we want to send to the server as a JSON object. First, we specify the model, which is meta-llama/llama-3.2-3b-instruct:free. (You can change this to any available model on OpenRouter.) Then we pass the messages to the model. The messages have different roles: system and user. When the role is set to system, the message should be a set of high-level instructions, like the system prompt, which is what we pass in this message. When the role is set to user, it corresponds to the query or prompt we send to the model. Thus, this is where we feed the input sequence and ask the model to predict the next set of values.

When the request is made, the server returns a response, which we parse as a JSON object using response.json(). Then we extract the model's answer and parse it as a list because we expect the output to be a list of future values.

Because Llama-3.2 is especially good at following instructions, we don't need to write lengthy code for processing the output and defining safeguards in case it's not as we expect.

### 8.6.3 Making predictions

When this function is defined, we can run it to generate predictions for each store. The predictions are plotted as shown in figure 8.7.

**Listing 8.17 Forecasting with Llama-3.2**

```
llama_preds_store1 = prompt_forecast(
    df=data.query("Store == 1"),
    horizon=8,
    context_len=16,
    target_col='Weekly_Sales'
)
llama_preds_store2 = prompt_forecast(
    df=data.query("Store == 2"),
    horizon=8,
    context_len=16,
    target_col='Weekly_Sales'
)
llama_preds_store3 = prompt_forecast(
    df=data.query("Store == 3"),
    horizon=8,
    context_len=16,
    target_col='Weekly_Sales'
)
llama_preds_store4 = prompt_forecast(
    df=data.query("Store == 4"),
    horizon=8,
    context_len=16,
    target_col='Weekly_Sales'
)

all_preds = [llama_preds_store1, llama_preds_store2, llama_preds_store3,
➥llama_preds_store4]
```

```
preds_df = combine_predictions(all_preds,
                               start_date='11-02-2012',
                               horizon=8,
                               freq='W-FRI',
                               model_name='Llama')
```

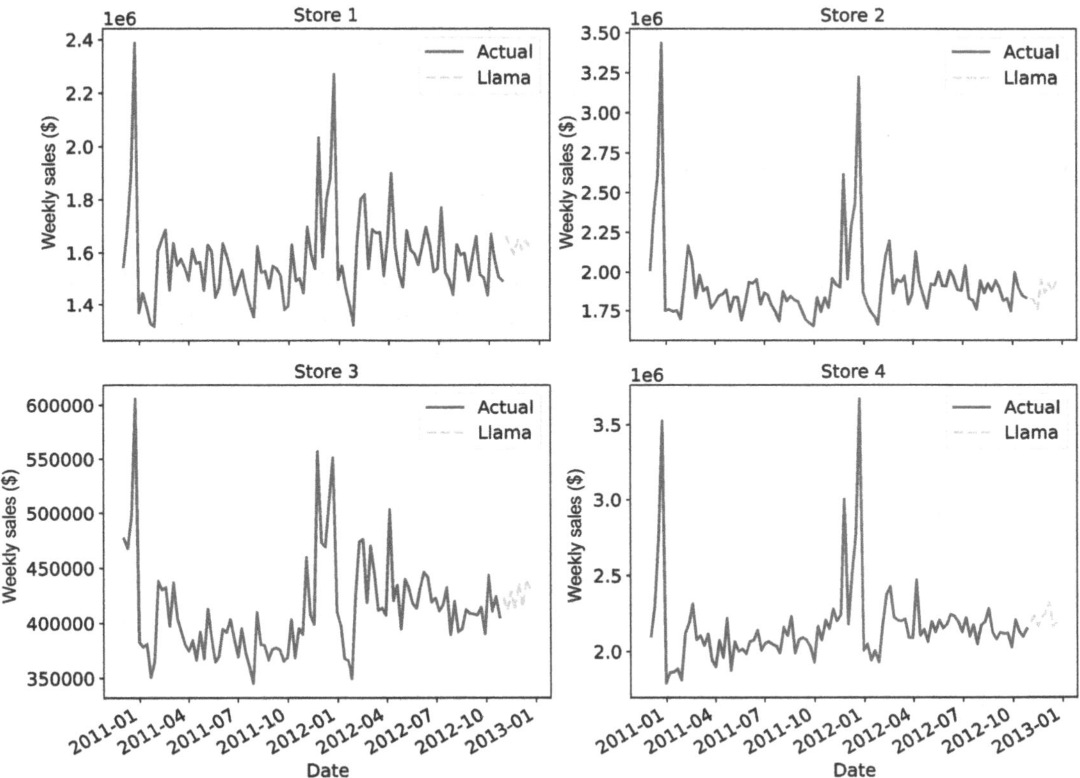


**Figure 8.7 Zero-shot predictions from Llama-3.2**

In the plot, the predictions for store 1 don't look reasonable given the historical data. But we don't know the actual values for those dates, so we can't evaluate the performance of the model.

## 8.7 Cross-validating with Llama-3.2

Let's run cross-validation to evaluate the performance of Llama-3.2 and compare it to that of Flan-T5. To perform cross-validation, we adapt the function we used with Flan-T5 to use the following `prompt_forecast` function. The rest of the logic stays the same.

**Listing 8.18 Cross-validation with Llama-3.2**

```
def cross_validation_prompt(df, h, n_windows, target_col):

    preds = []

    for i in range(n_windows, 0, -1):
        input_df = df.iloc[:-(h * i)]

        forecast = prompt_forecast(input_df,
                                   horizon=h,
                                   context_len=h,
                                   target_col=target_col)

        preds.extend(forecast)

    return preds
```

Now we run the cross-validation function. Again, we do it only for store 1 so we can compare performance with Flan-T5. The predictions are plotted as shown in figure 8.8.

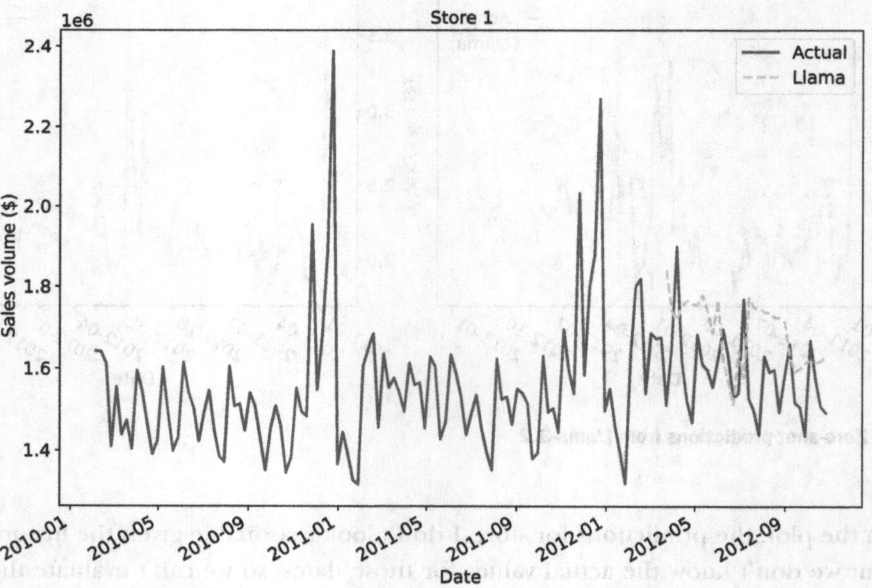


**Figure 8.8 Predictions from cross-validation with Llama-3.2 Here, the predictions seem to be off.**

**Listing 8.19 Running cross-validation**

```
store1_cv = cross_validation_prompt(
    data.query("Store == 1"),
    h=8,
```

```
    n_windows=4,
    target_col='Weekly_Sales'
)
```

The predictions don't look good because they're fairly far from the actual values, especially toward the end of the sequence. In figure 8.9, we compare the performance of Llama-3.2 to the performance of Flan-T5. Let's also compare it with all previous models in table 8.2.

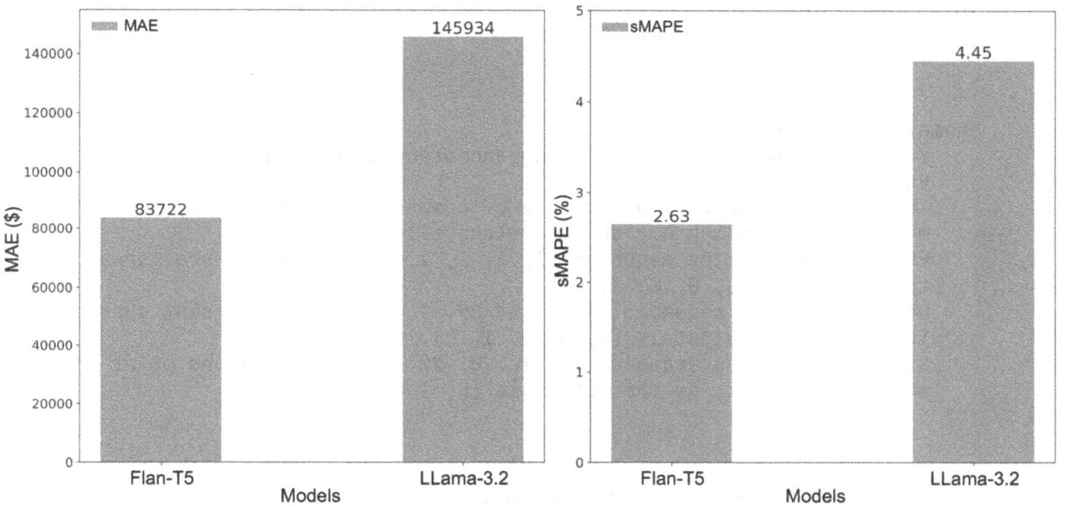


**Figure 8.9 Comparing the performance of Flan-T5 and Llama-3.2 from cross-validation. Here, Flan-T5 performs much better than Llama-3.2 because it achieves lower scores on both performance metrics. Lower is better.**

**Table 8.2 Performance metrics of foundation models in cross-validation over four windows of eight weeks**

| Model | MAE | sMAPE (%) |
|---|---|---|
| TimeGPT (fine-tuned) | 63544 | 2.04 |
| Lag-Llama (fine-tuned) | 72990 | 2.29 |
| Chronos (fine-tuned) | 63811 | 1.99 |
| Moirai + exog | 82041 | 2.57 |
| TimesFM | 64578 | 2.02 |
| Flan-T5 | 83721 | 2.62 |
| Llama-3.2 | 145934 | 4.45 |

In figure 8.9 and table 8.2, we see that Flan-T5 achieves much better results than Llama-3.2 in predicting the sales of store 1 because it achieves lower MAE and sMAPE scores. In fact, up to this point, Llama-3.2 achieved the worst performance on this particular task. Thus, although Llama-3.2 is a bigger model than Flan-T5 base and requires less code to interact with, its zero-shot forecasting performance falls short in this scenario.

## 8.8 Detecting anomalies with Llama-3.2

Finally, let's use Llama-3.2 to detect anomalies in time-series data. We use the dataset on taxi rides that we used in previous chapters.

### 8.8.1 Modifying the system prompt

First, we modify the system prompt to explain to the model how it should identify anomalies in time series.

**Listing 8.20 Setting the system prompt for anomaly detection**

```
anomaly_system_prompt = """
    You are an expert at identifying anomalous points in a sequence of
    values.
    The user will provide a sequence of comma-separated values, and you
    must indicate which one are anomalous (1) or normal (0).
    For example, in the sequence: 1, 1, 1, 1, 1, all points are normal, so
    the output is [0, 0, 0, 0, 0].
    However, in the sequence: 1, 1, 1, 89, 1, there is one point abnormally
    large, so the output is [0, 0, 0, 1, 0].
    Similarly, in the sequence 20, 1, 20, 20, 20, there is one point
    abnormally small, so the output is [0, 1, 0, 0, 0]
"""
```

### 8.8.2 Defining a function for anomaly detection

Next, we define a function to perform anomaly detection when using LLMs through API calls in OpenRouter. The function follows the same logic we applied with Flan-T5, but we adapt it to make API requests.

**Listing 8.21 Function for anomaly detection with Llama-3.2**

```
def detect_anomalies_llama(
    df,
    value_col,
    chunk_size
):

    anomalies = []

    for i in range(0, len(df), chunk_size):        # Feeds the data in chunks
        chunk = df.iloc[i:i + chunk_size]
        values_str = ", ".join([f"{x:.2f}" for x in chunk[value_col]])

        response = requests.post(                   # Makes the API call
          url="https://openrouter.ai/api/v1/chat/completions",
          headers={
```

```
            "Authorization": f"Bearer {OPENROUTER_API_KEY}",
        },
        data=json.dumps({
            "model": "meta-llama/llama-3.2-3b-instruct:free",
            "messages": [
                {
                    "role": "system",
                     "content": anomaly_system_prompt
                },
              {
                "role": "user",
                "content": f"Label each point in the following sequence as
normal (0) or abnormal (1): {values_str}.
Just output the label."
              }
            ]

        })
    )

        response_json = response.json()
        content = response_json['choices'][0]['message']['content']
        content = content.strip()
        if not content.startswith('['):
            content = '[' + content
        if not content.endswith(']'):
            content = content + ']'
        anomaly_flags = json.loads(content)[:chunk_size]
        anomalies.extend(anomaly_flags)

    if len(anomalies) < len(df):
        anomalies.extend([0] * (len(df) - len(anomalies)))

    return anomalies
```

**Ensures that the final number of labels matches the length of the input dataset**

We recognize the same logic that we applied before because we feed chunks of data at a time to avoid sending long sequences to the model. Then we make the API call, process the output, and make sure that the number of predicted labels matches the number of data points in the input series.

### 8.8.3 Running anomaly detection with Llama-3.2

Now we can run the function and plot the labeled anomalies as shown in figure 8.10.

**Listing 8.22 Running anomaly detection with Llama-3.2**

```
llama_anomaly_flag = detect_anomalies_llama(df_anomaly, 'value', 40)
```

The figure shows the anomalies labeled by the model as diamonds. Clearly, the model is labeling too many points as anomalous. This result means that recall is high but precision is low, making the F1 Score low as well. The model detected all actual anomalies but also mislabeled many normal points as anomalies.

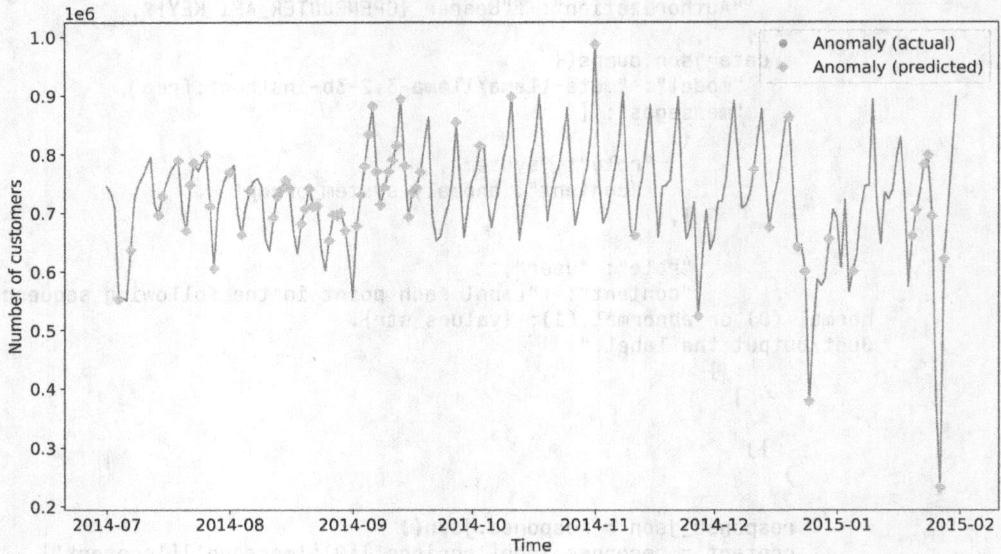


**Figure 8.10 Anomaly detection with Llama-3.2**

### 8.8.4 Evaluating anomaly detection

Figure 8.11 compares the F1 Scores of all the models we've tried for anomaly detection.

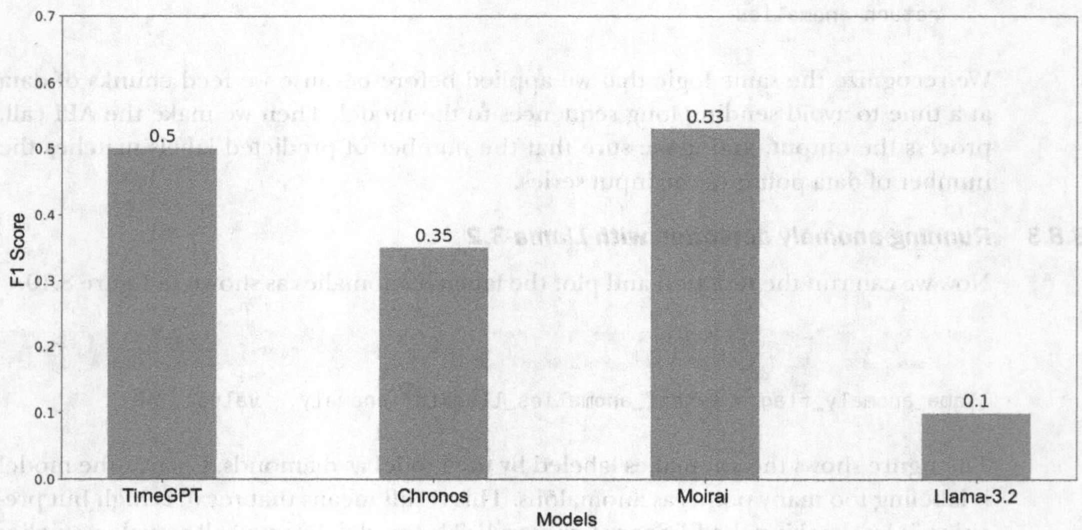


**Figure 8.11 F1 Scores of the foundation models we've tested for anomaly detection. Higher is better.**

We're not surprised to see that Llama-3.2 is the worst-performing model for anomaly detection because figure 8.10 showed that it mislabeled way too many points as anomalies. Therefore, Moirai is the best model for this particular dataset because it achieved the highest F1-score.

## 8.9 Next steps

In this chapter, we experimented with zero-shot forecasting using LLMs. Although these models are not specifically built to handle time-series data, we can use different prompting techniques to adapt their generative capabilities to time-series data. This implies framing our forecasting problem as a language task, formulating it as a question, and asking the language model to answer it.

Table 8.3 updates our table of foundation models.

**Table 8.3 Pros and cons of each foundation forecasting model**

| Model | Pros | Cons | When to use |
|---|---|---|---|
| TimeGPT | Easy and fast to use<br>Comes with many native functions<br>Works on any device, regardless of hardware<br>Free plan | Paid product for a certain usage<br>Model may not be available if the server is down. | Forecasting on long and short horizons with exogenous features.<br>You need to fine-tune but do not have the local resources. |
| Lag-Llama | Open source model<br>Free to use | Awkward to use because we must clone the repository<br>Speed of inference depends on our hardware. | Quick proof of concept<br>Ideal for research-oriented projects |
| Chronos | Open source model<br>Free to use<br>Can be installed as a Python package | Speed and accuracy depend on our hardware.<br>Fine-tuning requires cloning the repository.<br>We must define some functions manually. | Forecasting on horizons shorter than 64 time steps<br>Forecasting series without strong trends |
| TimesFM | Open source model<br>Free to use<br>Can be installed as a Python package<br>Supports exogenous features | Only the largest model is available.<br>Restrictive requirements for use (16 GB of RAM, Linux-based system to install dependencies)<br>Knowledge of JAX is required for fine-tuning.<br>Cannot perform anomaly detection because it is a deterministic model | Ideal for deterministic forecasting in which prediction intervals are not required<br>You want to feed a long input series. |

**Table 8.3 Pros and cons of each foundation forecasting model (*continued*)**

| Model | Pros | Cons | When to use |
|---|---|---|---|
| Moirai | Open source model<br>Free to use<br>Supports exogenous features<br>Can be installed as a Python package | Speed and accuracy depend on the hardware.<br>We must define helper functions when not working entirely with GluonTS. | You have exogenous features.<br>Forecasting on horizons shorter than 256 time steps |
| Large language models (Flan-T5 and Llama-3.2) | Possible to use free LLMs<br>Interacting through natural language feels intuitive, | Not built to handle time-series data<br>Requires lengthy code to preprocess the input and extract the values from the output<br>Requires a lot of computation power for local setups | You already have access to an LLM.<br>You need a natural language interface for forecasting.<br>You know how to develop prompts and safeguards for edge cases. |

Throughout this chapter, we've seen that it's possible to use LLMs for time series forecasting. But keep in mind that they're not meant to handle forecasting tasks. Using LLMs for forecasting is like using a fork to eat ice cream. It may work, but other models and tools are better suited to the task. Also, having to write lengthy code to preprocess the input and extract the values from the output is not ideal. Finally, LLMs are usually much larger models than the large time models that we've explored; setting them up locally requires a lot of computation power, which may not be available to everyone.

Although an off-the-shelf LLM may not be the best tool for time-series forecasting, we can reprogram it slightly to make it better for this task. We explore this topic in chapter 9.

## Summary

- LLMs are foundation models in natural language processing that can handle natural language tasks such as question answering and text classification.
- Because LLMs are trained for language tasks, we can frame the forecasting problem as a language task to use LLMs. This involves building a prompt and asking the model to predict the next set of values from an input sequence.
- To interact with LLMs, we use prompting. Few-shot and chain-of-thought prompts usually produce the best results.
- We can work with LLMs both locally and via API calls.
- LLMs can perform forecasting tasks, but they weren't built for this purpose, which may result in poor performances.

# 9 Reprogramming an LLM for forecasting

**_This chapter covers_**

- Discovering the architecture of Time-LLM
- Forecasting with Time-LLM
- Applying Time-LLM to anomaly detection

In chapter 8, we applied large language models (LLMs) directly to forecasting tasks. Although it's possible to use LLMs to make forecasts and detect anomalies, they're still ill suited to time-series forecasting because they were not specifically trained for this type of task. To overcome this hurdle, researchers have proposed Time-LLM, a framework that reprograms existing large language models for time-series forecasting [1].

Time-LLM is not a foundation model but a tool that allows us to repurpose off-the-shelf LLMs for time-series forecasting. As we'll see in this chapter, Time-LLM is effectively a multimodal model; we can feed it both historical time-series data and a textual prompt to provide context about our time series and obtain forecasts.

A model is *multimodal* when it supports different types of data. If we can feed an image and text to a model to get a certain output, for example, that model is multimodal. This type of model is especially useful when we want to enrich our forecasts with contextual data and have enough computing resources to reprogram an LLM.

## 9.1 Discovering Time-LLM

Much like Chronos, which we explored in chapter 5, Time-LLM is a framework that reprograms existing LLMs for time-series forecasting. Because a reprogramming step is required, we can use only open source language models. Figure 9.1 shows the general architecture of Time-LLM.

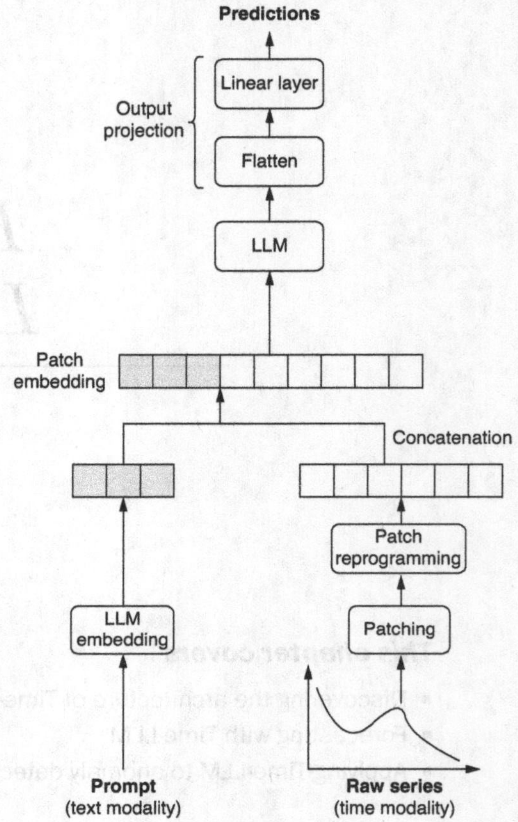


**Figure 9.1 General architecture of Time-LLM. (Right) The raw series is fed to the framework and undergoes patching before entering the patch-reprogramming phase. (Left) A prompt is used to provide context about the data. The prompt and reprogrammed patches are joined as a patch embedding, which is sent to the LLM. Then the output is projected to create a forecast for our series.**

The figure shows the multimodality characteristic of Time-LLM, which takes as input both a text prompt and a time series. The time series undergoes patching and patch reprogramming so we can align the modality of our time series (numbers) with the modality of the LLM (text). We will study this step in detail in section 9.1.1. A textual prompt can provide context about the series; it's used as a prefix to the final patch embedding that's sent to the LLM. Finally, the output of the LLM is passed through a projection step, which flattens the output, and a linear layer maps the output embedding to numeric forecasts.

Unlike Chronos, in which existing pretrained models allow us to perform zero-shot forecasting, Time-LLM has no pretrained model. As a result, we have to perform patch reprogramming, a task that involves some training time. As we will see later in section 9.2, depending on the size of the LLM and the availability of computing resources, training time can be extensive.

### 9.1.1 Patch reprogramming

The critical portion of Time-LLM is patch reprogramming, which aligns the modality of the input with the modality of the LLM. We know that time series are represented by numbers, whereas LLMs operate with text. Therefore, patch reprogramming effectively translates the values of the series to a textual representation that the LLM understands.

First, the series is normalized and patched. This patching process is the same one that occurs in Moirai and TimesFM (chapters 6 and 7, respectively). Patching keeps local semantic information and reduces the computational burden by reducing the number of input tokens. The patches are embedded as an abstract representation and sent to the patch-reprogramming step, as illustrated in figure 9.2.

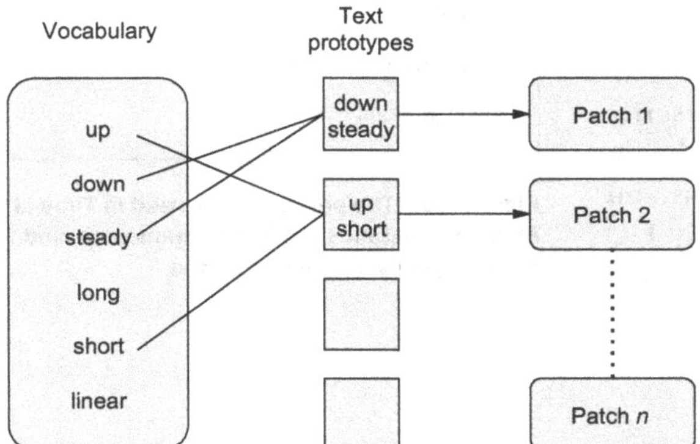


**Figure 9.2 Patch reprogramming**

In this step, a small set of words, called *vocabulary*, makes up learned text prototypes, which describe the information in a certain patch. In figure 9.2, the first text prototype describes patch 1 as "down steady," and the second text prototype describes patch 2 as "up short."

Although figure 9.2 shows a single text prototype assigned to each patch, other patches can be described by many text prototypes. Both text prototypes in the figure could be combined to describe a certain patch as "down steady then up short." Again, this step is critical in Time-LLM because it translates the input time series to a domain that the LLM understands, allowing us to use virtually any LLM for forecasting.

### 9.1.2 Discovering Prompt-as-Prefix

When the patches are reprogrammed, they're not sent to the LLM backbone immediately. First, they're prefixed with a prompt through a technique called *Prompt-as-Prefix*. To enrich the input to the LLM, the Prompt-as-Prefix technique complements patch reprogramming and allows the model to adapt better to forecasting time-series data.

This technique involves building a textual prompt to specify the task to the LLM and guide it to better results. As we saw in chapter 8, we interact with LLMs through prompts, and different prompts lead to different results. Thus, by providing background information on the series and specifying its domain, we can help the LLM forecast our series better. Figure 9.3 illustrates the prompt prefix used in Time-LLM.

The prompt prefix has three key components: context, task description, and input statistics. The following sections discuss these components in detail.

Prompt prefix

<|start_prompt|>

**Context**
This dataset tracks weekly sales in stores. Sales tend to be higher toward the end of the year.

**Task description**
Forecast the next *h* steps given the previous *input_size* steps information.

**Input statistics**
min value: <min_value>
max value: <max_value>
median value: <max_value>
the trend of the input is: <trend>
top 5 lags are: <top_5_lags>

<|end_prompt|>

**Figure 9.3 The prompt prefix used in Time-LLM. Elements in italics are input parameters, and values surrounded by <> are calculated.**

#### PROMPT CONTEXT

With the context, we can give general information about our series and specify its domain. As we know, series from different domains and frequencies behave differently. Figure 9.4 recreates the comparison we made in chapter 5.

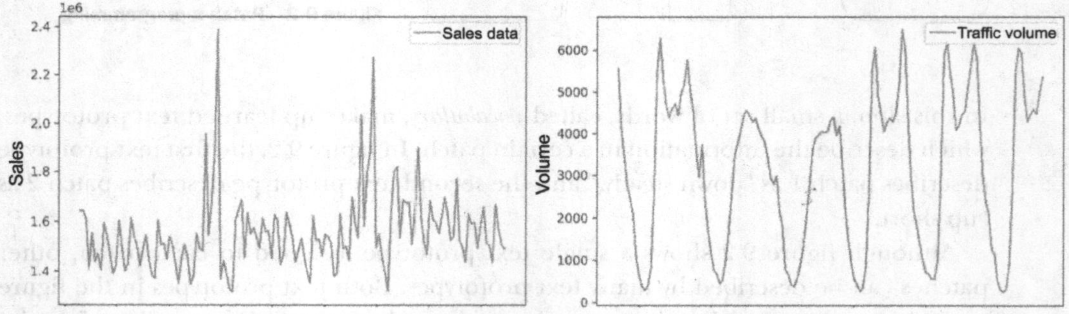


**Figure 9.4 Comparing weekly store sales (left) and daily traffic volume (right). Series from different domains at different frequencies exhibit different patterns.**

#### PROMPT DESCRIPTION

The prompt prefix in figure 9.3 includes a task description, which specifies what the LLM must accomplish. In this case, we want the model to forecast future time steps based on a certain input size.

#### PROMPT STATISTICS

Finally, the prompt contains statistics on the input series, such as the minimum and maximum values, the median, whether the series is increasing or decreasing over the entire history, and the top five lags. Identifying the top five lags is especially interesting because it involves applying the *fast Fourier transform*, an algorithm that maps a signal from the time domain to the frequency domain. In other words, it takes our time series and transforms it into a function of amplitude with respect to frequency. The frequencies with the largest amplitudes are considered the most important. This algorithm is useful for finding seasonal frequencies in data.

Consider the top five lags of a dataset in figure 9.5. This dataset tracks a household's hourly energy consumption.

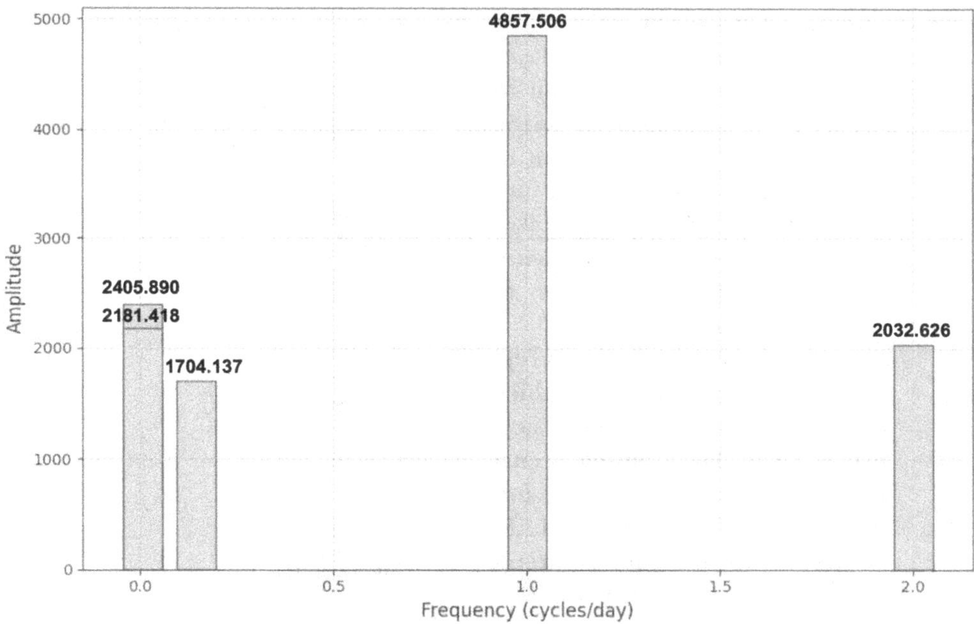


**Figure 9.5 The top five lags of a dataset tracking the hourly energy consumption of a household**

In this example, the top frequencies are 0.0051, 0.0058, 0.14, 1, and 2. To obtain the lags, we divide 24 by the frequency. We use 24 in the numerator because the plot reports cycles per day, but because the data is hourly, we must use the number of hours in a day, which is 24. When we carry out the operation for each frequency, we see the top five lags are 4705, 4137, 168, 24 and 12. We can interpret these lags as the most important seasonal cycles in the data. Lag 168, for example, indicates a weekly seasonality ($7 \times 24 = 168$). Similarly, lag 24 designates a daily seasonality, and lag 12 indicates a half-daily seasonality, meaning that a complete cycle occurs twice a day.

Time-LLM applies the fast Fourier transform internally to find the top five lags. This information helps the model find seasonal patterns in the data, which in turn helps it make better forecasts.

### 9.1.3 Making predictions

At this point, the patches are reprogrammed, and we've built a prompt prefix. Both are concatenated and sent to the LLM. The LLM is frozen, meaning that no training or fine-tuning is occurring. We feed the concatenated embedding to the LLM and get an output. That output is flattened and sent through a linear layer to project the abstract output to forecasts on the same scale as the original dataset. It's important to understand that the LLM is not fine-tuned. The training takes place in reprogramming patches and projecting the final output, as shown in figure 9.6.

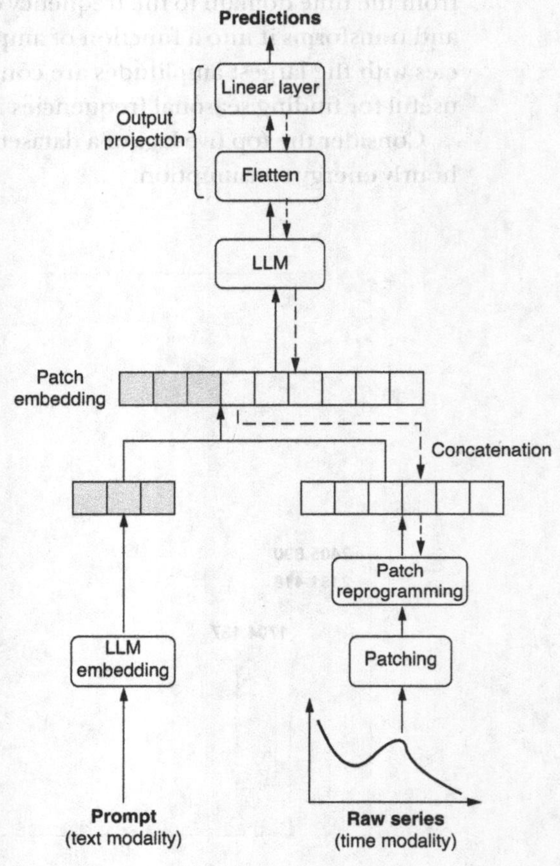


**Figure 9.6 Highlighting the training portion of Time-LLM**

In the figure, thick arrows represent the forward pass, and thick dashed arrows represent backpropagation. The training occurs in the patch-reprogramming and output-projection steps. The LLM is frozen; its parameters aren't being modified during training. Therefore, we effectively train the model to create better reprogrammed patches and output projection that minimize a certain loss function, such as the mean absolute error (MAE).

In other words, the model is trained to better describe patches of the series using natural language and to better project the LLM output to forecasts. We rely entirely on the zero-shot capabilities of the LLM, however.

## 9.2 Forecasting with Time-LLM

Now that we have a deep understanding of Time-LLM, let's apply it to our forecasting scenario. Luckily, forecasting with Time-LLM is easy because we use the `neuralforecast` library, the one we used in chapter 2 to build our own tiny foundation model using N-BEATS.

Again, we use our dataset on weekly store sales. Time-LLM supports only univariate forecasting, however, so we can't use any of the exogenous features available in the dataset.

### 9.2.1 Performing initial setup

We start by defining a prompt that describes the context of the dataset. This prompt will be added to the prompt prefix built internally in Time-LLM.

**Listing 9.1 Describing the context of the dataset**

```
prompt_prefix = """
    The dataset contains information on weekly sales in four different
    stores.
    Sales tend to increase towards the end of the year.
"""
```

Then we initialize the `TimeLLM` model the way we initialized N-BEATS in chapter 2.

**Listing 9.2 Initializing Time-LLM**

```
timellm = TimeLLM(
    h=8,
    input_size=16,
    d_llm=768,
    prompt_prefix=prompt_prefix,
    batch_size=16,
    windows_batch_size=16,
    max_steps=150
)
```

- `d_llm=768`: **This dimension changes depending on the LLM used. For GPT-2-small, the dimension is 768.**
- `prompt_prefix=prompt_prefix`: **Passes the context of the dataset**
- `max_steps=150`: **Defines the maximum number of steps to train patch reprogramming**

We don't specify any particular LLM because the default LLM is `GPT-2-small`. Also, we automatically fetch the tokenizer and configuration of the model to be used when reprogramming patches.

Technically, we can use any LLM with Time-LLM as long as it's available through Hugging Face along with its associated tokenizer and configuration file. (We used Hugging Face in chapter 8 to work with Flan-T5.) If we want to use `Llama-2-7b`, for example, we could specify

```
timellm = TimeLLM(
    h=8,
    input_size=16,
    llm="meta-llama/Llama-2-7b",
    d_llm=4096,
    prompt_prefix=prompt_prefix,
    batch_size=16,
    windows_batch_size=16,
    max_steps=150
)
```

We pass the URL for the model in Hugging Face, and the tokenizer and configuration files are automatically fetched.

**NOTE** Depending on the LLM, we must adjust the `d_llm` parameter accordingly. Each LLM has a specific hidden dimension, which we must pass to the model to enable it to train and work properly. GPT-2's hidden dimension is 768, and `Llama-2-7b`'s is 4096. If we use any other LLM, we must specify the correct hidden dimension. This information is easy to find through an internet search.

When the model is properly initialized, we can initialize the `NeuralForecast` object that will handle the entire training and forecasting logic, making sure to specify the frequency of the dataset. In this case, we have weekly data.

**Listing 9.3 Initializing the `NeuralForecast` object**

```
nf = NeuralForecast(
    models=[timellm],
    freq='W'
)
```

### 9.2.2 Generating forecasts

Finally, we can train Time-LLM and make predictions. During training, the model learns to reprogram patches and project the output of the LLM to optimize a certain loss function. In this case, the default loss function is the MAE.

To stay consistent with previous chapters, we keep the horizon to eight time steps. Also, because we're using `neuralforecast`, all stores will be forecasted automatically. Figure 9.7 shows the forecasts.

**Listing 9.4 Forecasting with Time-LLM**

```
df = data.drop(['Holiday_Flag', 'Temperature', 'Fuel_Price', 'CPI',
'Unemployment'], axis=1)     # Removes exogenous features because Time-LLM is univariate
nf.fit(                      # Trains the model for 150 steps
    df=df,
    time_col='Date',
    target_col='Weekly_Sales',
    id_col='Store'
)
preds = nf.predict()         # Makes predictions over the horizon
preds = preds.reset_index()
```

In the figure, the forecasts are mostly flat. We can't assess the quality of those predictions, however, because they're out of sample, and we can't compare them to actual values.

## 9.3 Cross-validating with Time-LLM

In this section, we'll perform cross-validation with Time-LLM to measure its performance. We'll use data only from store 1, and we'll use four windows of eight time steps

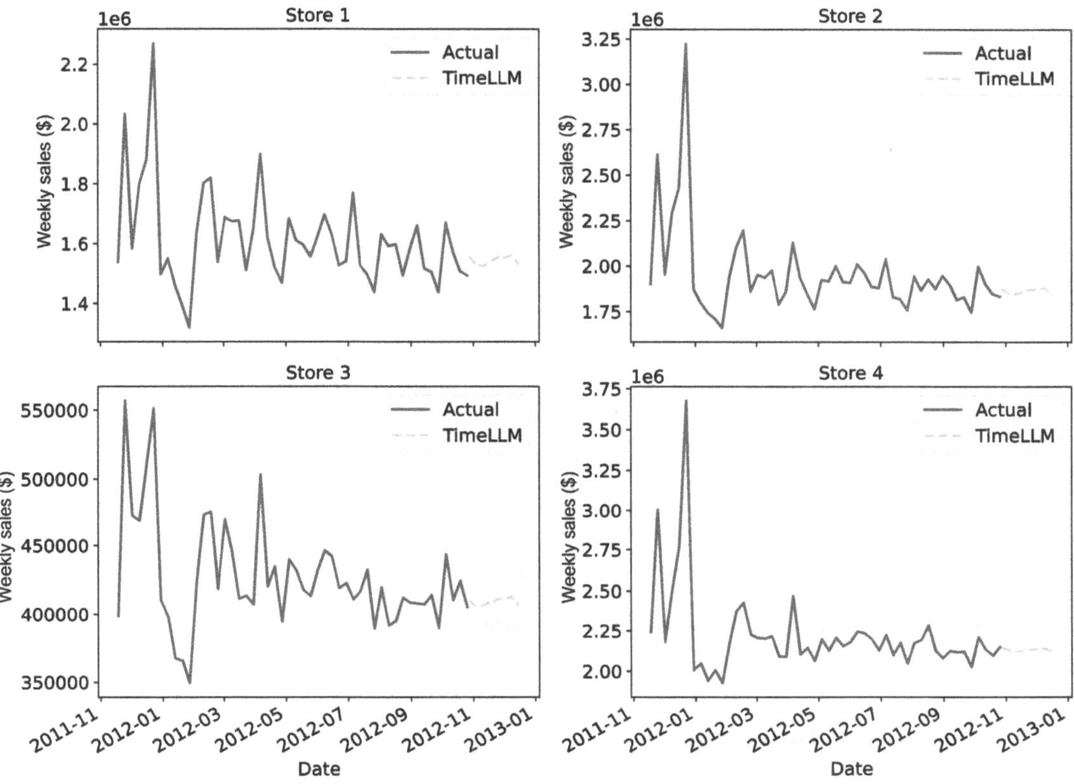


**Figure 9.7 Forecasting the weekly sales of four stores with Time-LLM**

each so that the model's performance is comparable to that of all previously explored models.

Because we're using `neuralforecast`, we can use the `cross_validation` method, as shown in the next listing. Figure 9.8 plots the result. The forecasts mostly overlap the actual values, which is a good sign.

**Listing 9.5 Cross-validation with Time-LLM**

```
store1_df = df.query("Store == 1")
cv_df = nf.cross_validation(
    df=store1_df,
    n_windows=4,
    step_size=8,
    refit=False,
    id_col='Store',
    target_col='Weekly_Sales',
    time_col='Date'
)
```

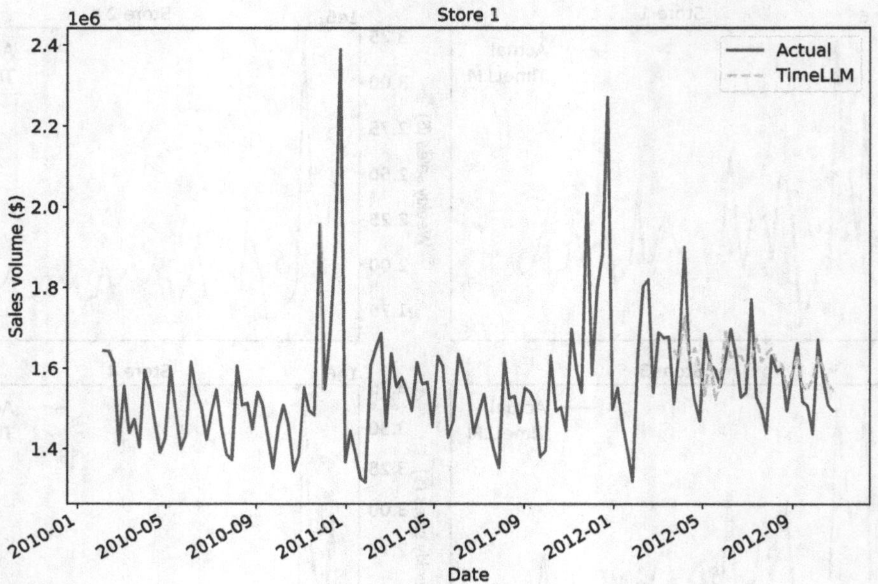


**Figure 9.8 Result of cross-validation with Time-LLM**

## 9.4 Evaluating Time-LLM

A visual assessment isn't enough, of course, so let's measure the MAE and symmetric mean absolute percentage error (sMAPE ). In table 9.1, we'll compare its performance to that of the other models explored so far.

**Listing 9.6 Evaluating Time-LLM**

```
test_df = cv_df.drop(['Date', 'cutoff'], axis=1)
evaluation = evaluate(
    test_df,
    metrics=[mae, smape],
    models=['TimeLLM'],
    target_col='Weekly_Sales',
    id_col='Store'
)
Evaluation
```

**Table 9.1 Performance metrics of foundation models in cross-validation over four windows of eight weeks**

| Model | MAE | sMAPE (%) |
|---|---|---|
| TimeGPT (fine-tuned) | 63544 | 2.04 |
| Lag-Llama (fine-tuned) | 72990 | 2.29 |
| Chronos (fine-tuned) | 63811 | 1.99 |

**Table 9.1 Performance metrics of foundation models in cross-validation over four windows of eight weeks (*continued*)**

| Model | MAE | sMAPE (%) |
|---|---|---|
| Moirai + exog | 82041 | 2.57 |
| TimesFM | 64578 | 2.02 |
| Flan-T5 | 83721 | 2.62 |
| Llama-3.2 | 138051 | 4.15 |
| Time-LLM | 80417 | 2.51 |

The evaluation shows an MAE of 80417$ and a sMAPE of 2.51%. This is better than using LLM directly, as we did in chapter 8, where Flan-T5 and Llama-3.2 achieved a sMAPE of 2.63% and 4.15%, respectively.

Although this is a single experiment on a single dataset, we see an advantage in reprogramming the LLM for forecasting and adapting it further rather than relying entirely on its text-completion capacity. This advantage comes at the expense of training for a certain number of steps, however. This training can take a significant amount of time, especially if we use a large model and train for many steps.

Thus, Time-LLM is a framework that reprograms readily available LLMs, but it requires some training steps, meaning that it has no zero-shot forecasting capability. Unlike the other models discussed in this book, Time-LLM always requires some training time.

## 9.5 Detecting anomalies with Time-LLM

With the implementation of `neuralforecast`, we can also use Time-LLM for anomaly detection. Specifically, we can combine cross-validation and conformal prediction intervals to get bounds and flag any actual values that fall outside the intervals as anomalies.

This method is similar to the one we used in TimeGPT (chapter 3), generating conformal predictions and using them to determine whether a value is an anomaly. This time, however, we have to set up the method ourselves. To do so, we must run cross-validation and refit the model at every window to calculate its conformal intervals. We'll set the maximum number of training steps to 10 to reduce the amount of time required to perform cross-validation. Increasing the number of training steps will likely yield better results but take significantly more time.

### 9.5.1 Detecting anomalies

To stay consistent with previous chapters, we use the dataset on daily taxi rides to detect anomalies in the last 184 time steps. But using conformal predictions in cross-validation requires an input size of 41 time steps, whereas only 31 are available. Thus, we detect over the last 160 time steps. Later, we pad the sequence with a default value to get metrics comparable to those of the other models.

Listing 9.7 Anomaly detection with Time-LLM

```
horizon = 20
input_size = 30

prediction_intervals = PredictionIntervals()     # Initializes conformal prediction intervals

prompt_prefix = """
    The dataset contains information on daily taxi rides in New York City.
    There is a weekly seasonality.
"""                                              # Describes the context of the dataset

timellm = TimeLLM(
    h=horizon,
    input_size=input_size,
    d_llm=768,
    prompt_prefix=prompt_prefix,
    batch_size=16,
    windows_batch_size=16,
    max_steps=10     # We can increase the maximum number of steps, but the process will take much longer to run.
)

nf = NeuralForecast(models=[timellm], freq='D')

anomaly_cv_df = nf.cross_validation(
    df=df_anomaly,
    n_windows=8,     # Runs eight rounds of cross-validation
    step_size=horizon,
    refit=True,      # Refits the model to estimate conformal prediction intervals
    prediction_intervals=prediction_intervals,     # Estimates conformal intervals
    level=[99],      # Uses a 99% interval. If a value is outside this bound, it will be an anomaly.
    target_col='value',
    time_col='timestamp'
)
```

In this listing, we set the horizon to `20` and the input size to `30`. These settings allow us to detect anomalies on the last 160 dates. To use conformal intervals, we use the `PredictionIntervals()` object in `neuralforecast`. This object automatically handles the estimation of the bounds given a confidence level.

Next, we define the context of the data and initialize the `TimeLLM` model as we did earlier. We use `max_steps=10` to speed the entire process. Using a larger value will likely lead to better results but take much longer to complete.

Finally, we run cross-validation. We use `refit=True`, which is required to estimate the conformal prediction intervals. We also use a level of `99` (percent), as specified in the `level` argument.

When cross-validation is done, we can flag actual values that fall outside the 99% prediction interval as anomalies. Figure 9.9 plots the result.

Listing 9.8 Flagging anomalies

```
anomaly_cv_df = anomaly_cv_df.reset_index()
anomaly_cv_df['anomaly'] = (
```

```
    (anomaly_cv_df['value'] < anomaly_cv_df['TimeLLM-lo-99']) | \
    (anomaly_cv_df['value'] > anomaly_cv_df['TimeLLM-hi-99'])
).astype(int)
```

A value is an anomaly if it is outside the 99% prediction interval.

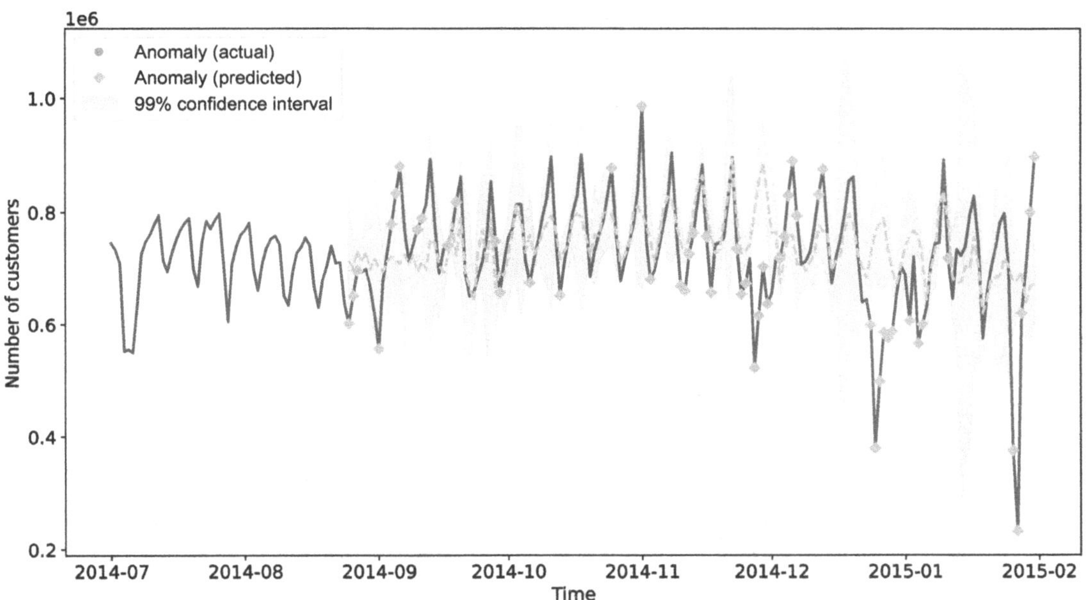


**Figure 9.9 Anomalies detected by Time-LLM using cross-validation and conformal intervals**

The model detected many false anomalies, which means that recall will be high but precision will be low. This may be due to the fact that we trained the model for only 10 steps for each window, resulting in poorly calibrated intervals. As a result, many values are falsely labeled as anomalies.

### 9.5.2 Evaluating anomaly detection

As mentioned earlier, we detected anomalies on the last 160 dates, but in previous chapters, we detected on 184 time steps. Thus, we pad the sequence of detected anomalies with a default value of `0`, indicating that values are normal. Then we can measure the precision, recall, and F1 Score and compare those metrics to those of other models, as shown in figure 9.10.

**Listing 9.9 Padding anomalies and evaluating**

```
n_pad_values = 184 - len(anomaly_cv_df)
pred_anomalies = np.pad(anomaly_cv_df['anomaly'].values, (n_pad_values, 0),
```

```
➥ 'constant')                    ◄── Padding with 0, indicating
                                      that values are normal
df_anomaly = df_anomaly[-184:]
df_anomaly['pred_anomaly'] = pred_anomalies
precision, recall, f1_score = evaluate_anomaly_detection(df_anomaly,
➥ 'pred_anomaly', 'is_anomaly')
```

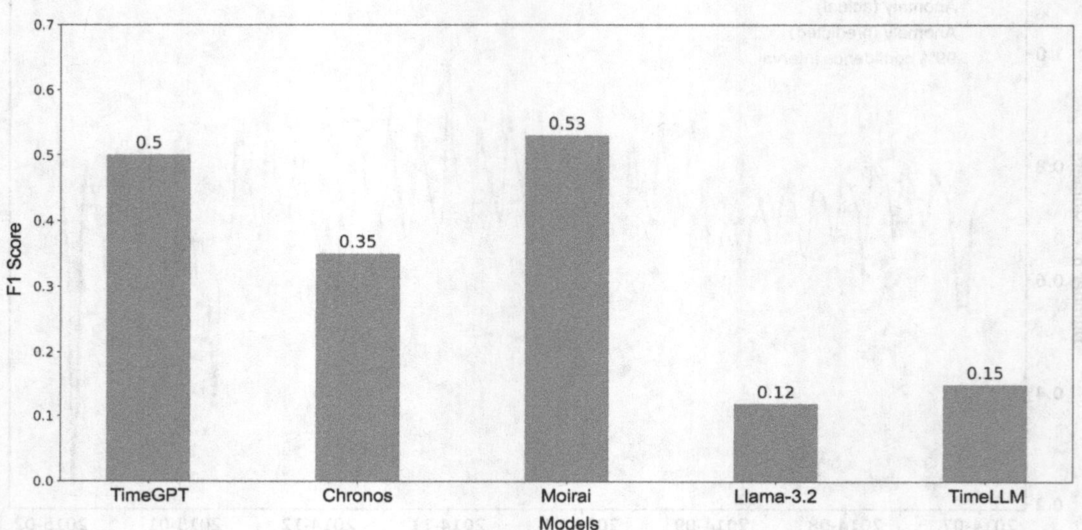


**Figure 9.10 F1 Score of all explored models in detecting anomalies of daily taxi rides. Higher is better.**

In figure 9.10, we can see that Time-LLM achieves a F1 Score of 0.15, which is slightly better than Llama-3.2's score but much worse than Moirai's and TimeGPT's scores. Keep in mind that we didn't train Time-LLM for many steps, which affected its performance.

## 9.6 Next steps

In this chapter, we explored Time-LLM, a framework that reprograms LLMs for time-series forecasting. It aligns the modality of time with the modality of text used to train LLMs by reprogramming patches of time series and learning text prototypes that best describe each patch, such as "short up then steady down."

Although this model is the first multimodal approach discussed in this book, a major drawback is that it must always be trained to reprogram patches; it has no true zero-shot forecasting capability. On the other hand, its implementation within `neuralforecast` makes it easy to use with minimal code.

Table 9.2 updates our summary table of foundation models.

**Table 9.2 Pros and cons of each foundation forecasting model**

| Model | Pros | Cons | When to use |
|---|---|---|---|
| TimeGPT | Easy and fast to use<br>Comes with many native functions<br>Works on any device, regardless of hardware<br>Free plan | Paid product for a certain usage<br>Model may not be available if the server is down. | Forecasting on long and short horizons with exogenous features.<br>You need to fine-tune but do not have the local resources. |
| Lag-Llama | Open source model<br>Free to use | Awkward to use because we must clone the repository<br>Speed of inference depends on our hardware. | Quick proof of concept<br>Ideal for research-oriented projects |
| Chronos | Open source model<br>Free to use<br>Can be installed as a Python package | Speed and accuracy depend on our hardware.<br>Fine-tuning requires cloning the repository.<br>We must define some functions manually. | Forecasting on horizons shorter than 64 time steps<br>Forecasting series without strong trends |
| Moirai | Open source model<br>Free to use<br>Supports exogenous features<br>Can be installed as a Python package | Speed and accuracy depend on the hardware.<br>We must define helper functions when not working entirely with GluonTS. | You have exogenous features.<br>Forecasting on horizons shorter than 256 time steps |
| TimesFM | Open source model<br>Free to use<br>Can be installed as a Python package<br>Supports exogenous features | Only the largest model is available.<br>Restrictive requirements for use (16 GB of RAM, Linux-based system to install dependencies)<br>Knowledge of JAX is required for fine-tuning.<br>Cannot perform anomaly detection because it is a deterministic model | Ideal for deterministic forecasting in which prediction intervals are not required<br>You want to feed a long input series. |
| LLMs (Flan-T5 and Llama-3.2) | Possible to use free LLMs<br>Interaction through natural language feels intuitive. | Not built to handle time-series data<br>Requires lengthy code to preprocess the input and extract the values from the output<br>Requires a lot of computation power for local setups | You already have access to an LLM.<br>You need a natural language interface for forecasting.<br>You know how to develop prompts and safeguards for edge cases. |

**Table 9.2 Pros and cons of each foundation forecasting model (*continued*)**

| Model | Pros | Cons | When to use |
|---|---|---|---|
| Time-LLM | Works with any open source language model<br>Available in `neuralforecast` | No true zero-shot forecasting capability<br>Univariate; does not support exogenous features<br>Always requires training | You want to provide context to the model with natural language.<br>You have resources to reprogram the LLM. |

At this point, we've explored several foundation models for time-series forecasting. We know how to work with models that are designed to handle time-series data, and we know how to adapt LLMs for time-series forecasting.

This is a great time to take a step back from exploring methods and complete a capstone project. This project, which is the topic of chapter 10, compares the performance of foundation models along with other data-specific methods.

This project will allow us to see the tradeoff in performance and speed between foundation models and data-specific models, and it also consolidates our learnings. We'll use a single dataset, so the project can't be seen as a benchmark. It's mostly an opportunity to test our knowledge and observe some of the tradeoffs.

## Summary

- Time-LLM is a framework that reprograms LLMs for time-series forecasting. It learns text prototypes that best describe patches of time series, thus aligning the time modality with the text modality.
- It uses the Prompt-as-Prefix technique to add context, instruction, and statistics to the input, helping the LLM perform better.
- Because the model must be reprogrammed through training, Time-LLM can't be used for zero-shot forecasting; some training steps always have to be completed.
- The model's availability in `neuralforecast` makes it easy to use and gives us access to all functionalities available in the package.

# Part 4

# Capstone project

To conclude this book, we complete a capstone project to solidify our learning. This project is the perfect opportunity to test the models we've studied in this book, comparing them with one another and with more traditional forecasting methods.

Chapter 10 focuses entirely on this capstone project and proposes a solution, although the project remains open-ended. The main takeaway is that now we have all the knowledge to test different methods and build a solid protocol to evaluate their performance and make an informed decision about which model performs best for our use case.

# 10 Capstone project: Forecasting daily visits to a blog

**This chapter covers**

- Making accurate predictions for the daily traffic volume to a blog's website
- Designing a robust protocol for model comparison and selection
- Evaluating the tradeoff between performance and inference speed

Congratulations on making it this far. Throughout this book, we've discovered and implemented many large time models, all of which have advantages and disadvantages. We've experimented with these models' zero-shot forecasting capabilities and fine-tuned them to specific scenarios.

Now we'll cement our learning with this capstone project. The goal of this chapter is to apply what we've learned throughout the book in a new scenario, using a new dataset. Although a suggested solution is provided, the main idea is for you to experiment with different approaches, design experiments, and adjust each model to try to generate the most accurate forecasts possible.

## 10.1 Introducing the use case

The goal of this project is to forecast the daily number of visitors to a blog's website. Here, to ensure that the data was not seen by any foundation model (because we now know that these models are trained on massive amounts of time-series data), I extracted the data from my blog (https://www.datasciencewithmarco.com/blog). The data starts on January 1, 2020, and ends on October 12, 2023. It compiles the daily number of visitors; it also includes an indicator showing when a new article is published and when a holiday occurs. Figure 10.1 plots the dataset.

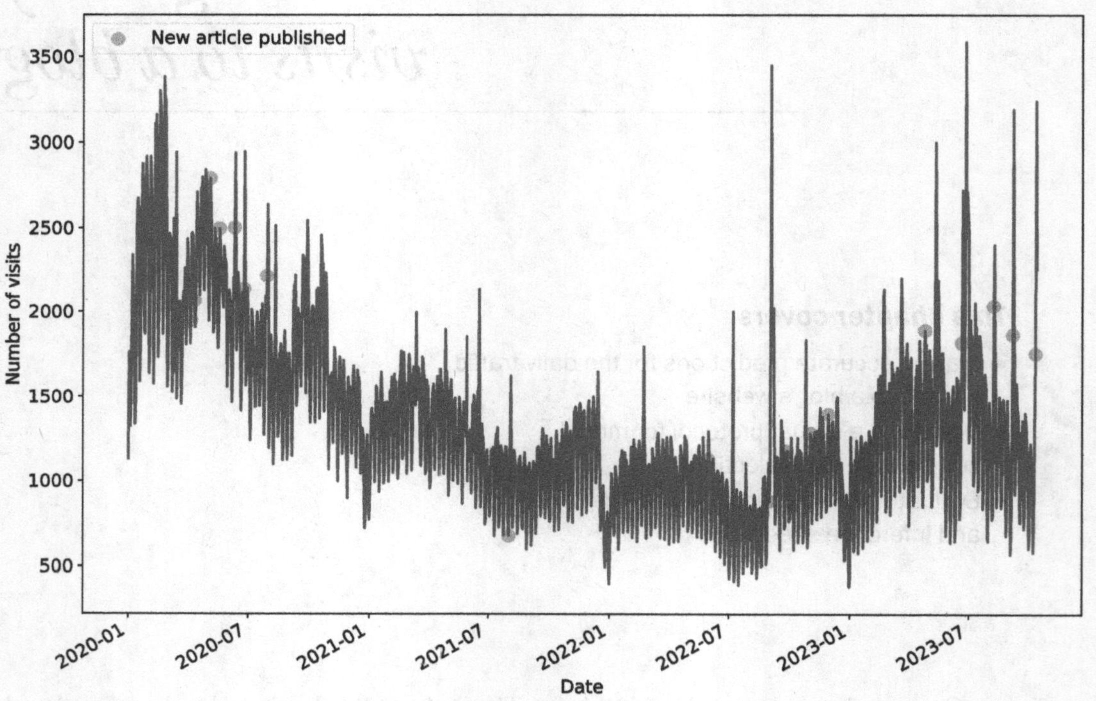


**Figure 10.1 Daily visits to my blog's website, from January 1, 2020, to October 12, 2023**

We can see when a new article was published, indicated by dots on the plot. We also see that traffic steadily decreased from 2020 because few new articles were being published. In 2022, more articles were written at a more consistent rate, resulting in increased traffic. Each new article is followed by a peak in traffic, which makes sense because new content usually drives more people to read the latest article.

In the figure, however, we can't distinguish the weekly seasonality. In fact, there were more visitors during weekdays than during weekends. This fact is more apparent when we zoom in on the dataset (figure 10.2).

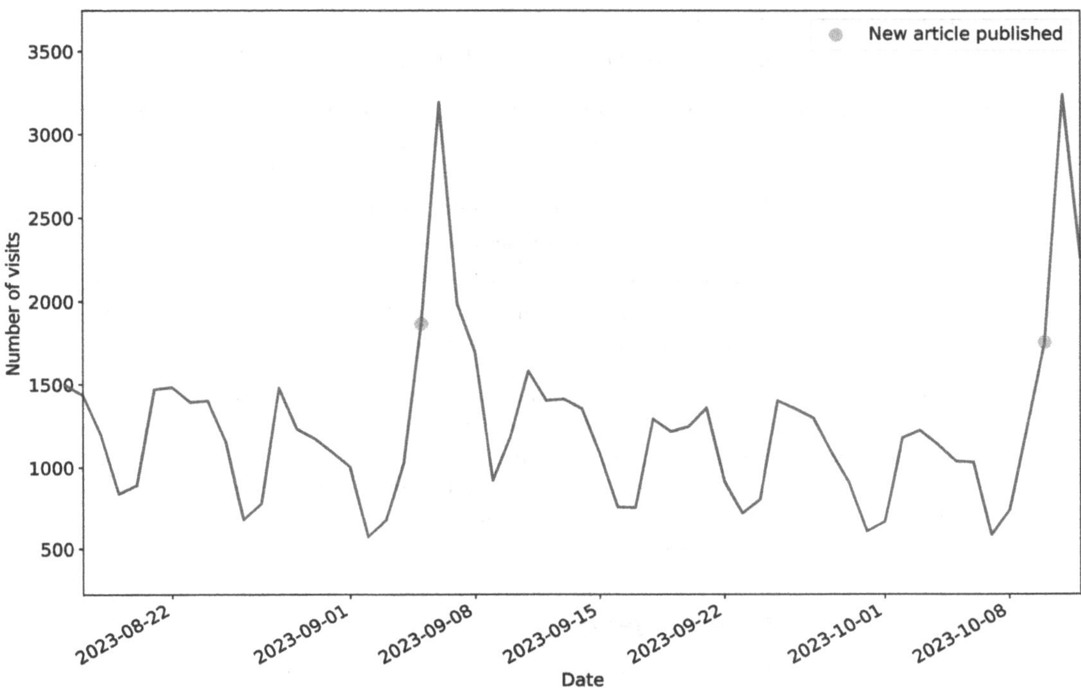


**Figure 10.2 Zooming in on the last 56 days of the dataset**

Now we clearly see the number of visitors decreasing during weekends and increasing during weekdays, indicating a weekly seasonality. Also, we see that on a day when a new article is published, the number of visitors increases that day and the following day before returning to a more normal pattern.

In this project, the objective is to forecast the number of daily visitors for the next seven days. To assess which model performs best, we'll perform cross-validation using 20 nonoverlapping windows of seven days, resulting in an evaluation over 140 data points. We'll use the mean absolute error (MAE) and the symmetric mean absolute percentage error (sMAPE) to evaluate our models as we've done throughout this book.

We'll take these steps to complete this capstone project:

1. Define the constants for the experiment
2. Use a naïve seasonal model as a baseline
3. Fit a seasonal autoregressive integrated moving average (SARIMA) model
4. Forecast with TimeGPT
5. Forecast with Chronos
6. Forecast with Moirai
7. Forecast with TimesFM

8. Forecast with Time-LLM
9. Evaluate the performances of the model using the MAE and sMAPE

We won't use Lag-Llama or another large language model (LLM) in the suggested approach. Lag-Llama isn't intended to be used in a production environment; it's designed for research, as discussed in chapter 4. As for LLMs, we've seen that they require lengthy code and ultimately aren't built for time-series forecasting (although it's possible to use them for that purpose, as discussed in chapter 8).

The best way to complete this task is to complete the project on your own and then refer to the chapter for the suggested approach. You can find the source code for this chapter and the dataset on GitHub at https://mng.bz/a9Q9.

> **NOTE** This project is not a benchmark. Any performance we get from this experiment is not indicative of the absolute performance of any model. This project is limited and works with a single dataset. Also, no model always performs best in every situation. Thus, the goal of this project is to implement a solid testing protocol to make the best choice of model. Focus on the methodology, not the performance of any model.

## 10.2 Walking through the project

This section provides a suggested approach to this project. The approach is suggested because the size of each model to use is subjective. Here, I present a solution that you can apply with reasonable computing power and without access to a graphics processing unit (GPU). If you have access to more power, more storage, and a GPU, feel free to use larger versions of the large time models, which tend to perform better at the cost of longer inference time.

The project measures the time it takes to complete the inference over the 20 cross-validation windows, so we can compare not only forecasting accuracy but also the time it takes to infer with a particular model.

### 10.2.1 Setting the constants

We start by importing the required packages for this experiment.

**Listing 10.1 Importing the packages**

```
import pandas as pd
import numpy as np
import matplotlib.pyplot as plt

from time import time

from utilsforecast.losses import mae, smape
from utilsforecast.evaluation import evaluate

import warnings
warnings.filterwarnings('ignore')
```

Other required packages will be imported as needed. Then we can read in the dataset and store it in a DataFrame.

**Listing 10.2 Reading the dataset**

```
df = pd.read_csv("../data/blog_traffic_daily.csv", parse_dates=["ds"])
```

Our DataFrame contains the date and the number of visitors. It has two extra columns that indicate whether an article was published and whether that day was a U.S. holiday.

Keep in mind that those features are known for certain in advance: the author of articles knows when they'll publish an article, and holiday dates are fixed. Therefore, those features can be accessed at the time of inference and used to inform the predictions.

Next, we define some constants that will be used throughout the project.

**Listing 10.3 Setting constants**

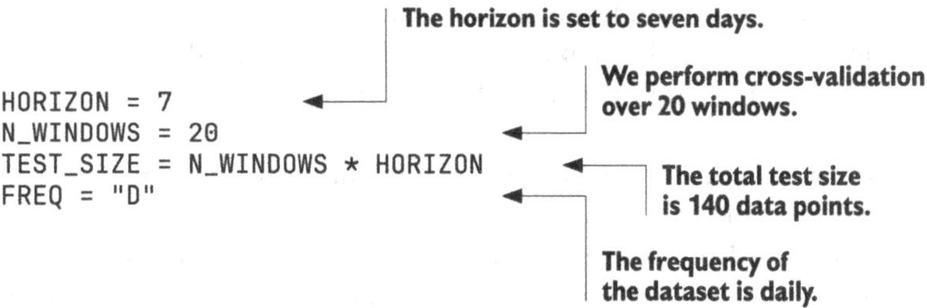


```
HORIZON = 7
N_WINDOWS = 20
TEST_SIZE = N_WINDOWS * HORIZON
FREQ = "D"
```

This code defines the constants that will be reused across models. The horizon is set to seven days, and we run cross-validation over 20 windows, which means that the test size covers 140 data points. Finally, the dataset has a daily frequency.

### 10.2.2 Forecasting with a seasonal naïve model

Here, baseline forecasts come from a seasonal naïve model. Given that we have a weekly seasonality with daily data, our season has a length, or period, of 7. Therefore, the naïve seasonal model repeats the last seven days into the future, acting as the baseline forecasts. To apply this model, we use its implementation in `statsforecast`.

**Listing 10.4 Baseline forecasts**

```
from statsforecast import StatsForecast
from statsforecast.models import SeasonalNaive

baseline_model = SeasonalNaive(season_length=7)
sf = StatsForecast(
    models=[baseline_model],
    freq=FREQ)
init = time()
baseline_cv_fcsts = sf.cross_validation(
```

**Imports the model**

**Specifies the season length (seven days)**

**Initializes the StatsForecast object and passes a list of models and the frequency of the data**

**Starts tracking the time it takes for inference**

```
    h=HORIZON,
    df=df,
    n_windows=N_WINDOWS,          Uses nonoverlapping windows
    step_size=HORIZON
)                                                          Reports the time it
print(f"Baseline time: {time() - init} seconds")           takes for inference
baseline_cv_fcsts.to_csv
➥ ("baseline_preds.csv", header=True, index=False)         (Optional) Saves the
                                                            forecasts as a CSV file
```

Working with `statsforecast` is similar to using `neuralforecast`, as we did in chapter 2. After initializing a model, we create an instance of the `StatsForecast` object, which takes a list of models and the frequency of the dataset. Then we can use the `cross_validation` function directly, specifying the horizon, number of windows, and `step_size`, which represents the distance between consecutive windows. We set `step_size` to the same value as the horizon to have nonoverlapping windows. That way, we don't forecast the same time step more than once, which would give more points to certain time steps during the evaluation, biasing the result.

Here, running inference with the naïve seasonal model took 0.08 seconds. This time is fast, which is expected because the model is not being trained but uses the last seven values as forecasts.

Optionally, we save the forecasts to a CSV file. That way, we don't have to run the entire experiment in a single shot, and we can come back to it and access the forecasts from previous models without rerunning them. In the solutions notebook in the repository and in this chapter, we assume that the predictions made with each model are saved in separate CSV files.

### 10.2.3 Forecasting with ARIMA

Now we fit an ARIMA model to our dataset. The ARIMA model is a fundamental statistical model in time-series forecasting. In chapter 7, TimesFM uses the ARMA model to generate synthetic data. The ARIMA model is like the ARMA model, but an integration order is added to account for nonstationary data.

In this case, we fit a seasonal ARIMA (SARIMA) model because there is a clear seasonal pattern in our dataset. I'll quickly explain the SARIMA model, although it's beyond the scope of this book, which assumes some comfort with traditional forecasting techniques. For more information on this model, I suggest reading *Time Series Forecasting in Python*, by Marco Peixeiro (Manning, 2021).

A SARIMA model is parametrized with $(p,d,q)$ and $(P,D,Q)$, where the uppercase letters are the seasonal counterparts of the lowercase letters. This means that $p$ is the autoregressive order, and $P$ is the seasonal autoregressive order. Similarly, $d$ is the order of integration, $D$ is the seasonal order of integration, $q$ is the order of the moving average portion, and $Q$ is the order of the seasonal moving average portion.

Thus, if $p = 1$ means that we include the first lag in the ARIMA equation, $P = 1$ means that we include the first multiple of the seasonal period, which is lag 7 in this case. The same logic applies to the other parameters.

Typically, we try different combinations of all parameters to minimize a certain metric, such as the Akaike information criterion (AIC), which balances model complexity and overfitting. Luckily for us, this entire process is automated using the `AutoARIMA` model from `statsforecast`.

**Listing 10.5 Fitting an `AutoARIMA` model**

```
from statsforecast.arima import ARIMASummary
from statsforecast.models import AutoARIMA

autoarima_model = AutoARIMA(season_length=7)
sf = StatsForecast(models=[autoarima_model], freq=FREQ)
init = time()
autoarima_cv_fcsts = sf.cross_validation(
    h=HORIZON,
    df=df,
    n_windows=N_WINDOWS,
    step_size=HORIZON
)
print(f"AutoARIMA time: {time() - init} seconds")
autoarima_cv_fcsts.to_csv("autoarima_preds.csv", header=True, index=False)
```

Prints the optimal parameter combination

This process took 223 seconds, which is slightly less than 4 minutes. This value considers the time it took to test different parameter combinations to find the best one. We can see the exact parameter combination by fitting the model on the training set and printing its summary.

**Listing 10.6 Printing the parameter combination of the `AutoARIMA` model**

```
sf.fit(df=df[:-TEST_SIZE])
print(ARIMASummary(sf.fitted_[0, 0].model_))
```

The training set excludes the last 140 time steps.

Prints the optimal parameter combination

Here, we get a `SARIMA(2,0,1)(0,1,1)` model, which means that $p=2$, $d=0$, $q=1$, $P=0$, $D=1$, and $Q=1$. At this point, we have baseline forecasts and forecasts from a statistical model.

### 10.2.4 Forecasting with TimeGPT

In this step, we use TimeGPT to forecast our scenario. To use TimeGPT, we need an API key, which should be stored in a `.env` file so we can load it and not have it appear in the code.

**Listing 10.7 Initializing the client for TimeGPT**

```
from dotenv import load_dotenv
from nixtla import NixtlaClient
```

```
load_dotenv()
nixtla_client = NixtlaClient()
```

Loads the API key stored in an .env file

Initializes the client to use TimeGPT

`NixtlaClient` comes with a cross-validation function that we can use directly. It also automatically detects and uses the exogenous features in the dataset. Further, because the model is not hosted locally, we can fine-tune it no matter what local resources we have.

**Listing 10.8 Cross-validating with TimeGPT**

```
init = time()
timegpt_cv_fcsts = nixtla_client.cross_validation(
    df=df,
    h=HORIZON,
    n_windows=N_WINDOWS,
    finetune_steps=50,
    finetune_loss="mae"
)
print(f"TimeGPT time: {time() - init} seconds")
timegpt_cv_fcsts.to_csv("timegpt_preds.csv", header=True, index=False)
```

This number is subjective. We can test with more or fewer steps.

We can optimize for only one metric or experiment with "smape."

In this case, it took a bit less than 52 seconds to fine-tune TimeGPT and perform cross-validation. One of the advantages of TimeGPT is that because the model isn't loaded locally, we're not limited by our hardware, and we get to use Nixtla's servers.

To further this experiment, we can run cross-validation without the exogenous features to determine whether including them improves or degrades performance. To do so, replace line 3 in listing 10.8 with `df=df.drop(["published", "is_holiday"], axis=1)`. Make sure to adjust the name of the CSV file in line 10 to avoid overwriting the previous results.

### 10.2.5 Forecasting with Chronos

Now we use Chronos to generate forecasts. Chronos expects tensors as input, so we need to format our input series accordingly. To do so, we reuse the function defined in chapter 5.

**Listing 10.9 Cross-validating with Chronos**

```
import torch
from chronos import ChronosPipeline

def cross_validation_chronos(df, h, n_windows, target_col):
    lows = []
    medians = []
    highs = []
    for i in range(n_windows, 0, -1):
        context = torch.tensor(df[target_col][:-(h * i)])
```

```
        predictions = pipeline.predict(
            context=context,
            prediction_length=h,
            num_samples=20,
        )
        low, median, high = np.quantile(predictions[0].numpy(), [0.1, 0.5,
        ➥ 0.9], axis=0)
        lows.extend(low)
        medians.extend(median)
        highs.extend(high)
    return lows, medians, highs
```

Next, we initialize the Chronos model and specify the model size we want. In this case, we're running the model on a CPU, so we use the small model.

**Listing 10.10 Initializing the Chronos model**

```
pipeline = ChronosPipeline.from_pretrained(
    "amazon/chronos-t5-small",          ◄── Feel free to specify any
    device_map="cpu",                       model size you want.
    torch_dtype=torch.bfloat16,
)
```

Finally, we generate predictions using the cross-validation function defined in listing 10.9.

**Listing 10.11 Forecasting with Chronos**

```
init = time()
_, medians, _ = cross_validation_chronos(
    df=df,
    h=HORIZON,
    n_windows=N_WINDOWS,
    target_col='y'
)
print(f"Chronos time: {time() - init} seconds")
```

This procedure took approximately 791 seconds, which is a bit more than 13 minutes. This is one of the longest inference times so far; the model is only making predictions.

We use the median as the point forecast from Chronos. We'll also use it in the evaluation step (section 10.2.9). When we work with probabilistic models, the median is often considered the point forecast, so we get a point prediction that is robust to skewed predicted distributions.

### 10.2.6 Forecasting with Moirai

In this step, we use the Moirai model to make predictions. Moirai relies on the `gluonts` package, so we need to format our dataset accordingly before feeding it to the model.

**Listing 10.12 Formatting the dataset with gluonts**

```
from gluonts.dataset.pandas import PandasDataset
from gluonts.dataset.split import split
from uni2ts.model.moirai import MoiraiForecast, MoiraiModule

df_to_gluon = df.copy()
df_to_gluon = df_to_gluon.set_index('ds')

ds = PandasDataset.from_long_dataframe(
    df_to_gluon,
    target='y',
    item_id='unique_id',
    feat_dynamic_real=["is_holiday", "published"]    ◄ Specifies the features the model can access at the time of inference
)
```

As mentioned at the start of this chapter, our features are easily known in advance, so we can reasonably use their future values to inform the forecasts.

Next, we use Moirai's built-in cross-validation functionality to generate different windows of predictions. Here, we redo the steps from chapter 6.

**Listing 10.13 Generating cross-validation windows**

```
train, test_template = split(
    ds, offset=-TEST_SIZE
)

test_data = test_template.generate_instances(
    prediction_length=HORIZON,
    windows=N_WINDOWS,
    distance=HORIZON
)
```

Next, we initialize the Moirai model and make predictions. Feel free to use a different model size or the newest Moirai architecture, which includes a mixture of experts. In this case, we use the original small model.

**Listing 10.14 Forecasting with Moirai**

```
model = MoiraiForecast(
    module=MoiraiModule.from_pretrained(f"Salesforce/moirai-1.0-R-small"),
    prediction_length=HORIZON,
    context_length=1000,    ◄ This value is subjective. The idea is to feed a sequence long enough that the model can extract temporal dependencies.
    patch_size="auto",
    num_samples=20,    ◄ We can increase this value to obtain a more precise distribution.
    target_dim=1,
    feat_dynamic_real_dim=ds.num_feat_dynamic_real,
    past_feat_dynamic_real_dim=ds.num_past_feat_dynamic_real,
```

```
)

predictor = model.create_predictor(batch_size=32)
init = time()
moirai_fcsts = predictor.predict(test_data.input)
moirai_fcsts = list(moirai_fcsts)
print(f"Moirai time: {time() - init} seconds")
```

This entire process took 18.53 seconds to complete, which is one of the fastest methods so far.

Moirai is a probabilistic model: it outputs a distribution of possible values. Because we're interested in point forecasts for this scenario, we need to take the median value for each time step.

**Listing 10.15 Extracting the median from Moirai**

```
all_samples = np.stack([forecast.samples
    for forecast in moirai_fcsts])          # Gets all output distribution for each time step
reshaped_samples = all_samples.reshape(20, -1)   # Reshapes so that we have 20 samples for all 140 time steps of the test set
moirai_medians = np.median(reshaped_samples, axis=0)   # Gets the median for each time step

moirai_fcsts_df = df[-TEST_SIZE:].copy()
moirai_fcsts_df['Moirai'] = moirai_medians
moirai_fcsts_df.to_csv("moirai_preds.csv", header=True, index=False)
```

### 10.2.7 Forecasting with TimesFM

The next model we'll try is TimesFM. For this portion of the experiment, the model was run in Google Colab on a CPU instance so that it ran in an environment similar to that of a local computer without GPU access.

The first step in using TimesFM is creating an instance of the model to specify its horizon. One drawback is that it we want to change the horizon, we must reinitialize the model.

**Listing 10.16 Initializing TimesFM**

```
import timesfm

tfm = timesfm.TimesFm(
    hparams=timesfm.TimesFmHparams(
        backend="cpu",                  # Uses a CPU backend to keep everything consistent with the other models
        per_core_batch_size=32,
        horizon_len=HORIZON,            # Sets the horizon
        num_layers=50,
        use_positional_embedding=False, # The model doesn't use positional encodings, so it is always False.
        context_len=2048,
    ),
```

```
    checkpoint=timesfm.TimesFmCheckpoint(
        huggingface_repo_id="google/timesfm-2.0-500m-pytorch"),
)
```

Then we reuse the cross-validation function defined in chapter 7.

**Listing 10.17 Cross-validating with TimesFM**

```
def cross_validation_timesfm(df, h, n_windows, target_col, freq):
    all_preds = []
    for i in range(n_windows, 0, -1):
        input_df = df.iloc[:-(h*i)]
        preds_df = tfm.forecast_on_df(
            inputs=input_df,
            freq=freq,
            value_name=target_col,
            num_jobs=-1
        )
        all_preds.append(preds_df)
    preds = pd.concat(all_preds, axis=0, ignore_index=True)
    return preds
```

Finally, we can make predictions using the model and the function defined in listing 10.17. We don't include exogenous features in this instance of TimesFM.

**Listing 10.18 Making predictions with TimesFM**

```
init = time()
timesfm_cv_fcsts = cross_validation_timesfm(
    df=df,
    h=HORIZON,
    n_windows=N_WINDOWS,
    target_col="y",
    freq=FREQ
)
print(f"TimesFM time: {time() - init}")
```

This took around 765 seconds to complete, which is a bit less than 13 minutes. For now, this is one of the longest inference times. If you ran this model in Colab, you can download the predictions as a CSV file.

**Listing 10.19 Downloading a CSV file from Colab**

```
from google.colab import files

timesfm_cv_fcsts.to_csv(
    "timsfm_preds.csv",
    index=False,
    header=True)                          ← Saves predictions to a CSV file
files.download('timsfm_preds.csv')        ← Downloads the CSV file locally
```

### 10.2.8 Forecasting with Time-LLM

The last model we'll apply is Time-LLM. Then we can evaluate all the models and choose the best.

Time-LLM uses an existing LLM but requires some training steps because it's reprogramming the model to handle time-series data. The process is streamlined by `neuralforecast`.

When initializing the model, we can optionally create a prompt to provide context to the model using natural language. In this case, we use the following prompt:

The dataset contains information on daily visits to a blog's website.

There is a weekly seasonality as more people visit the website during weekdays, and there are less visitors during the weekend.

Then we initialize the model. We're using the default GPT-2 model from OpenAI as the backbone LLM.

**Listing 10.20 Initializing Time-LLM**

```
from neuralforecast import NeuralForecast
from neuralforecast.models import TimeLLM
from neuralforecast.losses.pytorch import MAE

prompt_prefix = """
    The dataset contains information on daily visits to a blog's website.
    There is a weekly seasonality as more people visit the website during
      weekdays, and
    there are less visitors during the weekend.
"""

timellm = TimeLLM(
    h=HORIZON,
    input_size=2*HORIZON,
    d_llm=768,
    prompt_prefix=prompt_prefix,
    batch_size=16,
    windows_batch_size=16,
    max_steps=150
)

nf = NeuralForecast(
    models=[timellm],
    freq=FREQ
)
```

Finally, we run cross-validation using the built-in functionality in `neuralforecast`.

**Listing 10.21 Forecasting with Time-LLM**

```
init = time()
timellm_cv_fcsts = nf.cross_validation(
```

```
    df=df,
    n_windows=N_WINDOWS,
    step_size=HORIZON,
    refit=False,
)
print(f"Time-LLM time: {time() - init} seconds")
timellm_cv_fcsts.to_csv("timellm_preds.csv", header=True, index=False)
```

This process took 841 seconds, which is roughly 14 minutes. This model officially took the most time to run, but we're considering the time it takes to train the model because it's reprogramming the LLM. Because the model is large, it makes sense that it takes a long time to run. TimesFM and Chronos were slow, but they were performing zero-shot inference.

### 10.2.9 Evaluating all models

As mentioned at the start of the chapter, we'll evaluate the performance of each model using the MAE and sMAPE metrics. That way, if a model performs best on both metrics, we're more confident about designating it a champion model.

#### MEASURING THE PERFORMANCE

Assuming that all predictions from each model were saved in separate CSV files, we can combine everything into a single DataFrame so that we have the predictions from each model and the actual values.

**Listing 10.22 Combining all predictions with actual values**

```
baseline_cv_fcsts = pd.read_csv("baseline_preds.csv", parse_dates=["ds"])
autoarima_cv_fcsts = pd.read_csv("autoarima_preds.csv", parse_dates=["ds"])
timegpt_cv_fcsts = pd.read_csv("timegpt_preds.csv", parse_dates=["ds"])
timegpt_noexog_cv_fcsts = pd.read_csv("timegpt_noexog_preds.csv",
➥ parse_dates=["ds"])
chronos_cv_fcsts = pd.read_csv("chronos_preds.csv", parse_dates=["ds"])
moirai_cv_fcsts = pd.read_csv("moirai_preds.csv", parse_dates=["ds"])
timesfm_cv_fcsts = pd.read_csv("timesfm_preds.csv", parse_dates=["ds"])
timellm_cv_fcsts = pd.read_csv("timellm_preds.csv", parse_dates=["ds"])

test_df = df[-TEST_SIZE:].copy()

test_df = (test_df[["unique_id", "ds", "y"]]
    .merge(baseline_cv_fcsts[['ds', 'SeasonalNaive']], on='ds', how='left')
    .merge(autoarima_cv_fcsts[['ds', 'AutoARIMA']], on='ds', how='left')
    .merge(timegpt_cv_fcsts[['ds', 'TimeGPT']], on='ds', how='left')
    .merge(timegpt_noexog_cv_fcsts[['ds', 'TimeGPT']], on='ds', how='left')
    .merge(chronos_cv_fcsts[['ds', 'Chronos']], on='ds', how='left')
    .merge(moirai_cv_fcsts[['ds', 'Moirai']], on='ds', how='left')
    .merge(timesfm_cv_fcsts[['ds', 'timesfm']], on='ds', how='left')
    .merge(timellm_cv_fcsts[['ds', 'TimeLLM']], on='ds', how='left')
)
test_df = test_df.rename(columns={"timesfm": "TimesFM", "TimeGPT_x":
➥ "TimeGPT_exog", "TimeGPT_y": "TimeGPT"})
test_df.head()
```

All predictions are decimal numbers. In our scenario, however, decimal numbers don't make sense because we're tracking the number of visitors to a website, so let's cast all values as integers.

**Listing 10.23 Casting all values as integers**

```
forecast_cols = [col for col in test_df.columns
    if col not in ["unique_id", "ds", "y"]]
test_df[forecast_cols] = test_df[forecast_cols].astype(int)
```

Then we can calculate the MAE and sMAPE for each model. Table 10.1 contains the results, showing the best in bold.

**Listing 10.24 Evaluating all models**

```
evaluation = evaluate(
    test_df,
    metrics=[mae, smape],
)
Evaluation
```

**Table 10.1 MAE and sMAPE of all models used to forecast daily visitors to a website over 20 windows of seven days**

| Model | MAE | sMAPE (%) |
|---|---|---|
| Naïve seasonal | 325.37 | 10.53 |
| SARIMA + features | 258.76 | 8.39 |
| TimeGPT + features | 300.49 | 9.80 |
| TimeGPT | 249.05 | 8.04 |
| Chronos | 239.49 | 7.80 |
| Moirai + features | 328.08 | 11.82 |
| TimesFM | **230.44** | **7.35** |
| Time-LLM | 343.66 | 11.91 |

TimesFM achieves the lowest scores in both MAE and sMAPE. Therefore, it's the champion model for this scenario.

Interestingly, two models performed worse than even the simple naïve seasonal model: Moirai and Time-LLM. Time-LLM was trained for 150 steps, and it may not have been trained long enough to be performant in this situation. As for Moirai, we used the smallest model, and usually, larger models tend to perform better.

Another interesting aspect is that models that used features didn't perform as well as models that considered only past values of the series. Chronos, TimesFM, and TimeGPT achieved the best performances, whereas TimeGPT with exogenous features and Moirai performed worse, even though they had access to the future values of the exogenous features. We will investigate that result in more detail in the next section.

Finally, SARIMA performed better than some foundation models. This is not a big surprise due to the strong seasonality in the dataset.

#### INVESTIGATING THE PREDICTIONS

Let's investigate the predictions made by each model further by plotting them (figure 10.3).

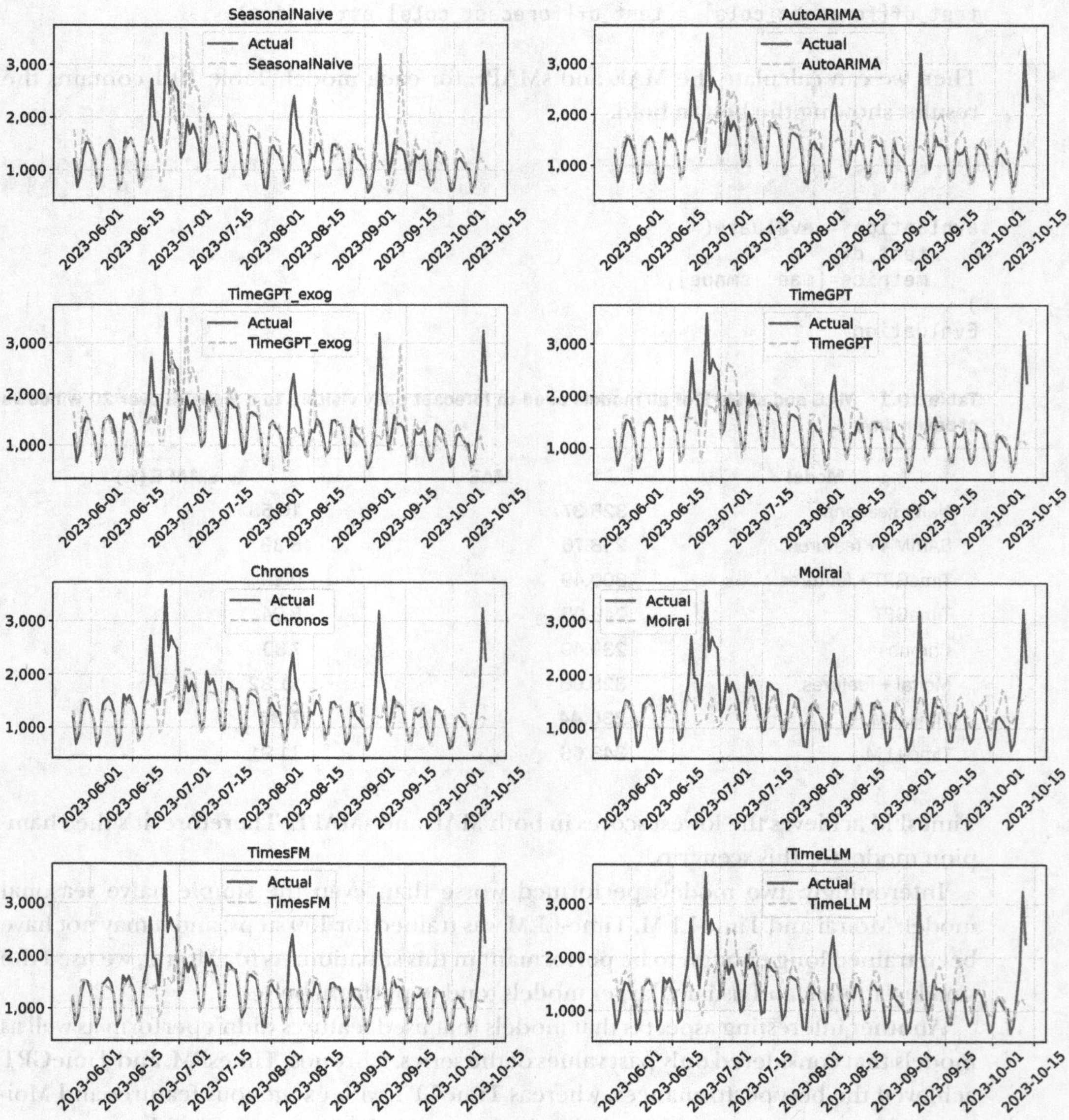


**Figure 10.3 Plotting the predictions of each model against the actual values**

First, TimeGPT with exogenous features is the only model that forecasted the peaks in visitors. But it seems that the model made the predictions a day too late, which hurt its performance. Unfortunately, we can't explain this behavior. Although Moirai also had access to the future values of the exogenous features, it was unable to predict the sudden peaks.

The predictions of Chronos and TimesFM are similar. Both underforecasted the same dates and failed to pick up the peaks in visitors. This result makes sense because they didn't use information from exogenous features, which could have resulted in better overall performances.

#### Comparing performance and inference time

The inference time varies greatly among models. In some situations, inference time is an important aspect of selecting a model, such as when we must obtain forecasts quickly with minimal latency to take action quickly. Let's plot the MAE against the inference time for each model (figure 10.4).

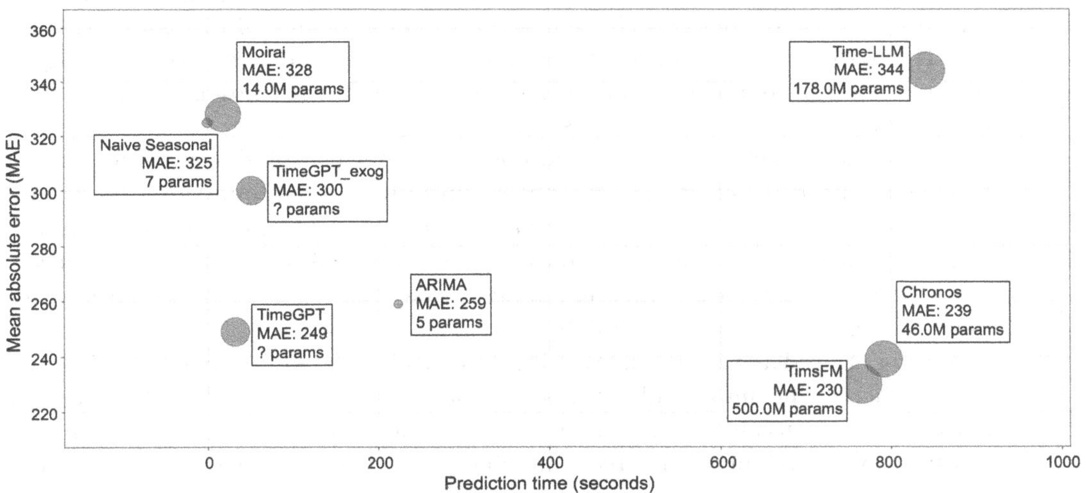


**Figure 10.4 Comparing the MAE to the inference time. The bubble size indicates the size of the model measured by the number of parameters. Interestingly, the most accurate models are also the slowest.**

The figure shows that TimeGPT and Moirai are the fastest foundation models in this scenario. TimeGPT has a bit of an unfair advantage, however, because the model is accessed via API and is likely running on servers with GPUs.

The slowest models, including TimesFM and Chronos, are also the most accurate. Again, using TimeGPT without exogenous features greatly improves its accuracy in this scenario, although it doesn't perform as well as Chronos and TimesFM in this experiment.

In an ideal world, we'd have a foundation model that is both fast at inference time and accurate, which would place it in the bottom-left corner of this plot. Based on figure 10.4, we could argue that TimeGPT without exogenous features fits this description.

Remember that this experiment is minimal and not a complete benchmark. Nevertheless, now you have all the knowledge you need to apply different foundation models and determine which one works best for your situation.

## 10.3 Staying up to date

In this book, we explored the concept of foundation models in time-series forecasting and experimented with its core concepts, such as pretraining and fine-tuning, when we built a tiny foundation model using N-BEATS.

Next, we covered the major contributions in the field and learned how to use TimeGPT, Lag-Llama, Chronos, Moirai, and TimesFM effectively. We learned their characteristics and how they were pretrained, and we implemented them for forecasting and anomaly detection. Then we explored LLMs as forecasting models. Although it's possible to use them for this task, they're not built for it.

Large time models are still in their early days. We're witnessing more work in that direction, and many new models came out during the writing of this book (Moment and Time-MoE, to name only two). But now you have all the necessary knowledge to read models' research papers, understand how they work, and (most important) implement them in your own datasets and scenarios.

Once again, I want to reiterate that there is no perfect solution to all forecasting problems. Although this is the romantic vision of building a foundation forecasting model, for now, no single model will perform best in all situations. I like to think of large time models as the new baselines. Whereas we used to fit statistical models or naïve models as baselines, foundation models make it easy to get zero-shot predictions that rival those of data-specific models.

Staying up to date with the latest advancements in the field of time-series forecasting is difficult. The amount of new research being published is overwhelming, and it doesn't always translate well to real-life scenarios. Thus, you can subscribe to my blog at https://www.datasciencewithmarco.com/blog, where I distill for you the latest research and apply it in a hands-on scenario so that you focus on the latest methods that actually work.

Thank you so much for taking the time to read this book. I hope that you enjoyed reading it as much as I enjoyed writing it. (I liked writing it a lot.)

# references


## Chapter 1

[1] D.D. Placido, "Toys 'R' Us AI-Generated Ad Controversy, Explained," *Forbes*, June 26, 2024. https://www.forbes.com/sites/danidiplacido/2024/06/26/the-toys-r-us-ai-generated-ad-controversy-explained/

[2] "What Is a Foundation Model? An Explainer for Non-Experts," *Stanford HAI*. https://hai.stanford.edu/news/what-foundation-model-explainer-non-experts

[3] A. Vaswani et al., "Attention Is All You Need," June 2017. https://arxiv.org/pdf/1706.03762

## Chapter 2

[1] B. Oreshkin, D. Carpov, N. Chapados, and Y. Bengio, "N-BEATS: Neural basis expansion analysis for interpretable time series forecasting," paper presented at ICLR 2020, June 29, 2024. https://arxiv.org/pdf/1905.10437

## Chapter 3

[1] A. Garza, C. Challu, and M. Mergenthaler-Canseco, "TimeGPT-1." https://arxiv.org/pdf/2310.03589

## Chapter 4

[1] K. Rasul et al., "Lag-Llama: Towards Foundation Models for Probabilistic Time Series Forecasting." https://arxiv.org/pdf/2310.08278

[2] "time-series-foundation-models/lag-llama," GitHub, June 30, 2024. https://github.com/time-series-foundation-models/lag-llama

### Chapter 5

[1] A. Fatir Ansari et al., "Chronos: Learning the Language of Time Series." https://arxiv.org/pdf/2403.07815

[2] "Exploring Transfer Learning with T5: the Text-To-Text Transfer Transformer," Google Research. https://research.google/blog/exploring-transfer-learning-with-t5-the-text-to-text-transfer-transformer/

### Chapter 6

[1] G. Woo, C. Liu, A. Kumar, C. Xiong, S. Savarese, and D. Sahoo, "Unified Training of Universal Time Series Forecasting Transformers," arXiv.org, 2024. https://arxiv.org/abs/2402.02592

[2] Y. Nie, N. H. Nguyen, P. Sinthong, and J. Kalagnanam, "A Time Series is Worth 64 Words: Long-term Forecasting with Transformers," arXiv.org, March 5, 2023. https://arxiv.org/abs/2211.14730

[3] X. Liu et al., "Moirai-MoE: Empowering Time Series Foundation Models with Sparse Mixture of Experts," arXiv.org, 2024. https://arxiv.org/abs/2410.10469

### Chapter 7

[1] A. Das, W. Kong, R. Sen, and Y. Zhou, "A decoder-only foundation model for time-series forecasting," arXiv.org, April 17, 2024. https://arxiv.org/abs/2310.10688

### Chapter 8

[1] H. Xue and F.D. Salim, "PromptCast: A New Prompt-based Learning Paradigm for Time Series Forecasting," arXiv.org, 2022. https://arxiv.org/abs/2210.08964

[2] H. Won Chung et al., "Scaling Instruction-Finetuned Language Models" https://arxiv.org/pdf/2210.11416

[3] Llama team, "The Llama 3 Herd of Models," Meta.com, July 23, 2024. https://mng.bz/MwpD

### Chapter 9

[1] M. Jin et al., "Time-LLM: Time Series Forecasting by Reprogramming Large Language Models," arXiv (Cornell University), October 2023. https://doi.org/10.48550/arxiv.2310.01728

# index

## A



## B



## C

## M



## N



## O



## P